The Plane Story

To Harvey Kurtzman
And my wife Ronnie
And children, Noah and Isabella

This Graphic Memoir is based on personal experiences, though the
names in certain cases have been changed and certain characters,
places, and incidents have been modified in the service of the story.

– Kevin Sacco

The Plane Story

Written and Illustrated by
Kevin Sacco

Lettering and Book Design by
Tom B. Long

Edits by
Justin Eisinger

ISBN: 978-1-60010-867-9

14 13 12 11   1 2 3 4

www.idwpublishing.com

IDW Publishing
Operations:
Ted Adams, CEO & Publisher
Greg Goldstein, Chief Operating Officer
Matthew Ruzicka, CPA, Chief Financial Officer
Alan Payne, VP of Sales
Lorelei Bunjes, Director of Digital Services
Jeff Webber, Director of ePublishing
AnnaMaria White, Dir., Marketing and Public
Relations
Dirk Wood, Dir., Retail Marketing
Marci Hubbard, Executive Assistant
Alonzo Simon, Shipping Manager
Angela Loggins, Staff Accountant
Cherrie Go, Assistant Web Designer

Editorial:
Chris Ryall, Chief Creative Officer, Editor-In-
Chief
Scott Dunbier, Senior Editor, Special Projects
Andy Schmidt, Senior Editor
Justin Eisinger, Senior Editor, Books
Kris Oprisko, Editor/Foreign Lic.
Denton J. Tipton, Editor
Tom Waltz, Editor
Mariah Huehner, Editor
Carlos Guzman, Assistant Editor
Bobby Curnow, Assistant Editor

Design:
Robbie Robbins, EVP/Sr. Graphic Artist
Neil Uyetake, Senior Art Director
Chris Mowry, Senior Graphic Artist
Amauri Osorio, Graphic Artist
Gilberto Lazcano, Production Assistant
Shawn Lee, Graphic artist

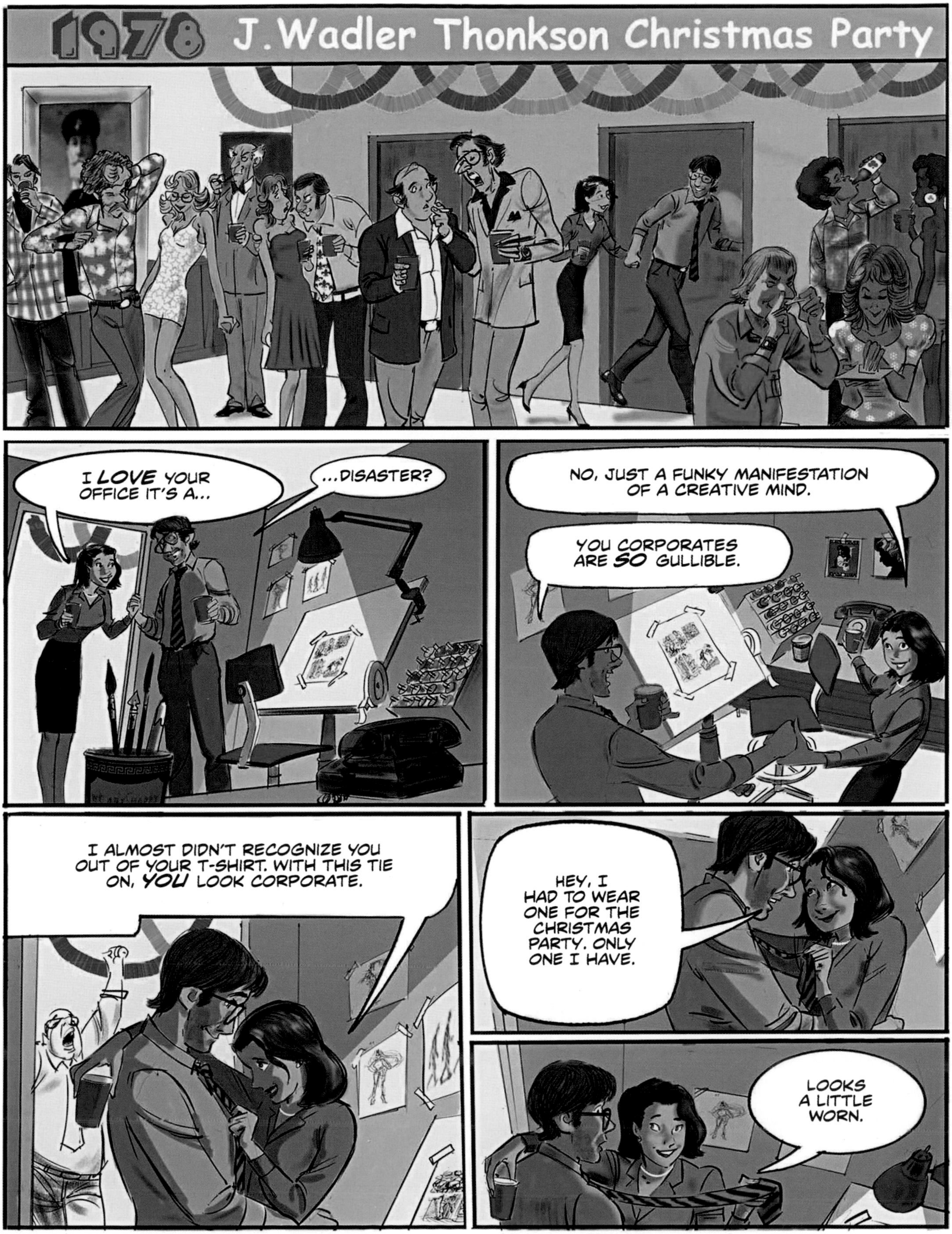
1978 J. Wadler Thonkson Christmas Party
I LOVE YOUR OFFICE IT'S A...
...DISASTER?
NO, JUST A FUNKY MANIFESTATION OF A CREATIVE MIND.
YOU CORPORATES ARE SO GULLIBLE.
I ALMOST DIDN'T RECOGNIZE YOU OUT OF YOUR T-SHIRT. WITH THIS TIE ON, YOU LOOK CORPORATE.
HEY, I HAD TO WEAR ONE FOR THE CHRISTMAS PARTY. ONLY ONE I HAVE.
LOOKS A LITTLE WORN.

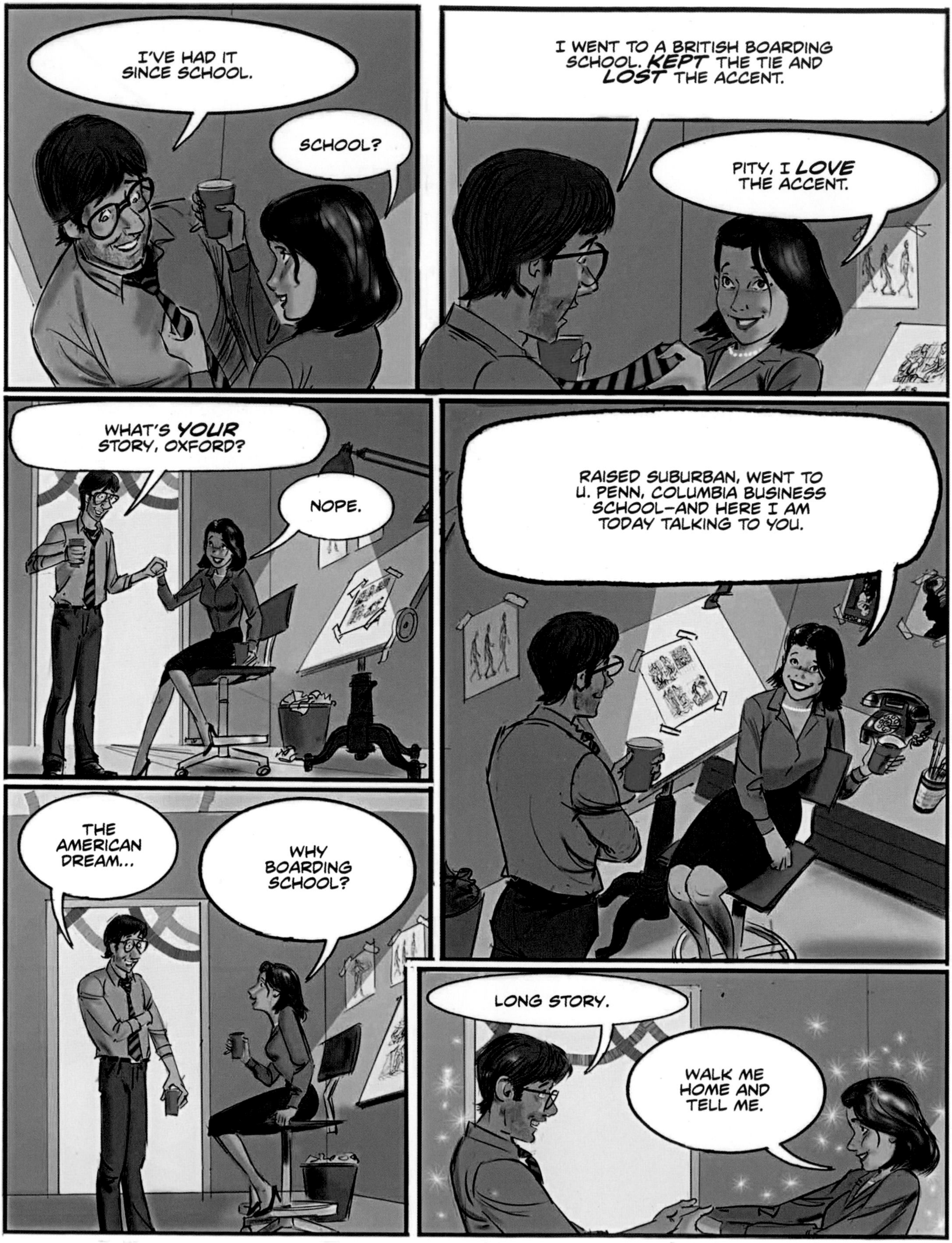
I'VE HAD IT SINCE SCHOOL.
SCHOOL?
I WENT TO A BRITISH BOARDING SCHOOL. KEPT THE TIE AND LOST THE ACCENT.
PITY, I LOVE THE ACCENT.
WHAT'S YOUR STORY, OXFORD?
NOPE.
RAISED SUBURBAN, WENT TO U. PENN, COLUMBIA BUSINESS SCHOOL—AND HERE I AM TODAY TALKING TO YOU.
THE AMERICAN DREAM...
WHY BOARDING SCHOOL?
LONG STORY.
WALK ME HOME AND TELL ME.

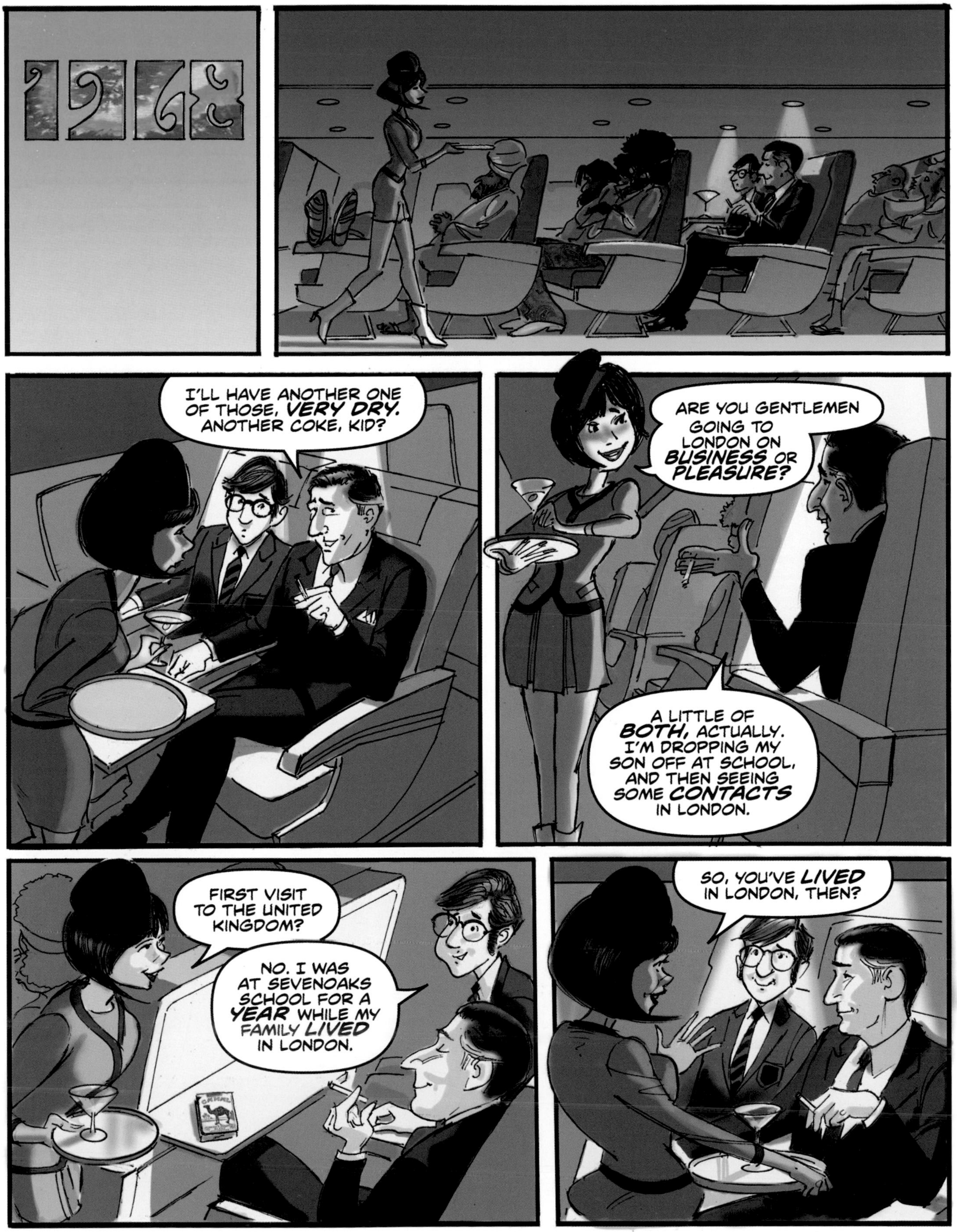
1963
I'LL HAVE ANOTHER ONE OF THOSE, VERY DRY. ANOTHER COKE, KID?
ARE YOU GENTLEMEN GOING TO LONDON ON BUSINESS OR PLEASURE?
A LITTLE OF BOTH, ACTUALLY. I'M DROPPING MY SON OFF AT SCHOOL, AND THEN SEEING SOME CONTACTS IN LONDON.
FIRST VISIT TO THE UNITED KINGDOM?
NO. I WAS AT SEVENOAKS SCHOOL FOR A YEAR WHILE MY FAMILY LIVED IN LONDON.
SO, YOU'VE LIVED IN LONDON, THEN?

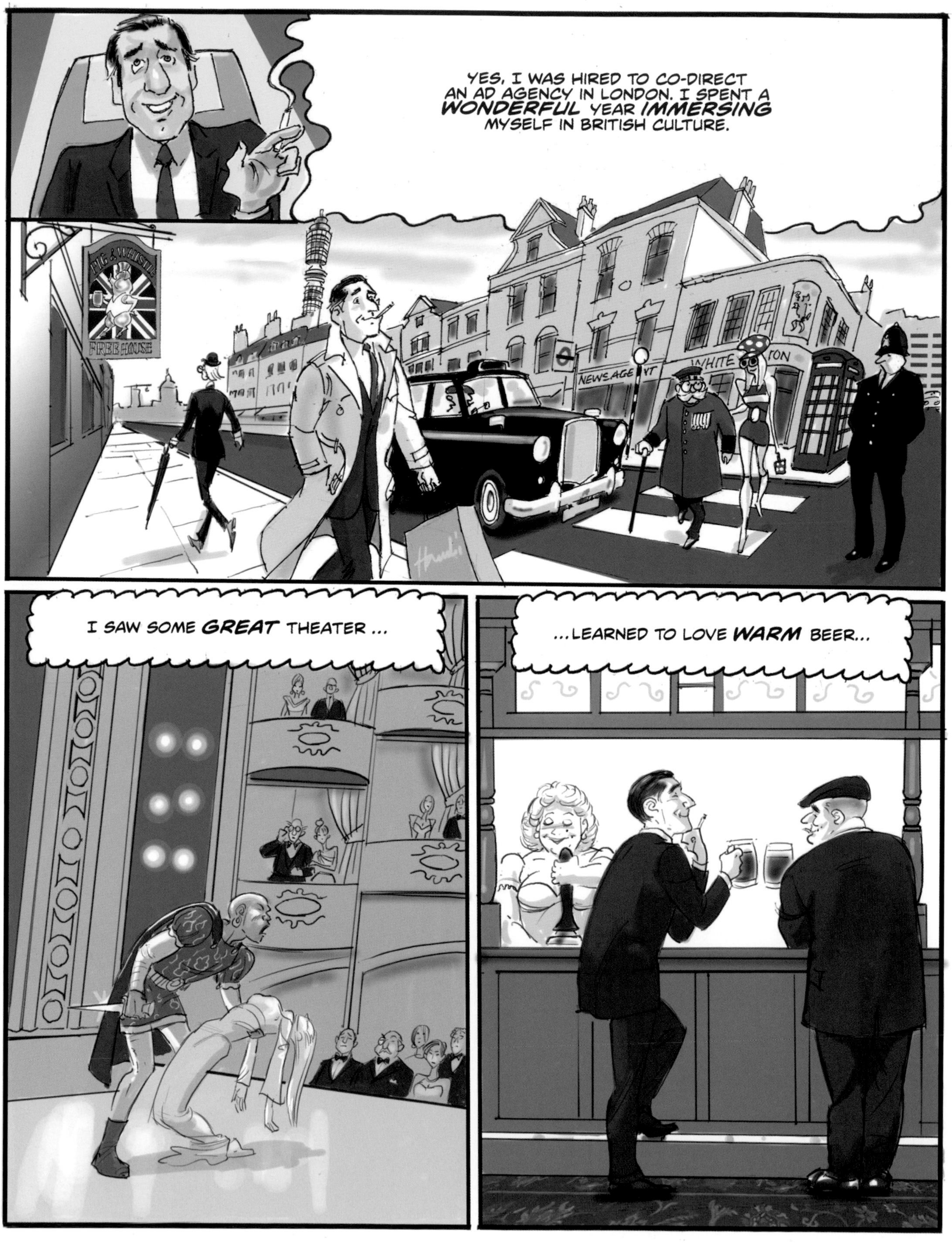

YES, I WAS HIRED TO CO-DIRECT AN AD AGENCY IN LONDON. I SPENT A WONDERFUL YEAR IMMERSING MYSELF IN BRITISH CULTURE.
I SAW SOME GREAT THEATER ...
...LEARNED TO LOVE WARM BEER...

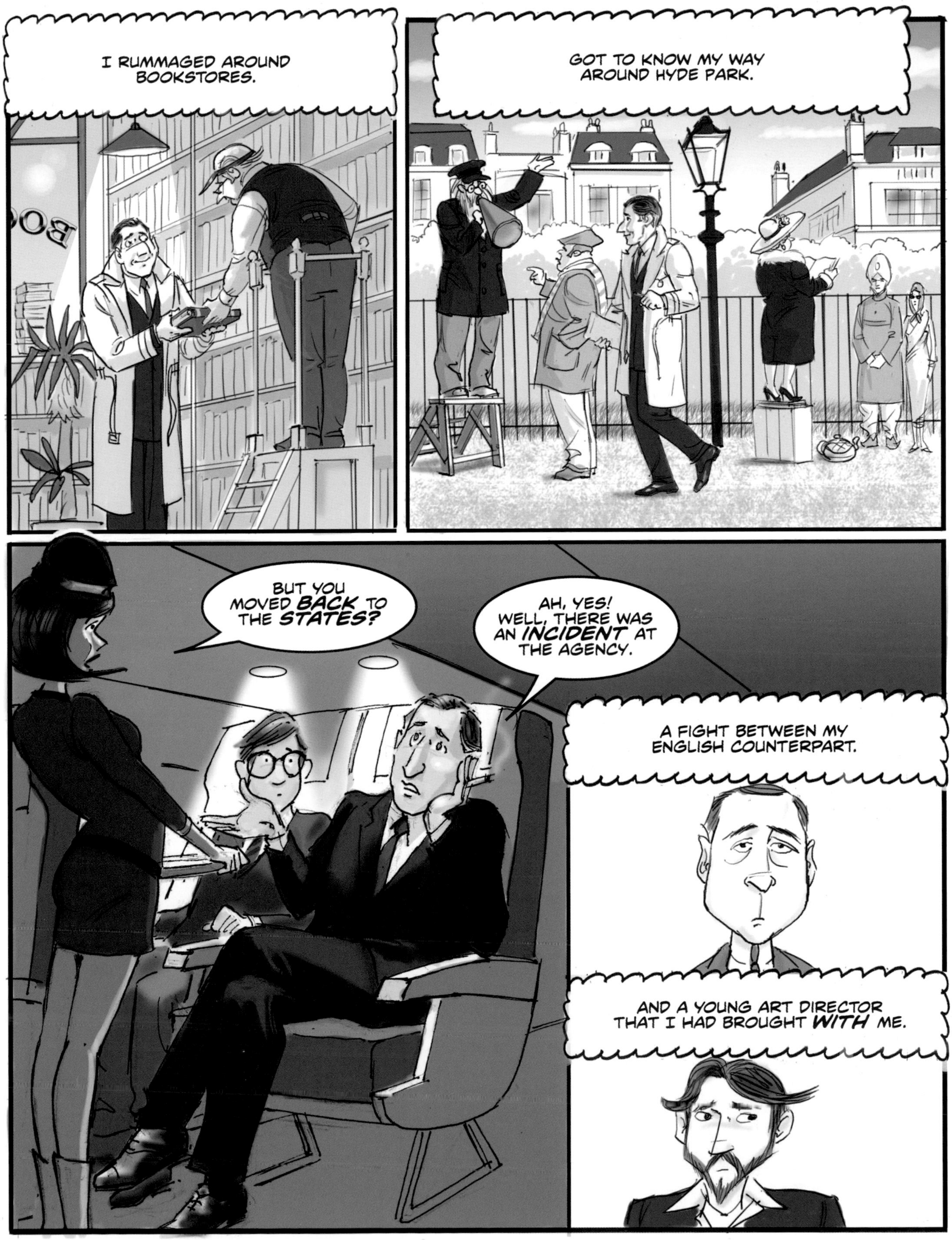

I RUMMAGED AROUND BOOKSTORES.
GOT TO KNOW MY WAY AROUND HYDE PARK.
BUT YOU MOVED BACK TO THE STATES?
AH, YES! WELL, THERE WAS AN INCIDENT AT THE AGENCY.
A FIGHT BETWEEN MY ENGLISH COUNTERPART.
AND A YOUNG ART DIRECTOR THAT I HAD BROUGHT WITH ME.

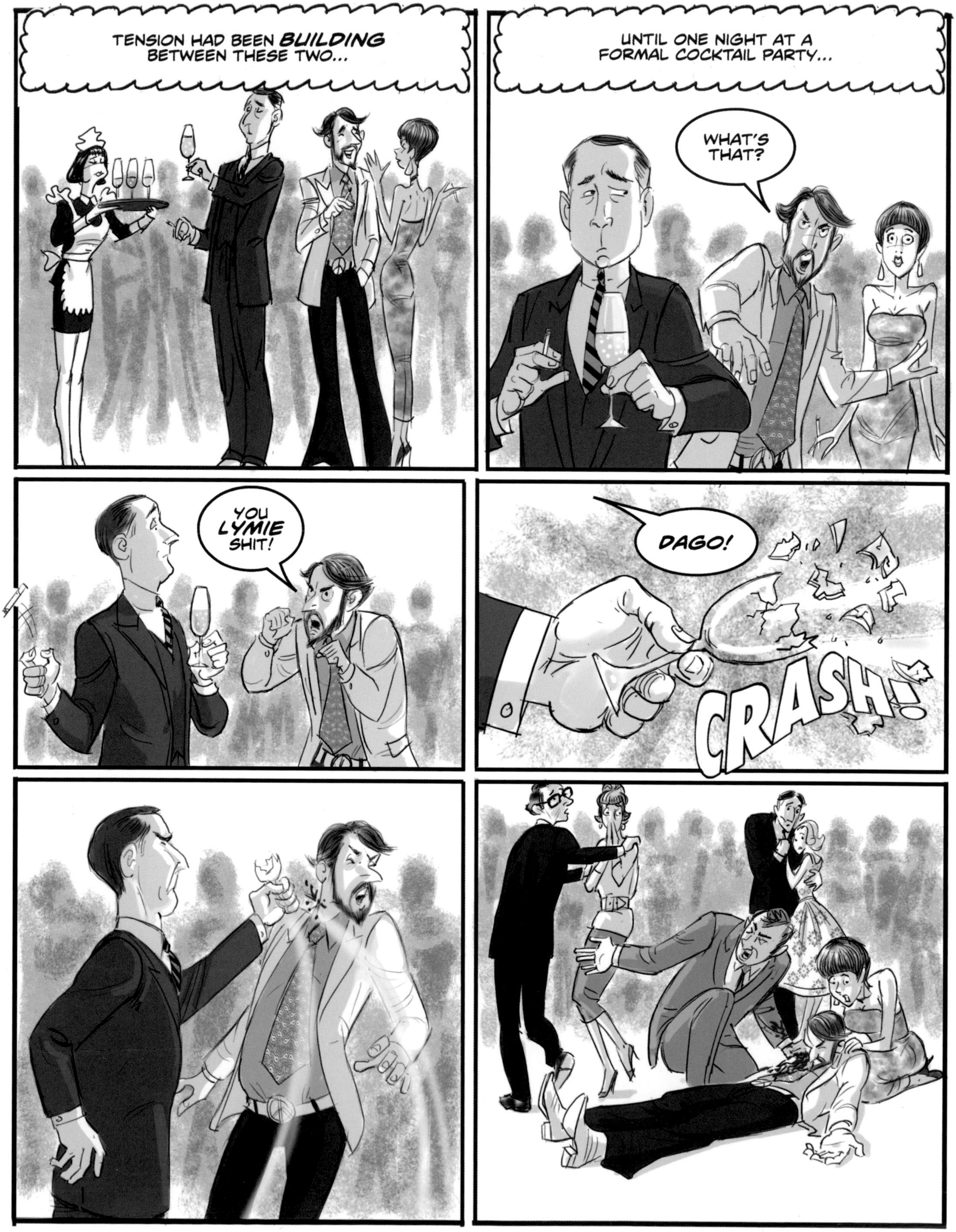
TENSION HAD BEEN BUILDING BETWEEN THESE TWO...
UNTIL ONE NIGHT AT A FORMAL COCKTAIL PARTY...
WHAT'S THAT?
YOU LYMIE SHIT!
DAGO!
CRASH!

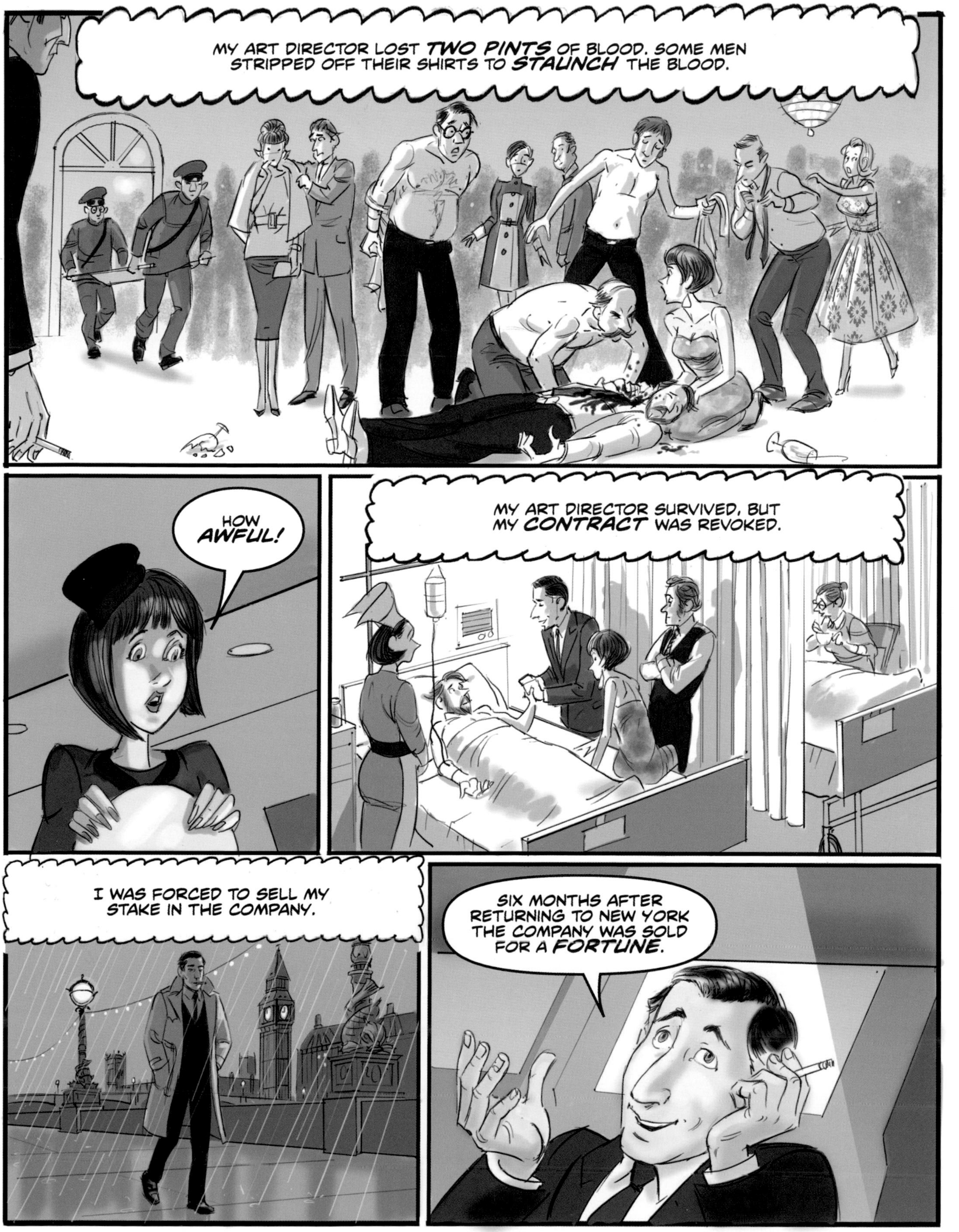
MY ART DIRECTOR LOST TWO PINTS OF BLOOD. SOME MEN STRIPPED OFF THEIR SHIRTS TO STAUNCH THE BLOOD.
HOW AWFUL!
MY ART DIRECTOR SURVIVED, BUT MY CONTRACT WAS REVOKED.
I WAS FORCED TO SELL MY STAKE IN THE COMPANY.
SIX MONTHS AFTER RETURNING TO NEW YORK THE COMPANY WAS SOLD FOR A FORTUNE.

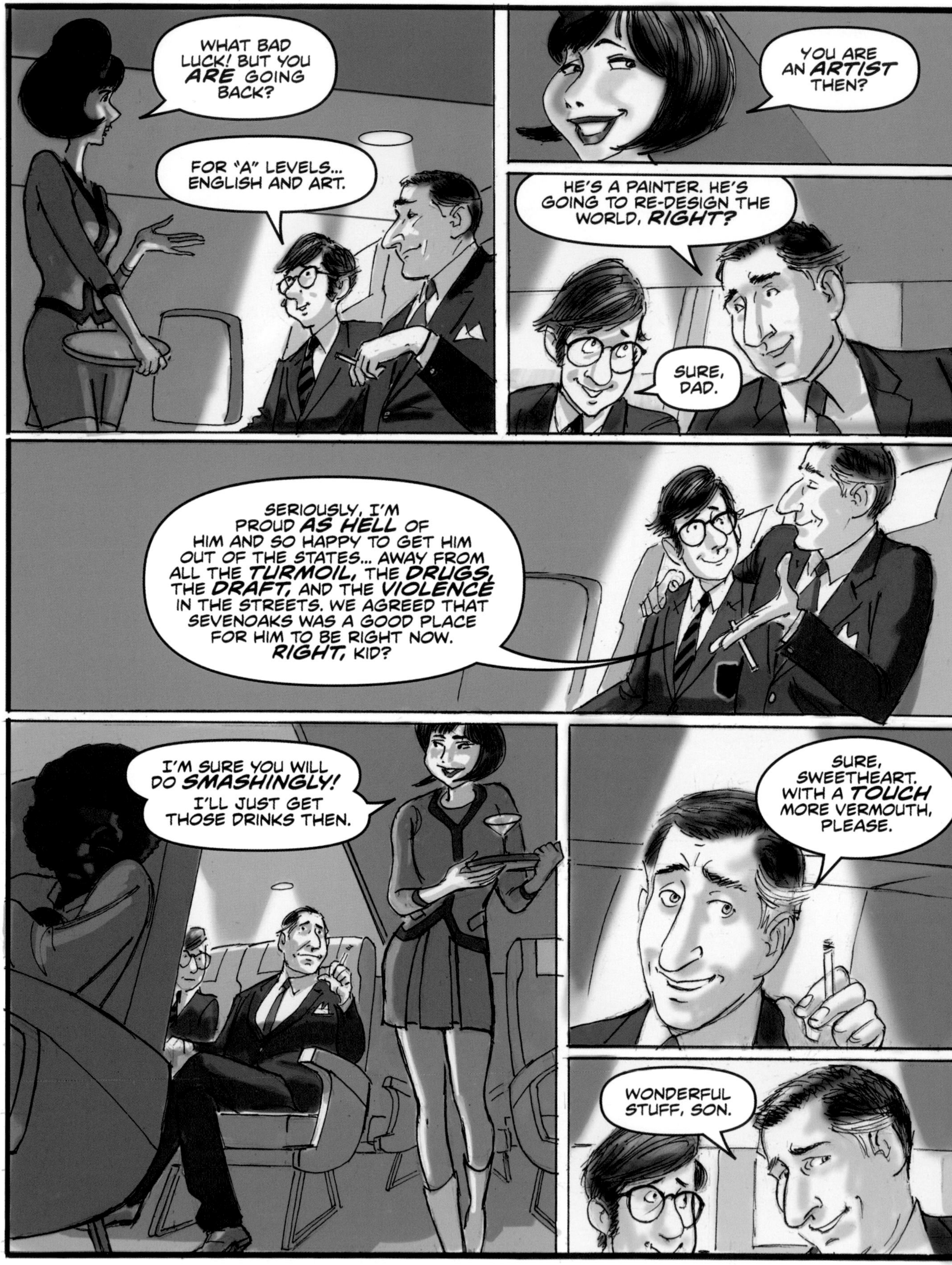
WHAT BAD LUCK! BUT YOU ARE GOING BACK?
FOR "A" LEVELS... ENGLISH AND ART.
YOU ARE AN ARTIST THEN?
HE'S A PAINTER. HE'S GOING TO RE-DESIGN THE WORLD, RIGHT?
SURE, DAD.
SERIOUSLY, I'M PROUD AS HELL OF HIM AND SO HAPPY TO GET HIM OUT OF THE STATES... AWAY FROM ALL THE TURMOIL, THE DRUGS, THE DRAFT, AND THE VIOLENCE IN THE STREETS. WE AGREED THAT SEVENOAKS WAS A GOOD PLACE FOR HIM TO BE RIGHT NOW. RIGHT, KID?
I'M SURE YOU WILL DO SMASHINGLY! I'LL JUST GET THOSE DRINKS THEN.
SURE, SWEETHEART. WITH A TOUCH MORE VERMOUTH, PLEASE.
WONDERFUL STUFF, SON.

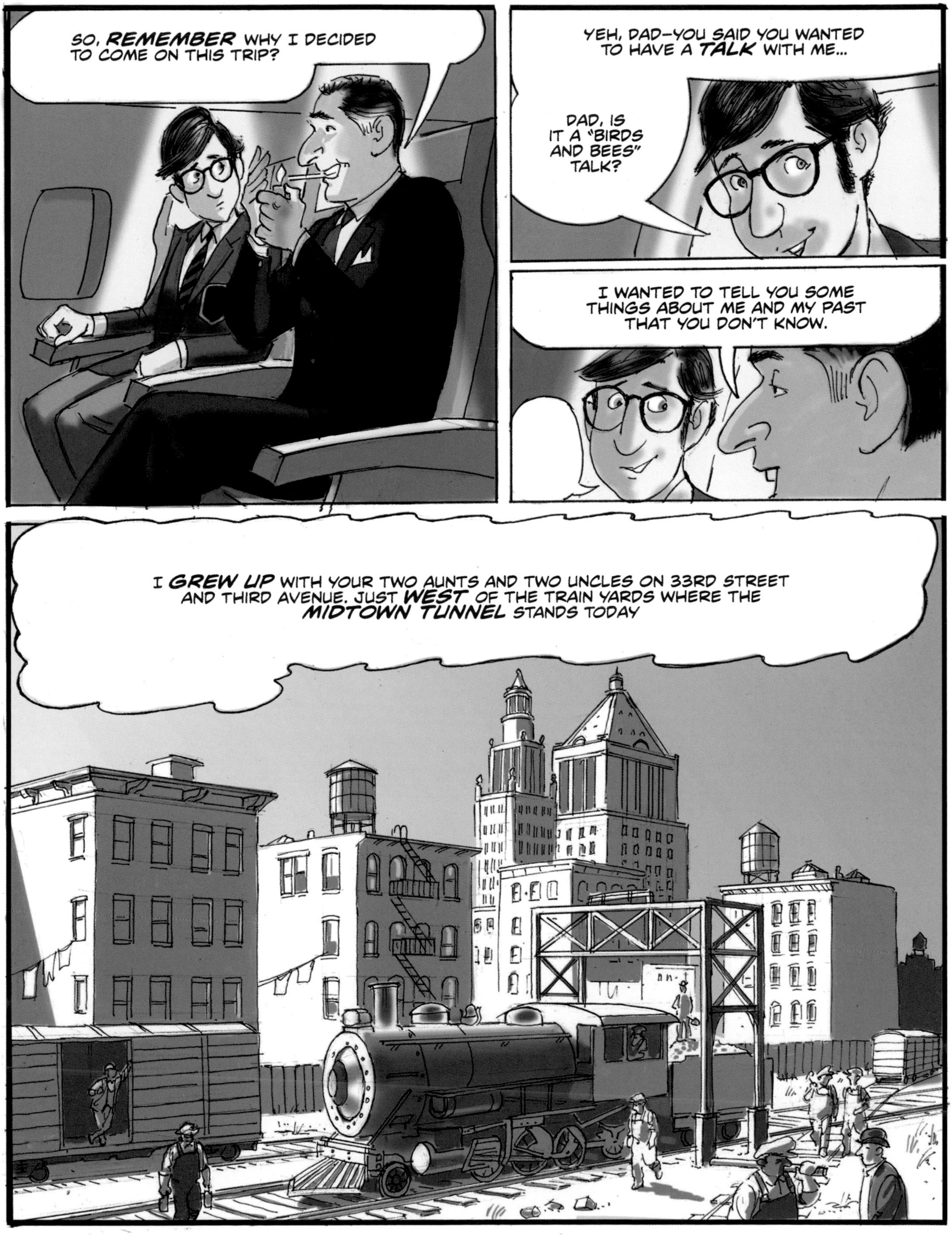
SO, REMEMBER WHY I DECIDED TO COME ON THIS TRIP?
YEH, DAD—YOU SAID YOU WANTED TO HAVE A TALK WITH ME...
DAD, IS IT A "BIRDS AND BEES" TALK?
I WANTED TO TELL YOU SOME THINGS ABOUT ME AND MY PAST THAT YOU DON'T KNOW.
I GREW UP WITH YOUR TWO AUNTS AND TWO UNCLES ON 33RD STREET AND THIRD AVENUE. JUST WEST OF THE TRAIN YARDS WHERE THE MIDTOWN TUNNEL STANDS TODAY

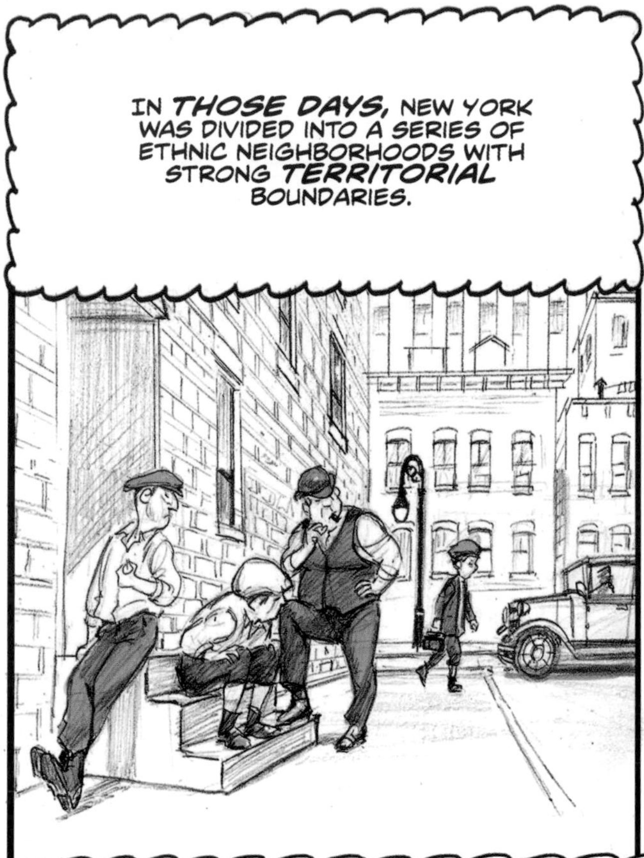
IN THOSE DAYS, NEW YORK WAS DIVIDED INTO A SERIES OF ETHNIC NEIGHBORHOODS WITH STRONG TERRITORIAL BOUNDARIES.

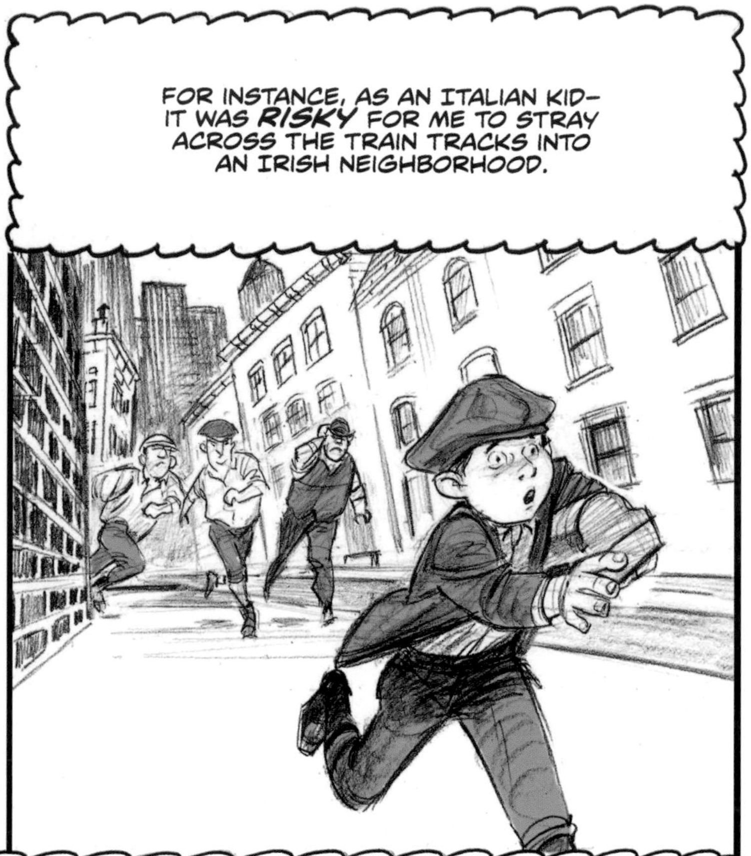
FOR INSTANCE, AS AN ITALIAN KID-IT WAS RISKY FOR ME TO STRAY ACROSS THE TRAIN TRACKS INTO AN IRISH NEIGHBORHOOD.

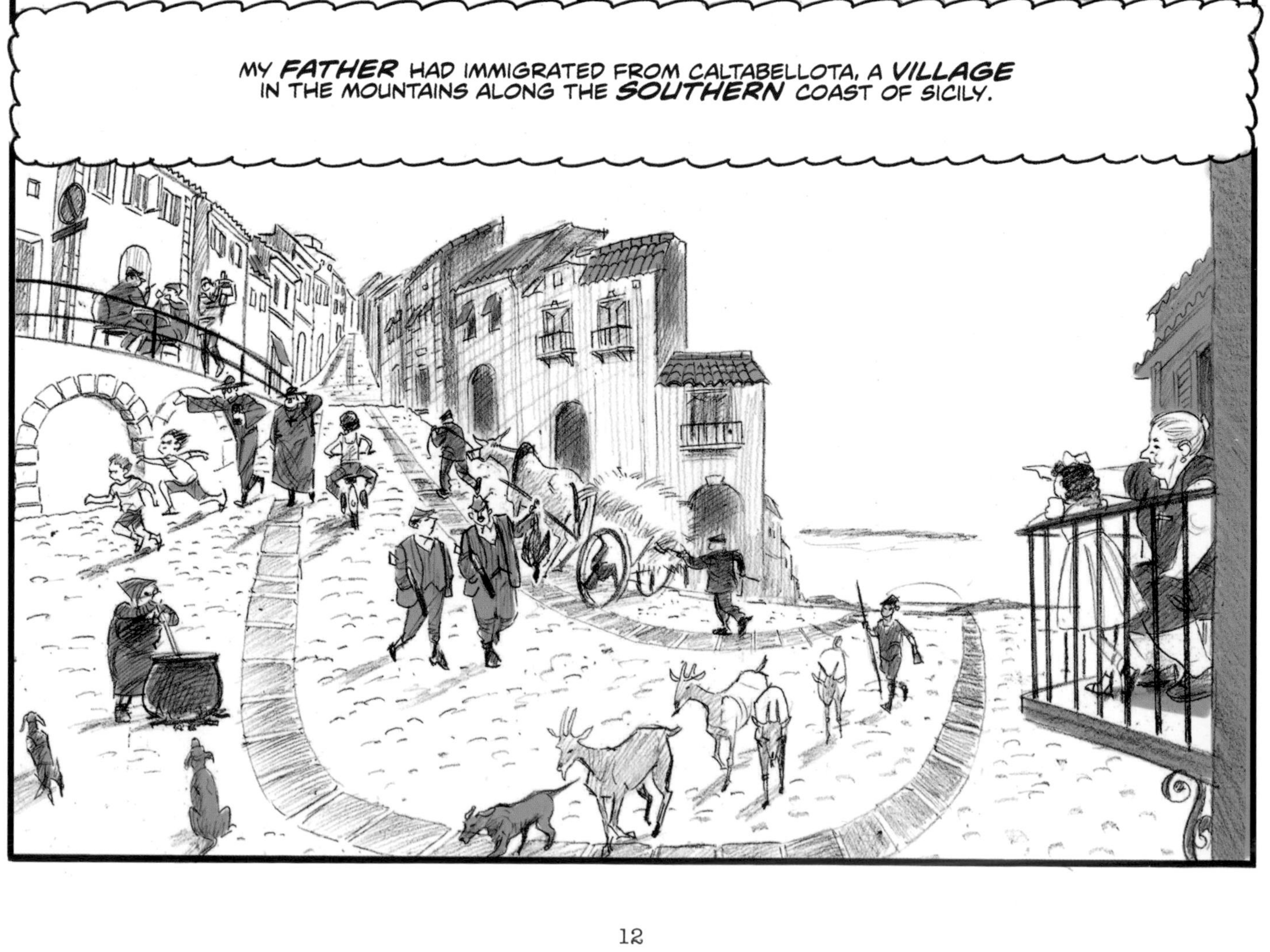
MY FATHER HAD IMMIGRATED FROM CALTABELLOTA, A VILLAGE IN THE MOUNTAINS ALONG THE SOUTHERN COAST OF SICILY.

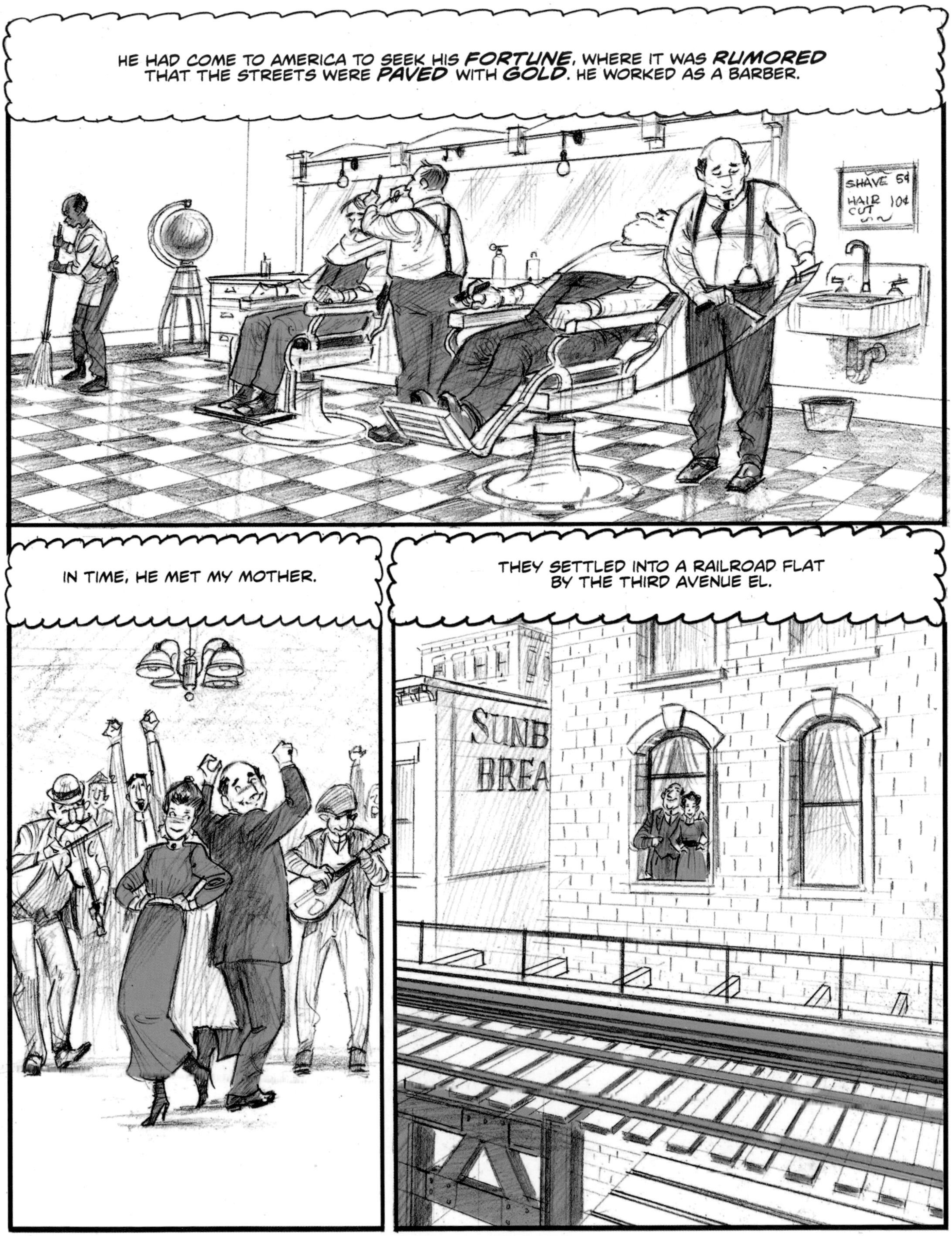

HE HAD COME TO AMERICA TO SEEK HIS ***FORTUNE***, WHERE IT WAS ***RUMORED*** THAT THE STREETS WERE ***PAVED*** WITH ***GOLD***. HE WORKED AS A BARBER.
SHAVE 5¢
HAIR CUT 10¢
IN TIME, HE MET MY MOTHER.
THEY SETTLED INTO A RAILROAD FLAT BY THE THIRD AVENUE EL.
SUNB
BREA

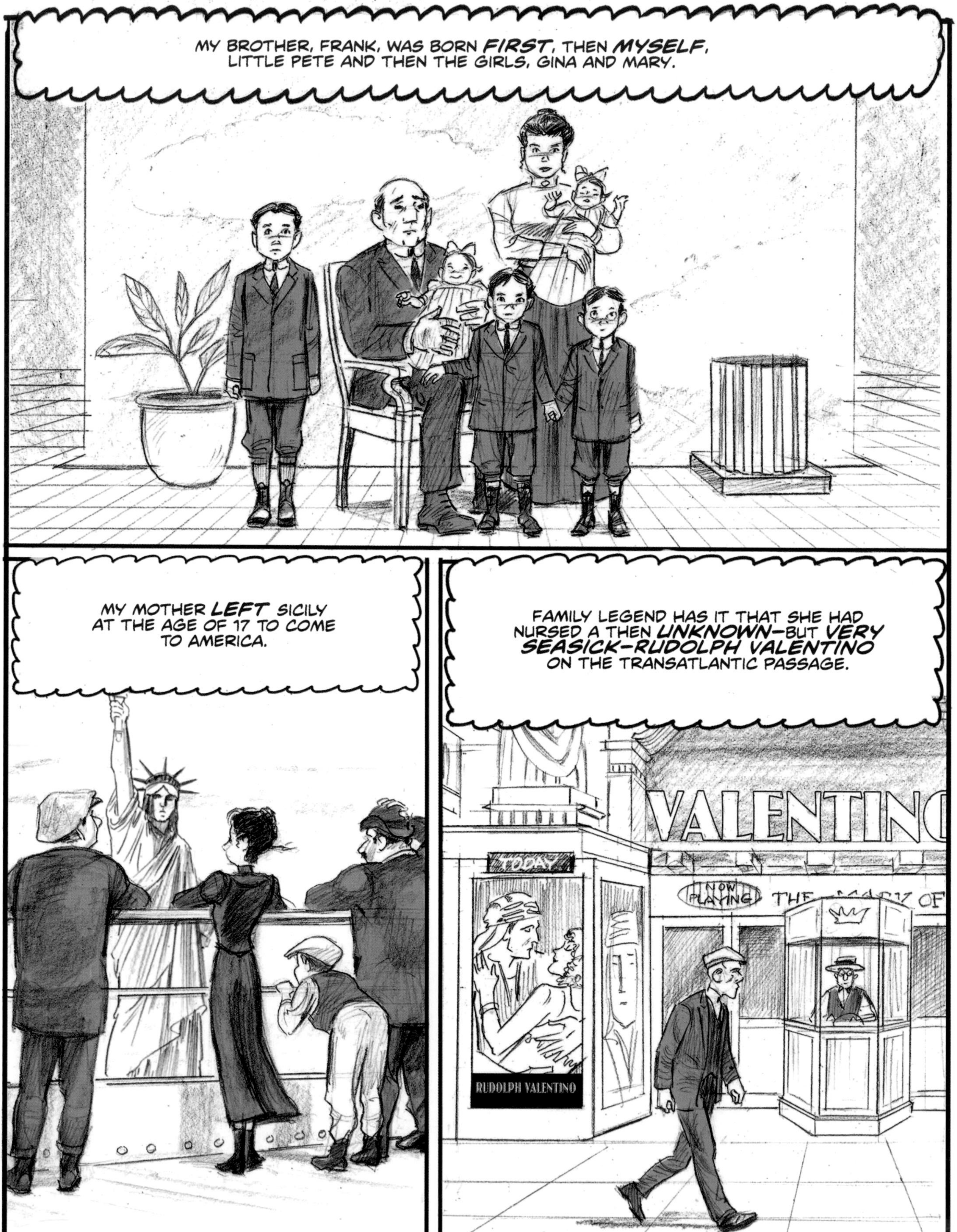
MY BROTHER, FRANK, WAS BORN FIRST, THEN MYSELF, LITTLE PETE AND THEN THE GIRLS, GINA AND MARY.
MY MOTHER LEFT SICILY AT THE AGE OF 17 TO COME TO AMERICA.
FAMILY LEGEND HAS IT THAT SHE HAD NURSED A THEN UNKNOWN—BUT VERY SEASICK—RUDOLPH VALENTINO ON THE TRANSATLANTIC PASSAGE.
VALENTINO
TODAY
NOW PLAYING
RUDOLPH VALENTINO

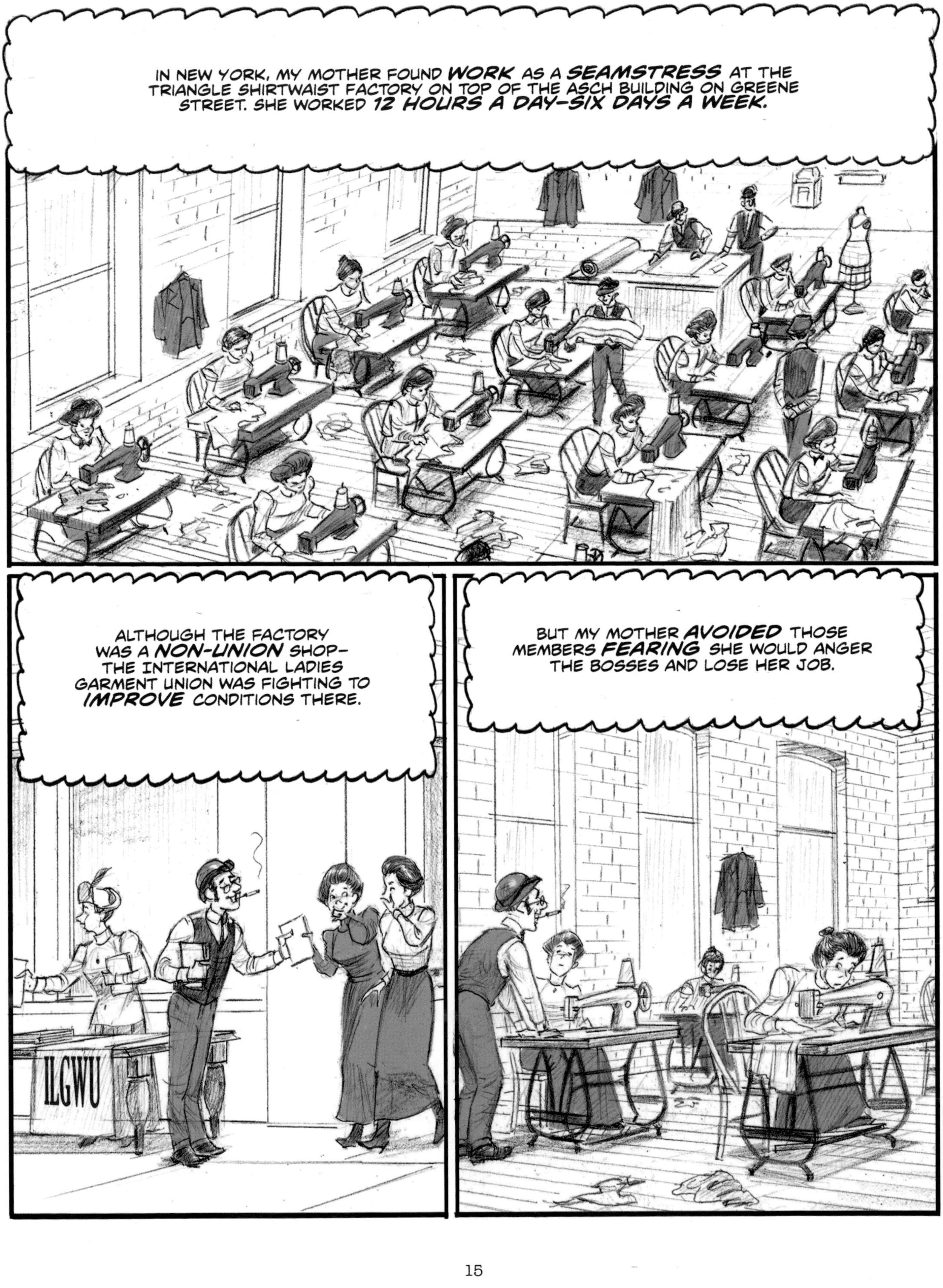
IN NEW YORK, MY MOTHER FOUND WORK AS A SEAMSTRESS AT THE TRIANGLE SHIRTWAIST FACTORY ON TOP OF THE ASCH BUILDING ON GREENE STREET. SHE WORKED 12 HOURS A DAY-SIX DAYS A WEEK.
ALTHOUGH THE FACTORY WAS A NON-UNION SHOP- THE INTERNATIONAL LADIES GARMENT UNION WAS FIGHTING TO IMPROVE CONDITIONS THERE.
ILGWU
BUT MY MOTHER AVOIDED THOSE MEMBERS FEARING SHE WOULD ANGER THE BOSSES AND LOSE HER JOB.

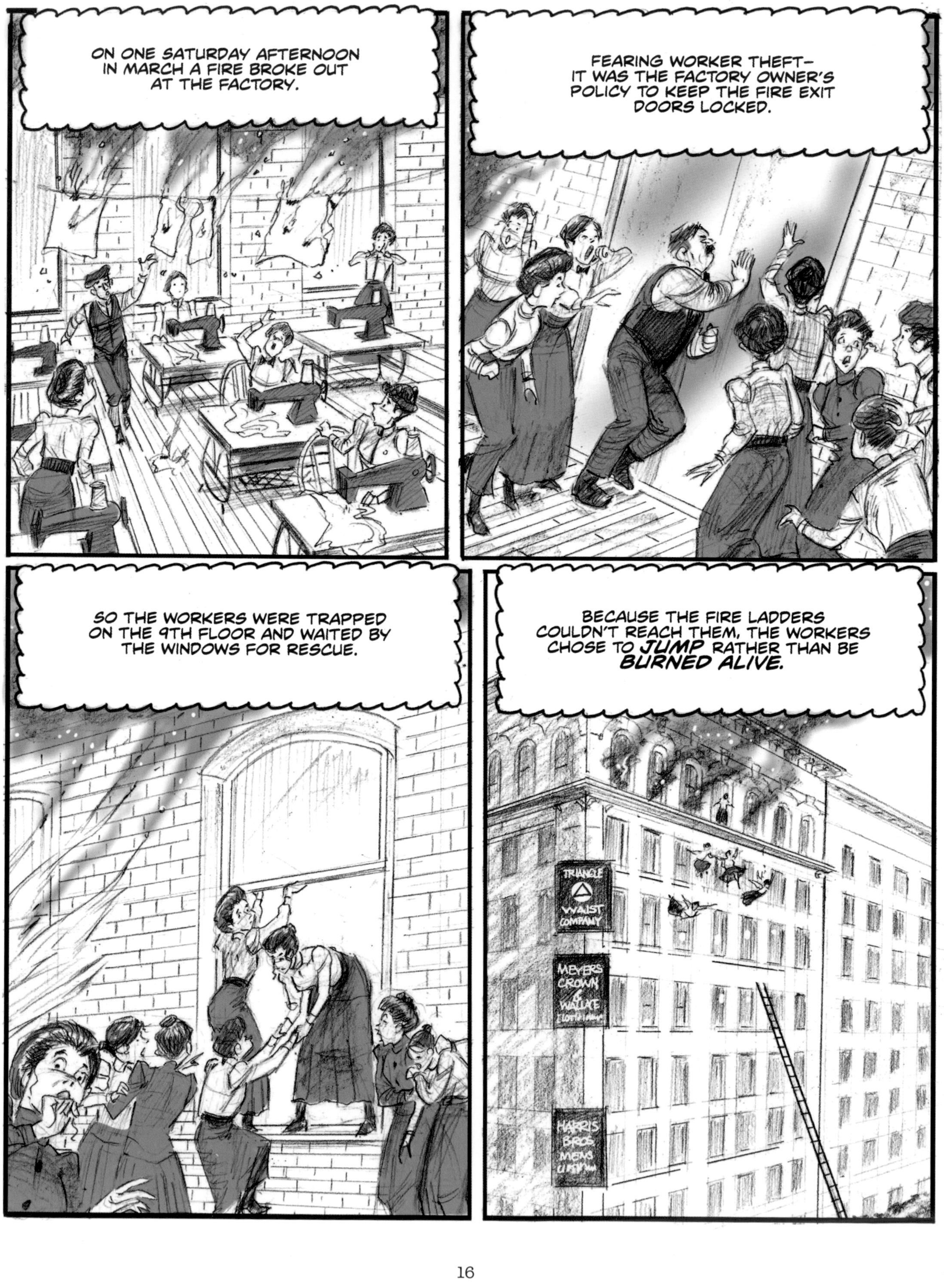
ON ONE SATURDAY AFTERNOON IN MARCH A FIRE BROKE OUT AT THE FACTORY.
FEARING WORKER THEFT— IT WAS THE FACTORY OWNER'S POLICY TO KEEP THE FIRE EXIT DOORS LOCKED.
SO THE WORKERS WERE TRAPPED ON THE 9TH FLOOR AND WAITED BY THE WINDOWS FOR RESCUE.
BECAUSE THE FIRE LADDERS COULDN'T REACH THEM, THE WORKERS CHOSE TO ***JUMP*** RATHER THAN BE ***BURNED ALIVE.***
TRIANGLE
WAIST COMPANY
MEYERS CROWN & WALLACE
HARRIS BROS. MENS

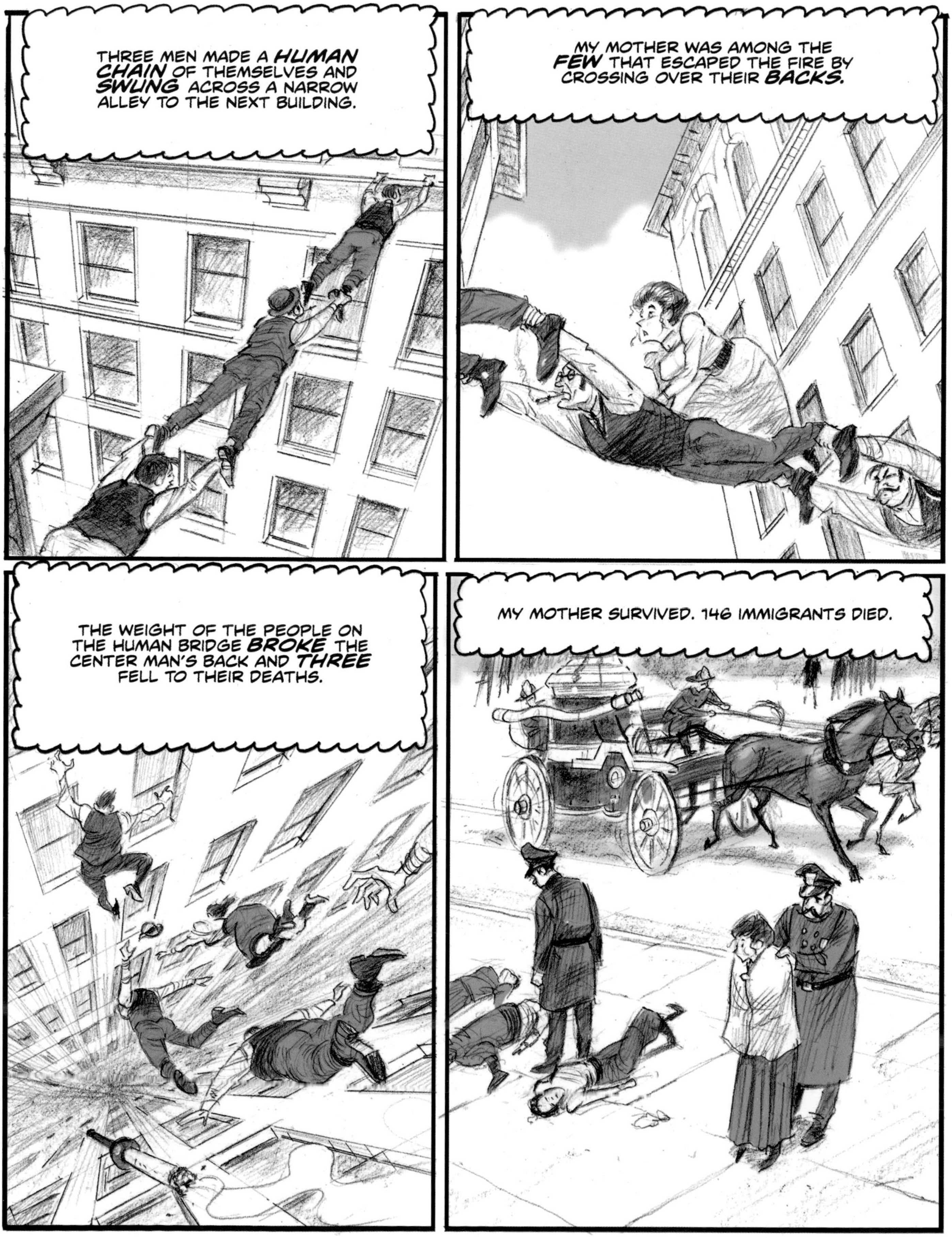
THREE MEN MADE A HUMAN CHAIN OF THEMSELVES AND SWUNG ACROSS A NARROW ALLEY TO THE NEXT BUILDING.
MY MOTHER WAS AMONG THE FEW THAT ESCAPED THE FIRE BY CROSSING OVER THEIR BACKS.
THE WEIGHT OF THE PEOPLE ON THE HUMAN BRIDGE BROKE THE CENTER MAN'S BACK AND THREE FELL TO THEIR DEATHS.
MY MOTHER SURVIVED. 146 IMMIGRANTS DIED.

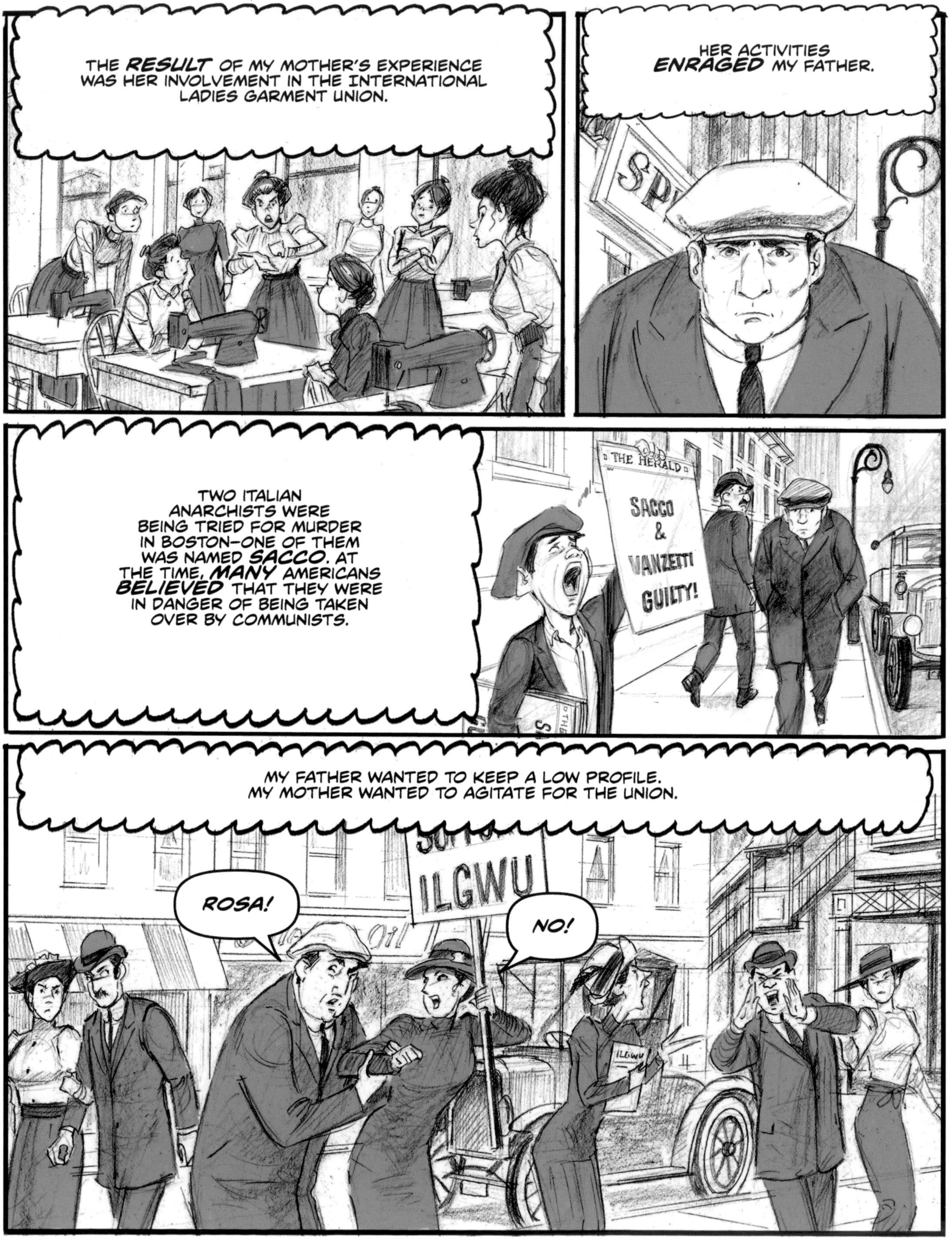
THE RESULT OF MY MOTHER'S EXPERIENCE WAS HER INVOLVEMENT IN THE INTERNATIONAL LADIES GARMENT UNION.
HER ACTIVITIES ENRAGED MY FATHER.
SP
TWO ITALIAN ANARCHISTS WERE BEING TRIED FOR MURDER IN BOSTON—ONE OF THEM WAS NAMED SACCO. AT THE TIME, MANY AMERICANS BELIEVED THAT THEY WERE IN DANGER OF BEING TAKEN OVER BY COMMUNISTS.
THE HERALD
SACCO & VANZETTI GUILTY!
MY FATHER WANTED TO KEEP A LOW PROFILE. MY MOTHER WANTED TO AGITATE FOR THE UNION.
ILGWU
ROSA!
NO!
ILGWU

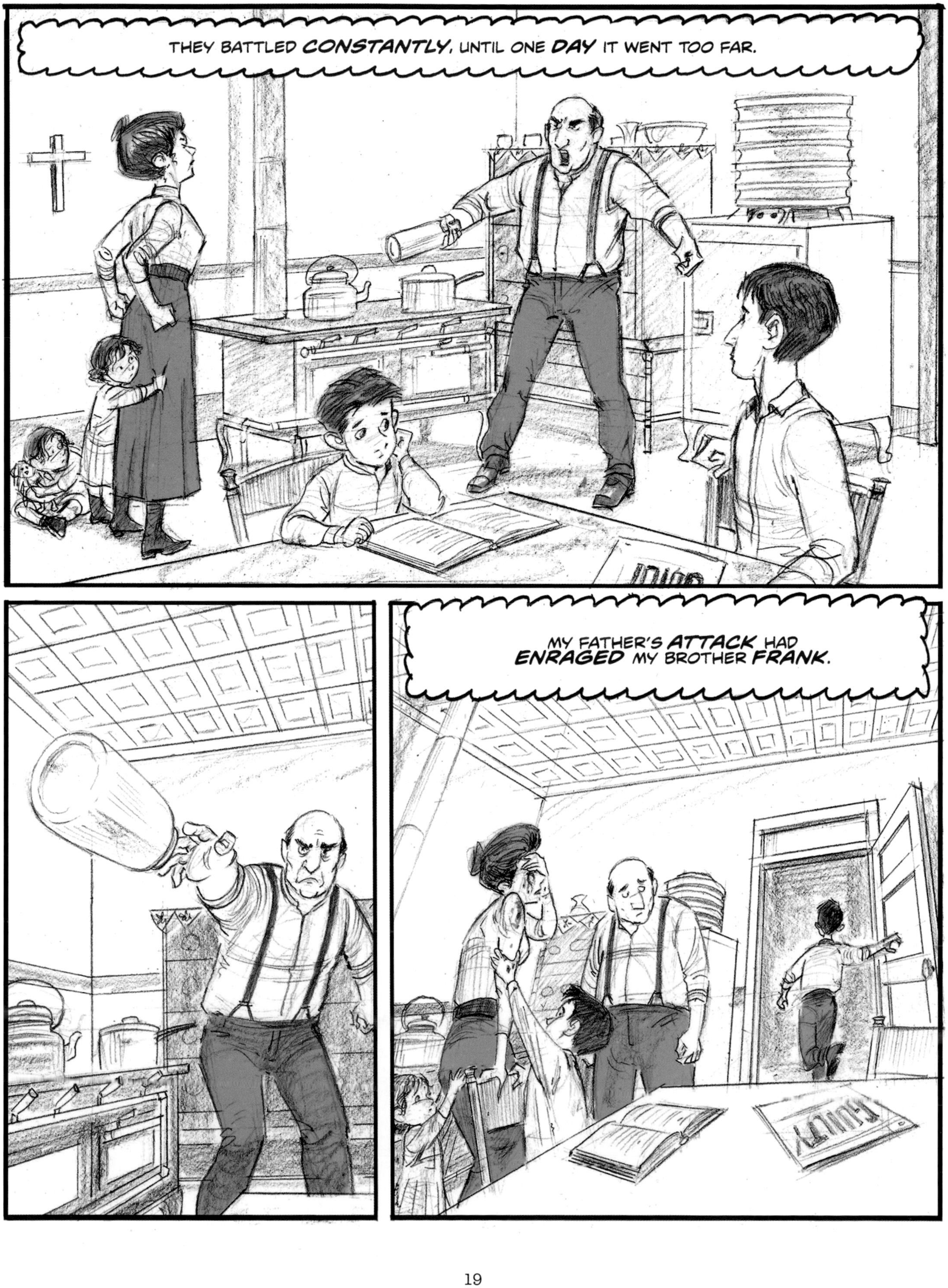
THEY BATTLED CONSTANTLY, UNTIL ONE DAY IT WENT TOO FAR.
MY FATHER'S ATTACK HAD ENRAGED MY BROTHER FRANK.

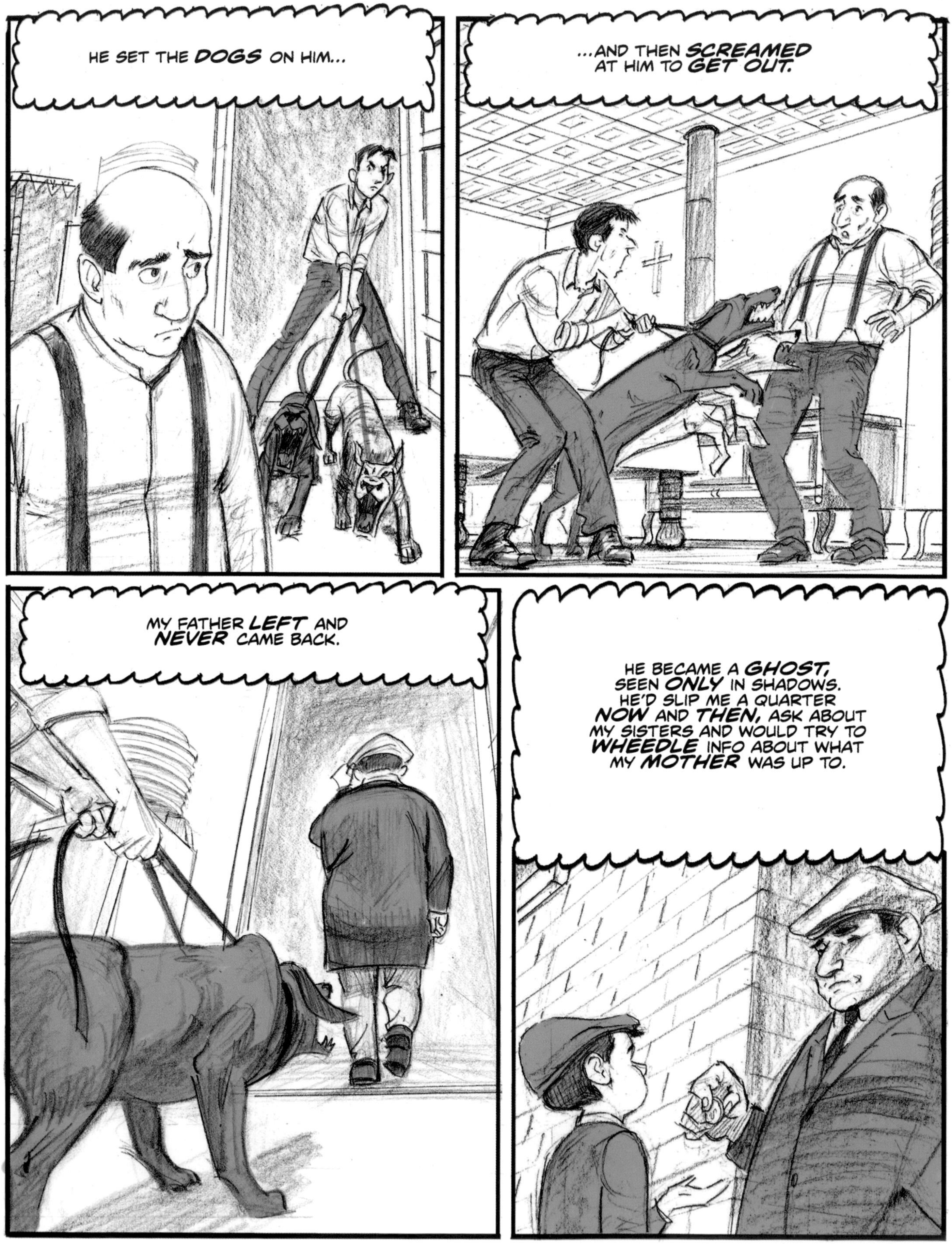
HE SET THE DOGS ON HIM...
...AND THEN SCREAMED AT HIM TO GET OUT.
MY FATHER LEFT AND NEVER CAME BACK.
HE BECAME A GHOST, SEEN ONLY IN SHADOWS. HE'D SLIP ME A QUARTER NOW AND THEN, ASK ABOUT MY SISTERS AND WOULD TRY TO WHEEDLE INFO ABOUT WHAT MY MOTHER WAS UP TO.

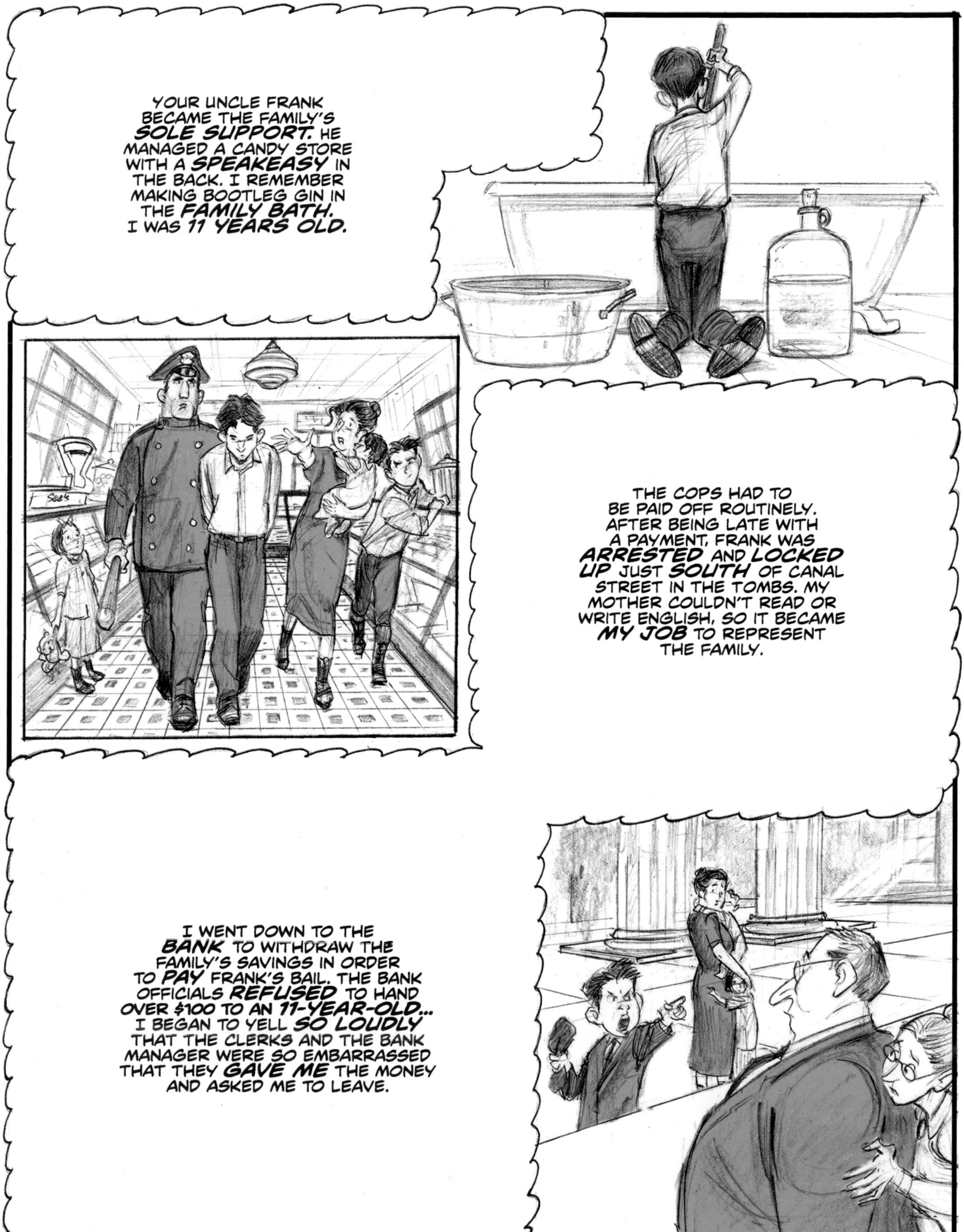
YOUR UNCLE FRANK BECAME THE FAMILY'S SOLE SUPPORT. HE MANAGED A CANDY STORE WITH A SPEAKEASY IN THE BACK. I REMEMBER MAKING BOOTLEG GIN IN THE FAMILY BATH. I WAS 11 YEARS OLD.
THE COPS HAD TO BE PAID OFF ROUTINELY. AFTER BEING LATE WITH A PAYMENT, FRANK WAS ARRESTED AND LOCKED UP JUST SOUTH OF CANAL STREET IN THE TOMBS. MY MOTHER COULDN'T READ OR WRITE ENGLISH, SO IT BECAME MY JOB TO REPRESENT THE FAMILY.
I WENT DOWN TO THE BANK TO WITHDRAW THE FAMILY'S SAVINGS IN ORDER TO PAY FRANK'S BAIL. THE BANK OFFICIALS REFUSED TO HAND OVER $100 TO AN 11-YEAR-OLD... I BEGAN TO YELL SO LOUDLY THAT THE CLERKS AND THE BANK MANAGER WERE SO EMBARRASSED THAT THEY GAVE ME THE MONEY AND ASKED ME TO LEAVE.

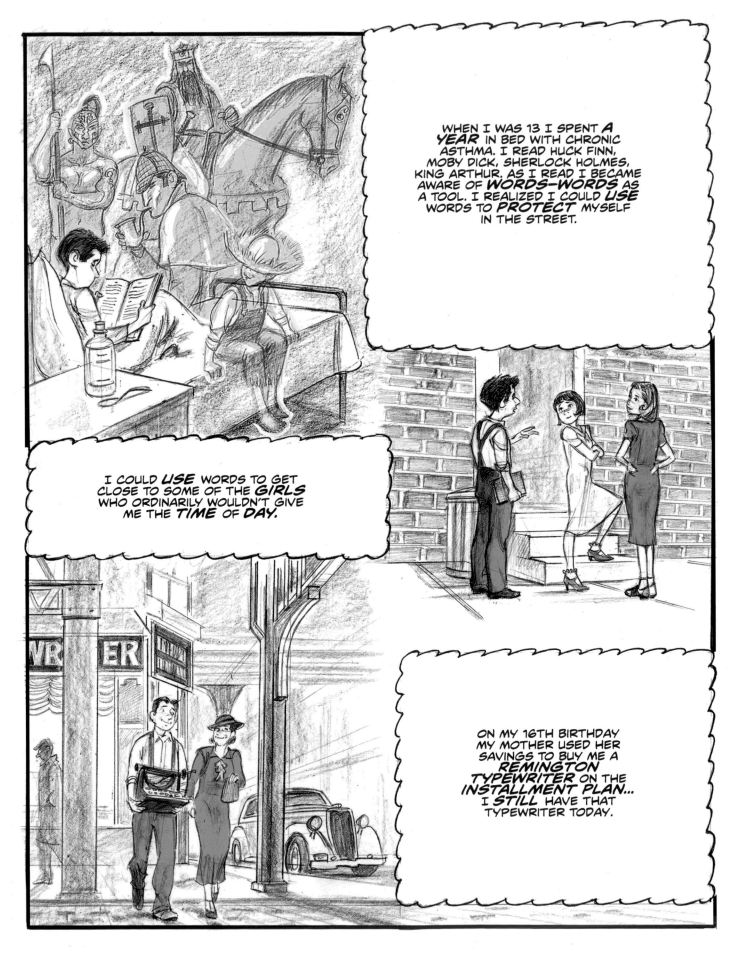

WHEN I WAS 13 I SPENT *A YEAR* IN BED WITH CHRONIC ASTHMA. I READ HUCK FINN, MOBY DICK, SHERLOCK HOLMES, KING ARTHUR. AS I READ I BECAME AWARE OF *WORDS—WORDS* AS A TOOL. I REALIZED I COULD *USE* WORDS TO *PROTECT* MYSELF IN THE STREET.

I COULD *USE* WORDS TO GET CLOSE TO SOME OF THE *GIRLS* WHO ORDINARILY WOULDN'T GIVE ME THE *TIME* OF *DAY*.

ON MY 16TH BIRTHDAY MY MOTHER USED HER SAVINGS TO BUY ME A *REMINGTON TYPEWRITER* ON THE *INSTALLMENT PLAN*... I *STILL* HAVE THAT TYPEWRITER TODAY.

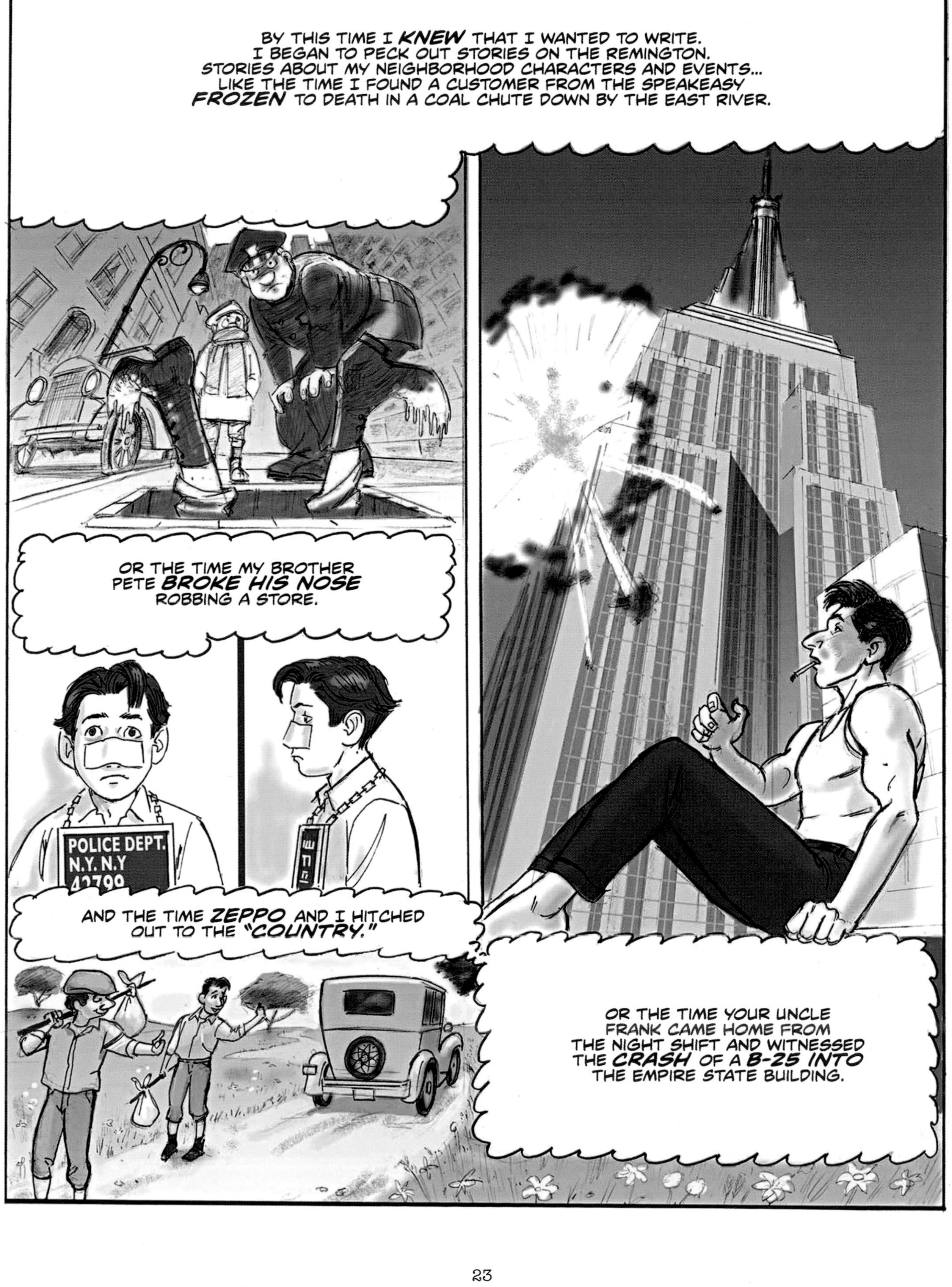
BY THIS TIME I KNEW THAT I WANTED TO WRITE. I BEGAN TO PECK OUT STORIES ON THE REMINGTON. STORIES ABOUT MY NEIGHBORHOOD CHARACTERS AND EVENTS... LIKE THE TIME I FOUND A CUSTOMER FROM THE SPEAKEASY FROZEN TO DEATH IN A COAL CHUTE DOWN BY THE EAST RIVER.
OR THE TIME MY BROTHER PETE BROKE HIS NOSE ROBBING A STORE.
POLICE DEPT.
N.Y. N.Y
AND THE TIME ZEPPO AND I HITCHED OUT TO THE "COUNTRY."
OR THE TIME YOUR UNCLE FRANK CAME HOME FROM THE NIGHT SHIFT AND WITNESSED THE CRASH OF A B-25 INTO THE EMPIRE STATE BUILDING.

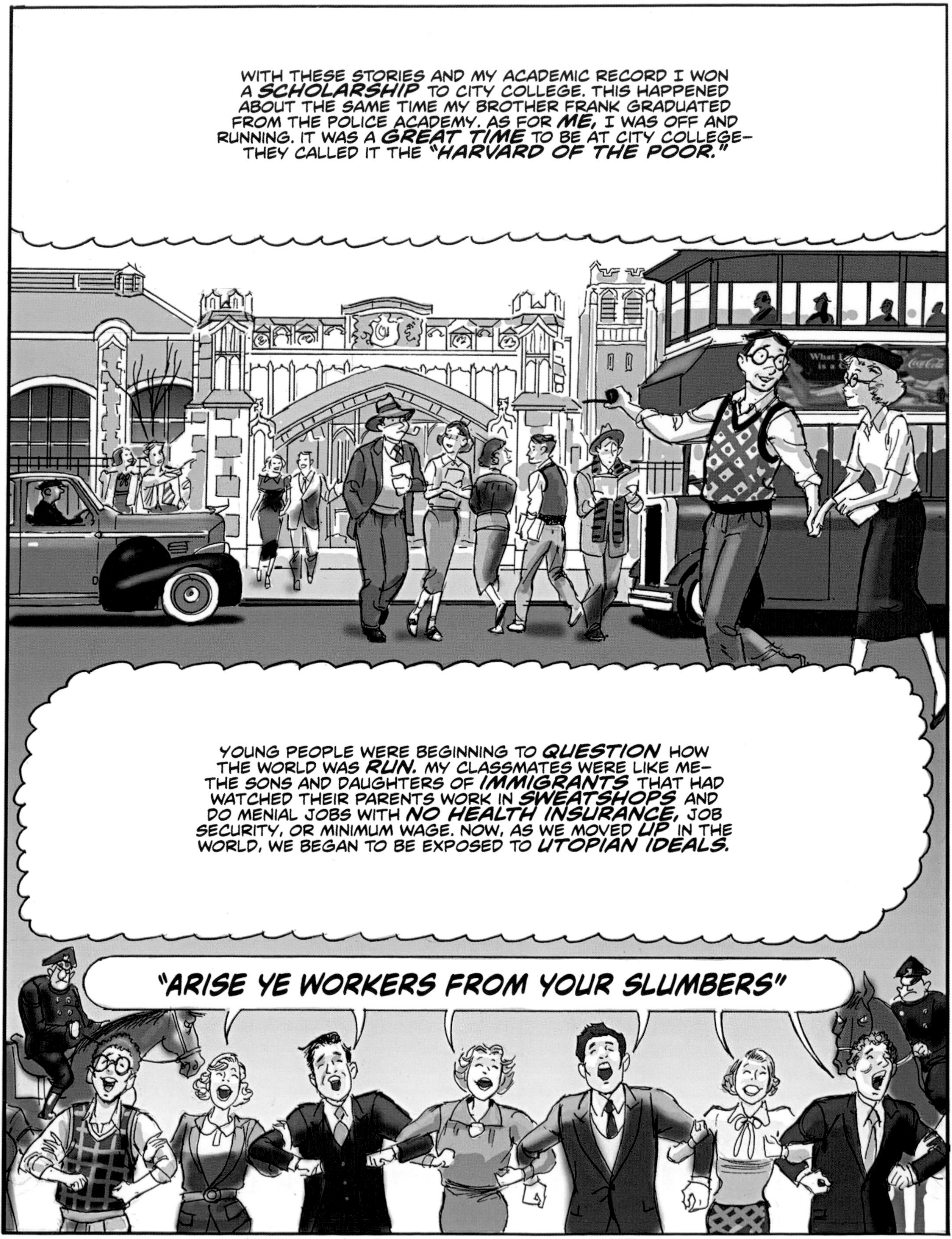
WITH THESE STORIES AND MY ACADEMIC RECORD I WON A SCHOLARSHIP TO CITY COLLEGE. THIS HAPPENED ABOUT THE SAME TIME MY BROTHER FRANK GRADUATED FROM THE POLICE ACADEMY. AS FOR ME, I WAS OFF AND RUNNING. IT WAS A GREAT TIME TO BE AT CITY COLLEGE– THEY CALLED IT THE "HARVARD OF THE POOR."
YOUNG PEOPLE WERE BEGINNING TO QUESTION HOW THE WORLD WAS RUN. MY CLASSMATES WERE LIKE ME– THE SONS AND DAUGHTERS OF IMMIGRANTS THAT HAD WATCHED THEIR PARENTS WORK IN SWEATSHOPS AND DO MENIAL JOBS WITH NO HEALTH INSURANCE, JOB SECURITY, OR MINIMUM WAGE. NOW, AS WE MOVED UP IN THE WORLD, WE BEGAN TO BE EXPOSED TO UTOPIAN IDEALS.
"ARISE YE WORKERS FROM YOUR SLUMBERS"

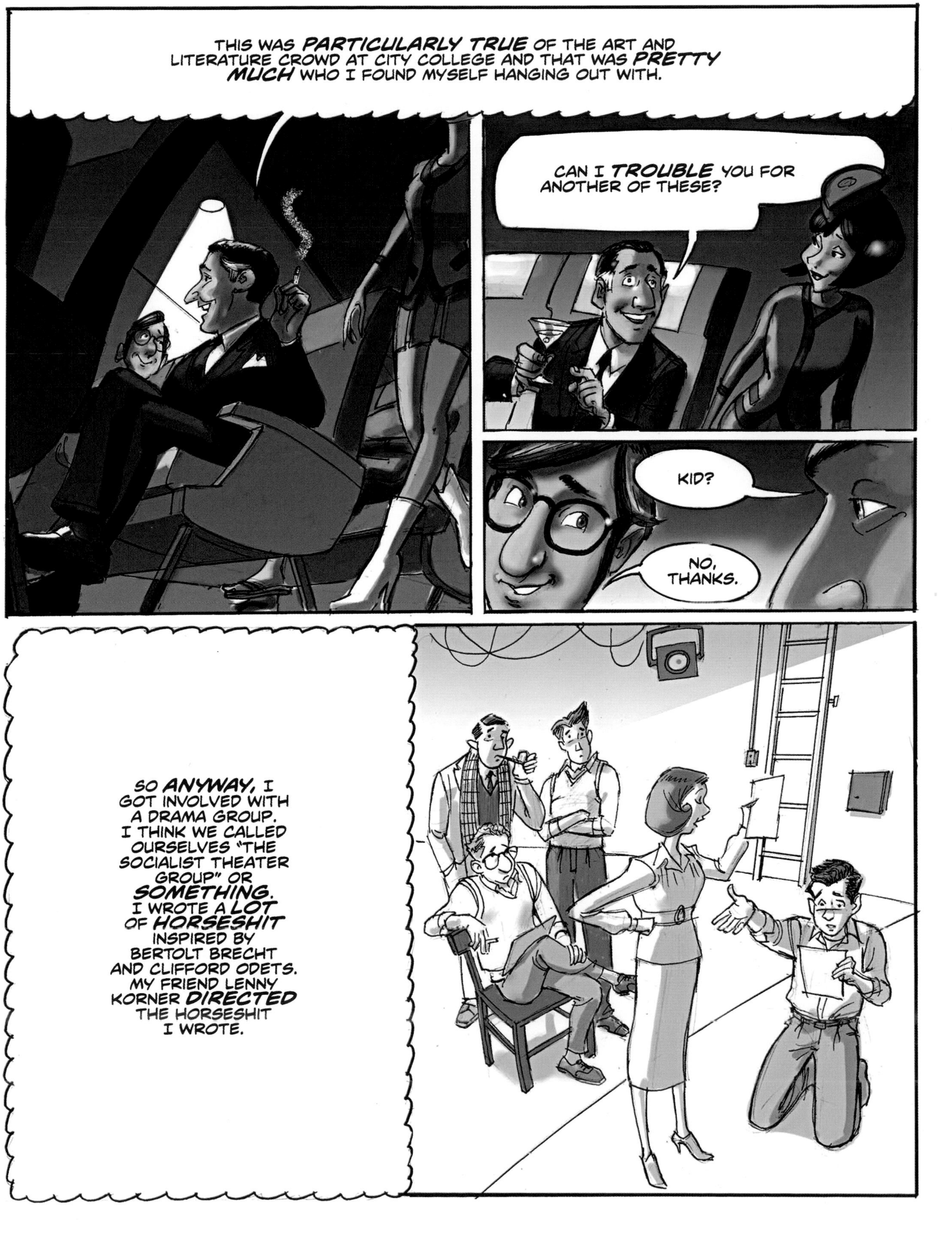
THIS WAS PARTICULARLY TRUE OF THE ART AND LITERATURE CROWD AT CITY COLLEGE AND THAT WAS PRETTY MUCH WHO I FOUND MYSELF HANGING OUT WITH.
CAN I TROUBLE YOU FOR ANOTHER OF THESE?
KID?
NO, THANKS.
SO ANYWAY, I GOT INVOLVED WITH A DRAMA GROUP. I THINK WE CALLED OURSELVES "THE SOCIALIST THEATER GROUP" OR SOMETHING. I WROTE A LOT OF HORSESHIT INSPIRED BY BERTOLT BRECHT AND CLIFFORD ODETS. MY FRIEND LENNY KORNER DIRECTED THE HORSESHIT I WROTE.

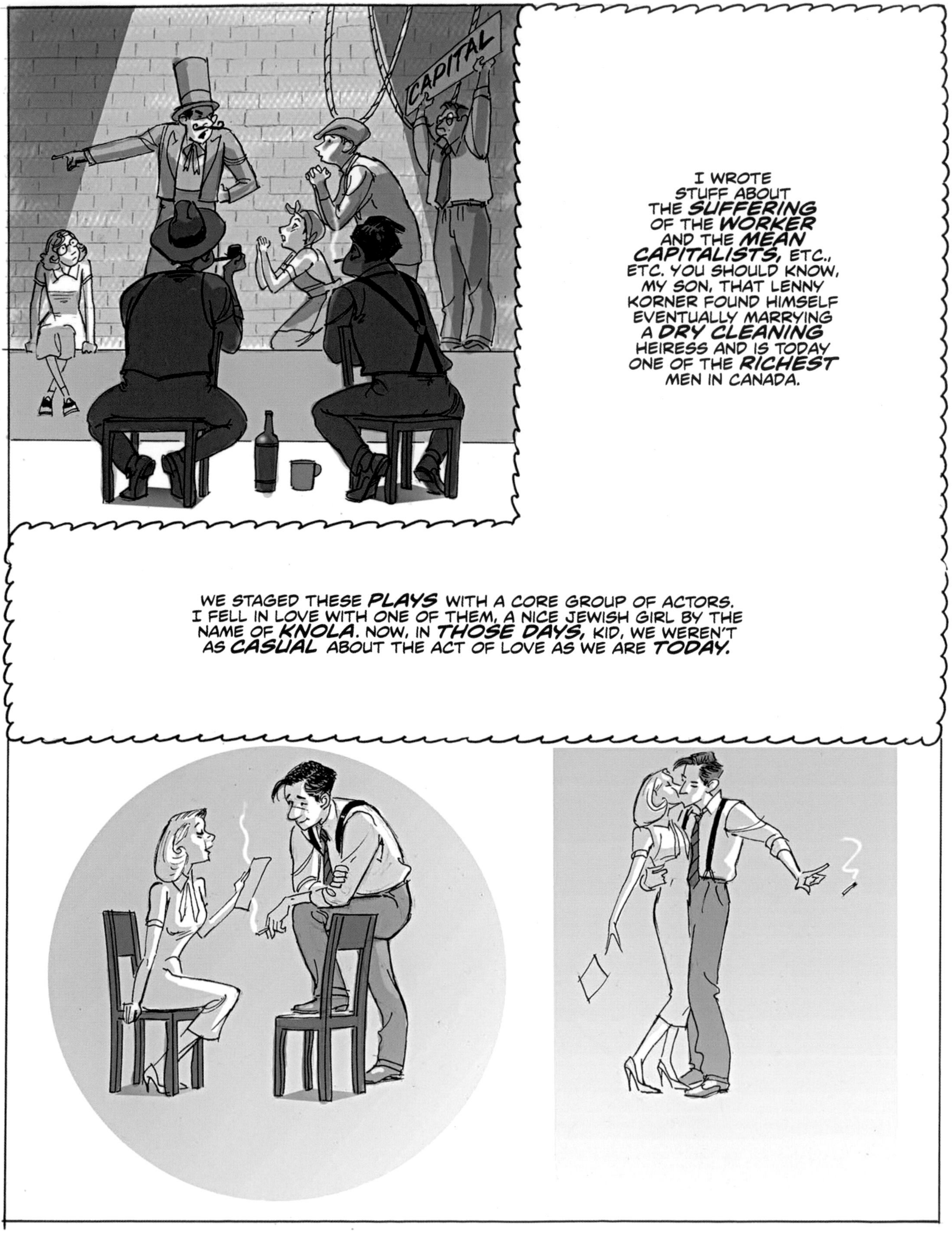
CAPITAL
I WROTE STUFF ABOUT THE SUFFERING OF THE WORKER AND THE MEAN CAPITALISTS, ETC., ETC. YOU SHOULD KNOW, MY SON, THAT LENNY KORNER FOUND HIMSELF EVENTUALLY MARRYING A DRY CLEANING HEIRESS AND IS TODAY ONE OF THE RICHEST MEN IN CANADA.
WE STAGED THESE PLAYS WITH A CORE GROUP OF ACTORS. I FELL IN LOVE WITH ONE OF THEM, A NICE JEWISH GIRL BY THE NAME OF KNOLA. NOW, IN THOSE DAYS, KID, WE WEREN'T AS CASUAL ABOUT THE ACT OF LOVE AS WE ARE TODAY.

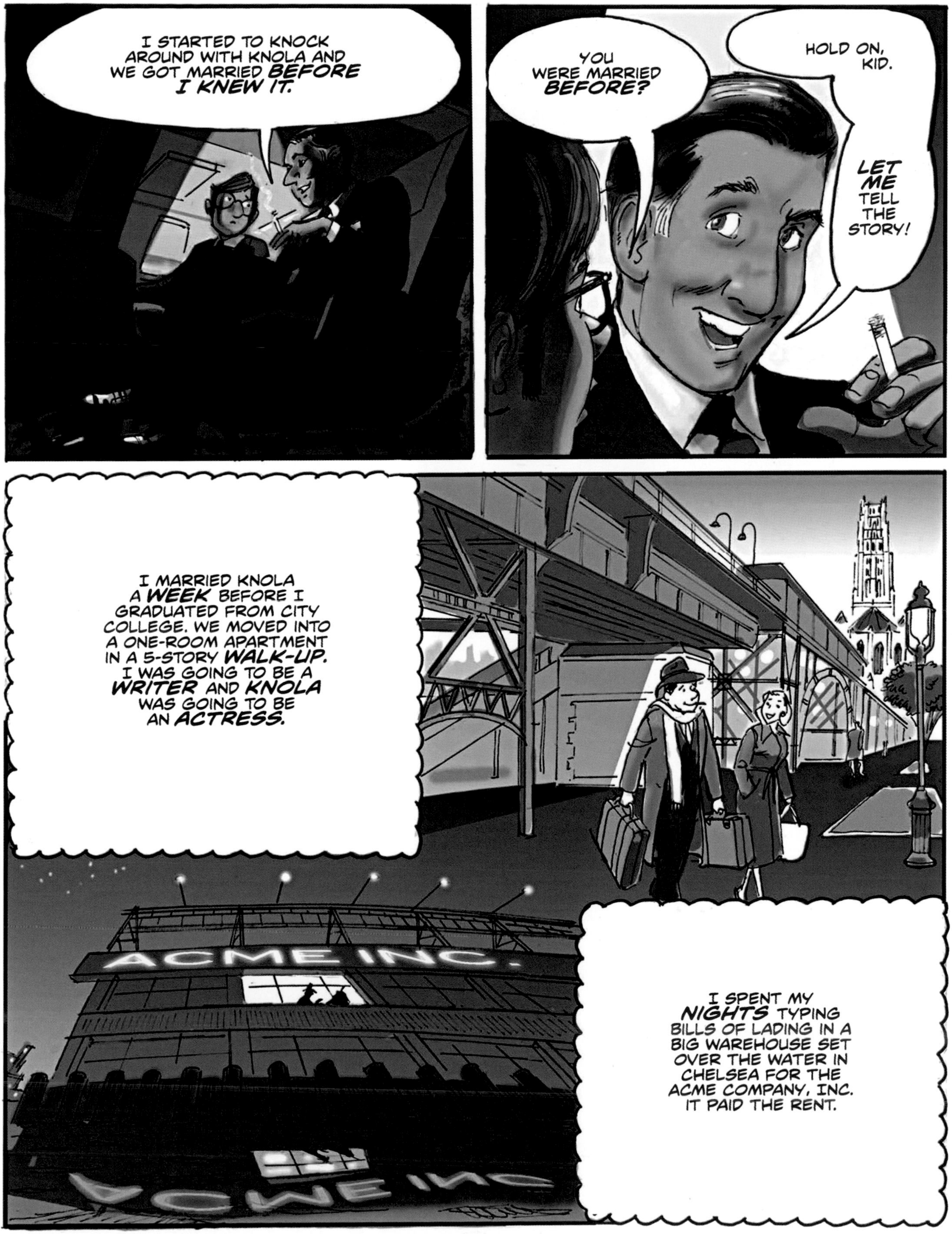
I STARTED TO KNOCK AROUND WITH KNOLA AND WE GOT MARRIED BEFORE I KNEW IT.
YOU WERE MARRIED BEFORE?
HOLD ON, KID.
LET ME TELL THE STORY!
I MARRIED KNOLA A WEEK BEFORE I GRADUATED FROM CITY COLLEGE. WE MOVED INTO A ONE-ROOM APARTMENT IN A 5-STORY WALK-UP. I WAS GOING TO BE A WRITER AND KNOLA WAS GOING TO BE AN ACTRESS.
ACME INC.
I SPENT MY NIGHTS TYPING BILLS OF LADING IN A BIG WAREHOUSE SET OVER THE WATER IN CHELSEA FOR THE ACME COMPANY, INC. IT PAID THE RENT.

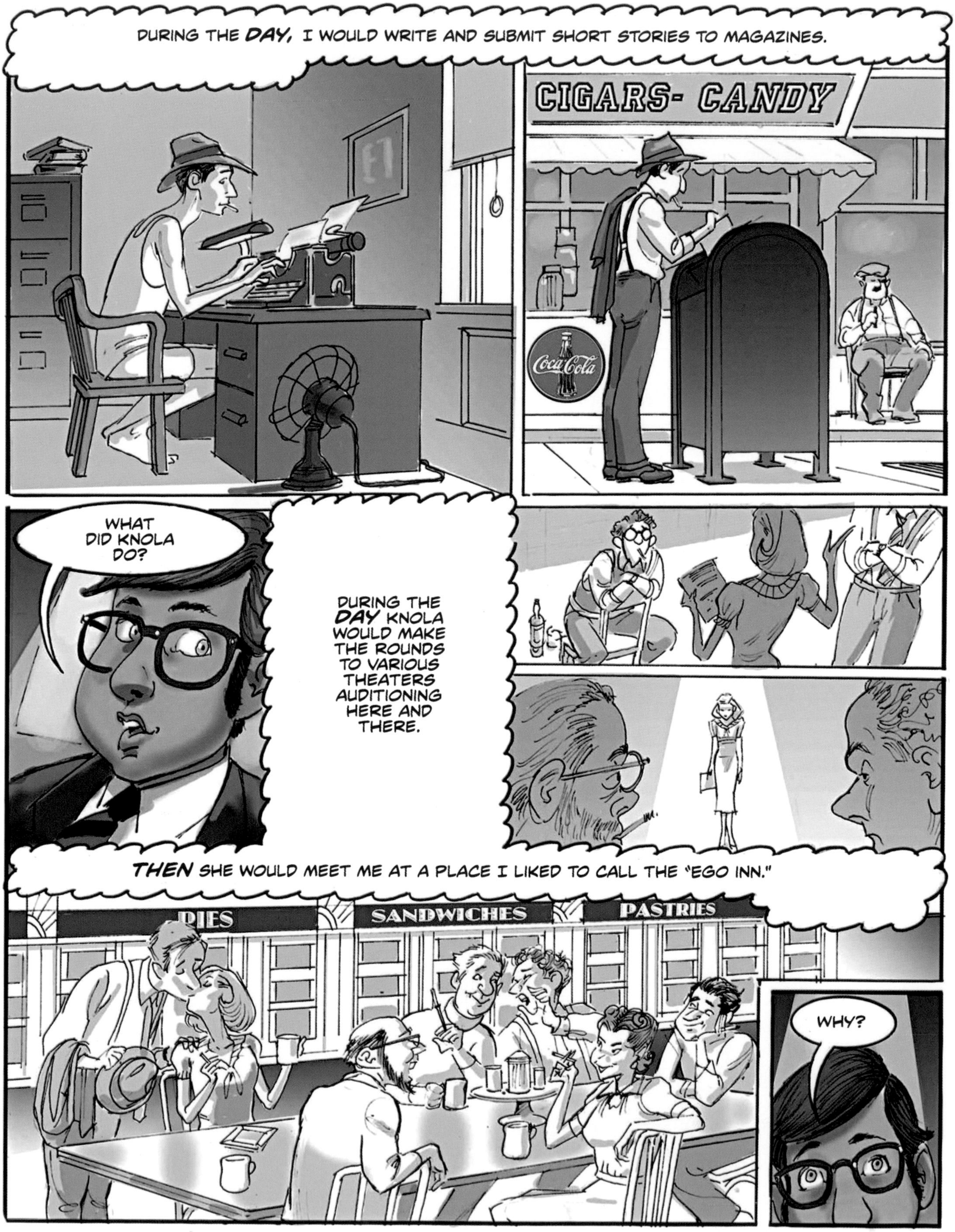
DURING THE DAY, I WOULD WRITE AND SUBMIT SHORT STORIES TO MAGAZINES.
CIGARS- CANDY
Coca-Cola
WHAT DID KNOLA DO?
DURING THE DAY KNOLA WOULD MAKE THE ROUNDS TO VARIOUS THEATERS AUDITIONING HERE AND THERE.
THEN SHE WOULD MEET ME AT A PLACE I LIKED TO CALL THE "EGO INN."
PIES
SANDWICHES
PASTRIES
WHY?

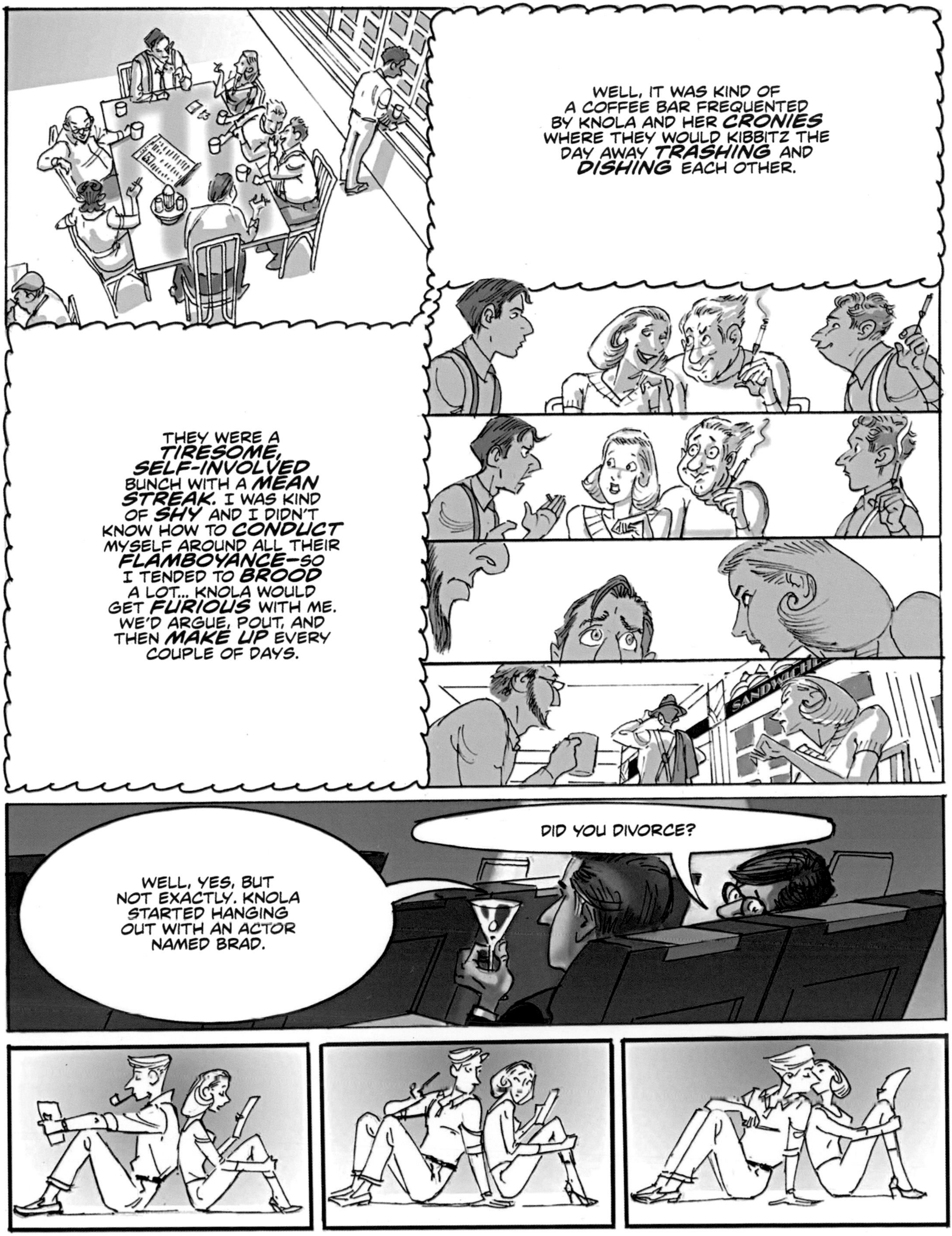
WELL, IT WAS KIND OF A COFFEE BAR FREQUENTED BY KNOLA AND HER CRONIES WHERE THEY WOULD KIBBITZ THE DAY AWAY TRASHING AND DISHING EACH OTHER.
THEY WERE A TIRESOME, SELF-INVOLVED BUNCH WITH A MEAN STREAK. I WAS KIND OF SHY AND I DIDN'T KNOW HOW TO CONDUCT MYSELF AROUND ALL THEIR FLAMBOYANCE–SO I TENDED TO BROOD A LOT... KNOLA WOULD GET FURIOUS WITH ME. WE'D ARGUE, POUT, AND THEN MAKE UP EVERY COUPLE OF DAYS.
SANDWICH
DID YOU DIVORCE?
WELL, YES, BUT NOT EXACTLY. KNOLA STARTED HANGING OUT WITH AN ACTOR NAMED BRAD.

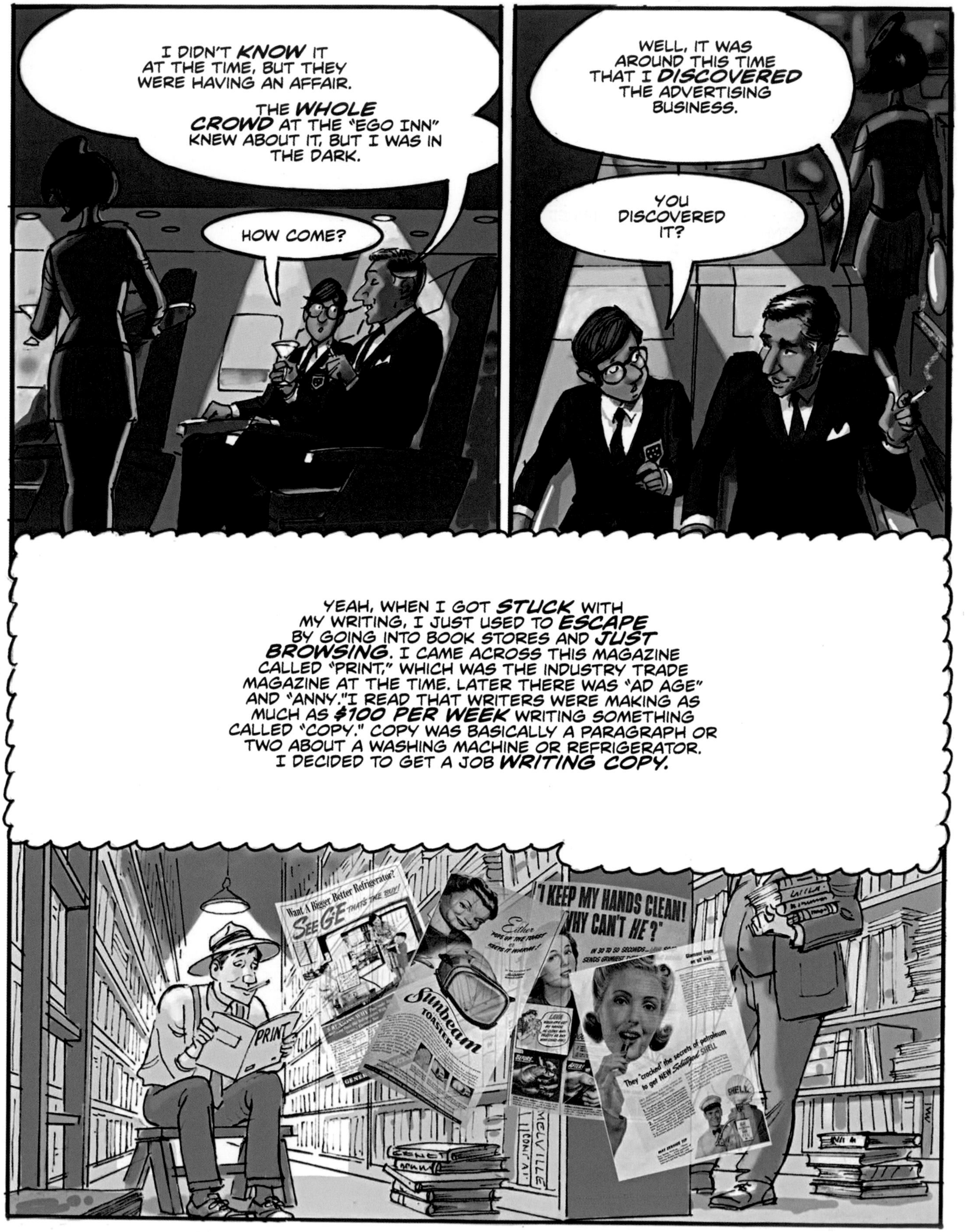
I DIDN'T KNOW IT AT THE TIME, BUT THEY WERE HAVING AN AFFAIR.
THE WHOLE CROWD AT THE "EGO INN" KNEW ABOUT IT, BUT I WAS IN THE DARK.
HOW COME?
WELL, IT WAS AROUND THIS TIME THAT I DISCOVERED THE ADVERTISING BUSINESS.
YOU DISCOVERED IT?
YEAH, WHEN I GOT STUCK WITH MY WRITING, I JUST USED TO ESCAPE BY GOING INTO BOOK STORES AND JUST BROWSING. I CAME ACROSS THIS MAGAZINE CALLED "PRINT," WHICH WAS THE INDUSTRY TRADE MAGAZINE AT THE TIME. LATER THERE WAS "AD AGE" AND "ANNY."I READ THAT WRITERS WERE MAKING AS MUCH AS $100 PER WEEK WRITING SOMETHING CALLED "COPY." COPY WAS BASICALLY A PARAGRAPH OR TWO ABOUT A WASHING MACHINE OR REFRIGERATOR. I DECIDED TO GET A JOB WRITING COPY.
Want A Bigger Better Refrigerator?
SEE GE
"I KEEP MY HANDS CLEAN! WHY CAN'T HE?"
Sunbeam TOASTER
PRINT
MELVILLE

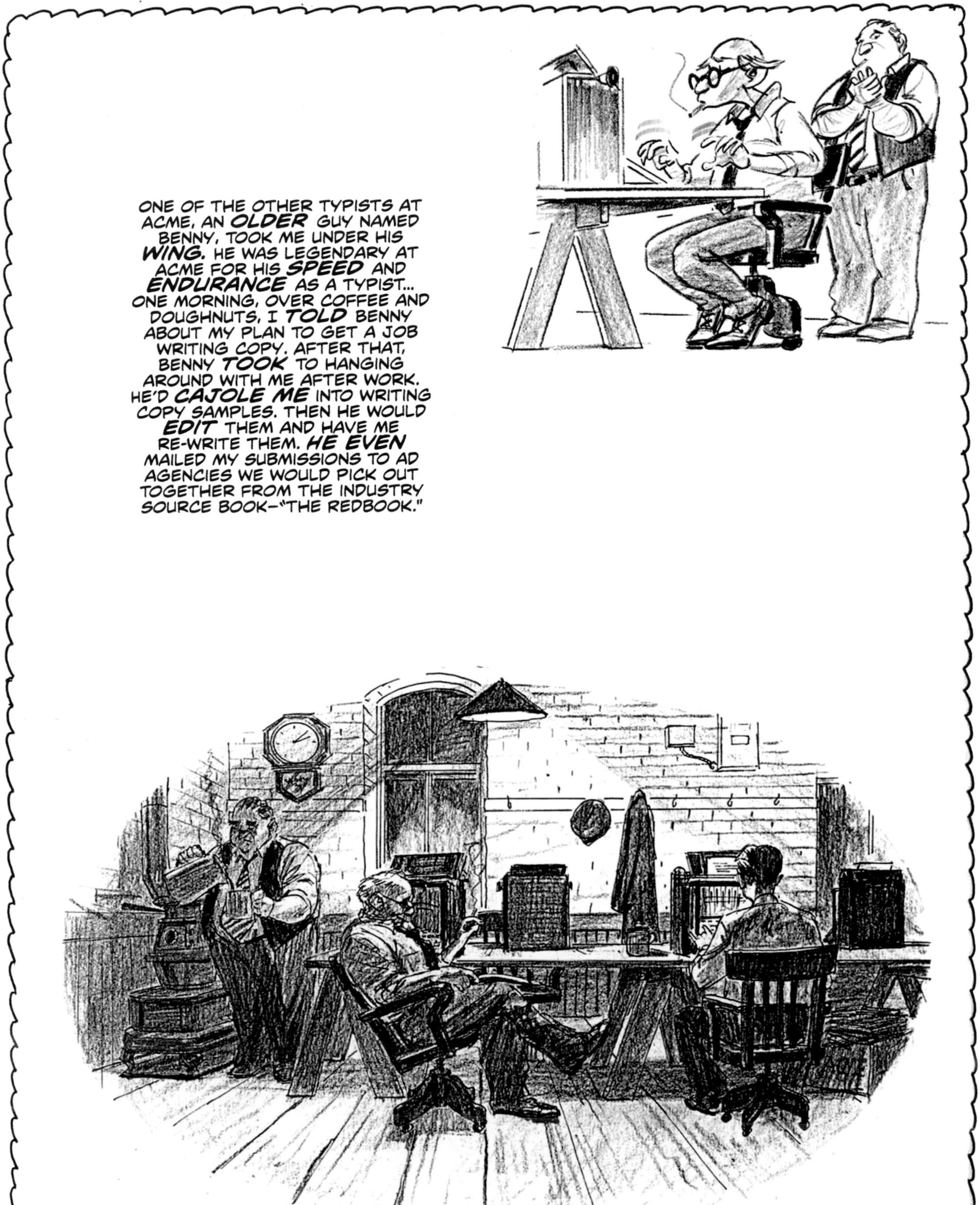
ONE OF THE OTHER TYPISTS AT ACME, AN OLDER GUY NAMED BENNY, TOOK ME UNDER HIS WING. HE WAS LEGENDARY AT ACME FOR HIS SPEED AND ENDURANCE AS A TYPIST... ONE MORNING, OVER COFFEE AND DOUGHNUTS, I TOLD BENNY ABOUT MY PLAN TO GET A JOB WRITING COPY. AFTER THAT, BENNY TOOK TO HANGING AROUND WITH ME AFTER WORK. HE'D CAJOLE ME INTO WRITING COPY SAMPLES. THEN HE WOULD EDIT THEM AND HAVE ME RE-WRITE THEM. HE EVEN MAILED MY SUBMISSIONS TO AD AGENCIES WE WOULD PICK OUT TOGETHER FROM THE INDUSTRY SOURCE BOOK—"THE REDBOOK."

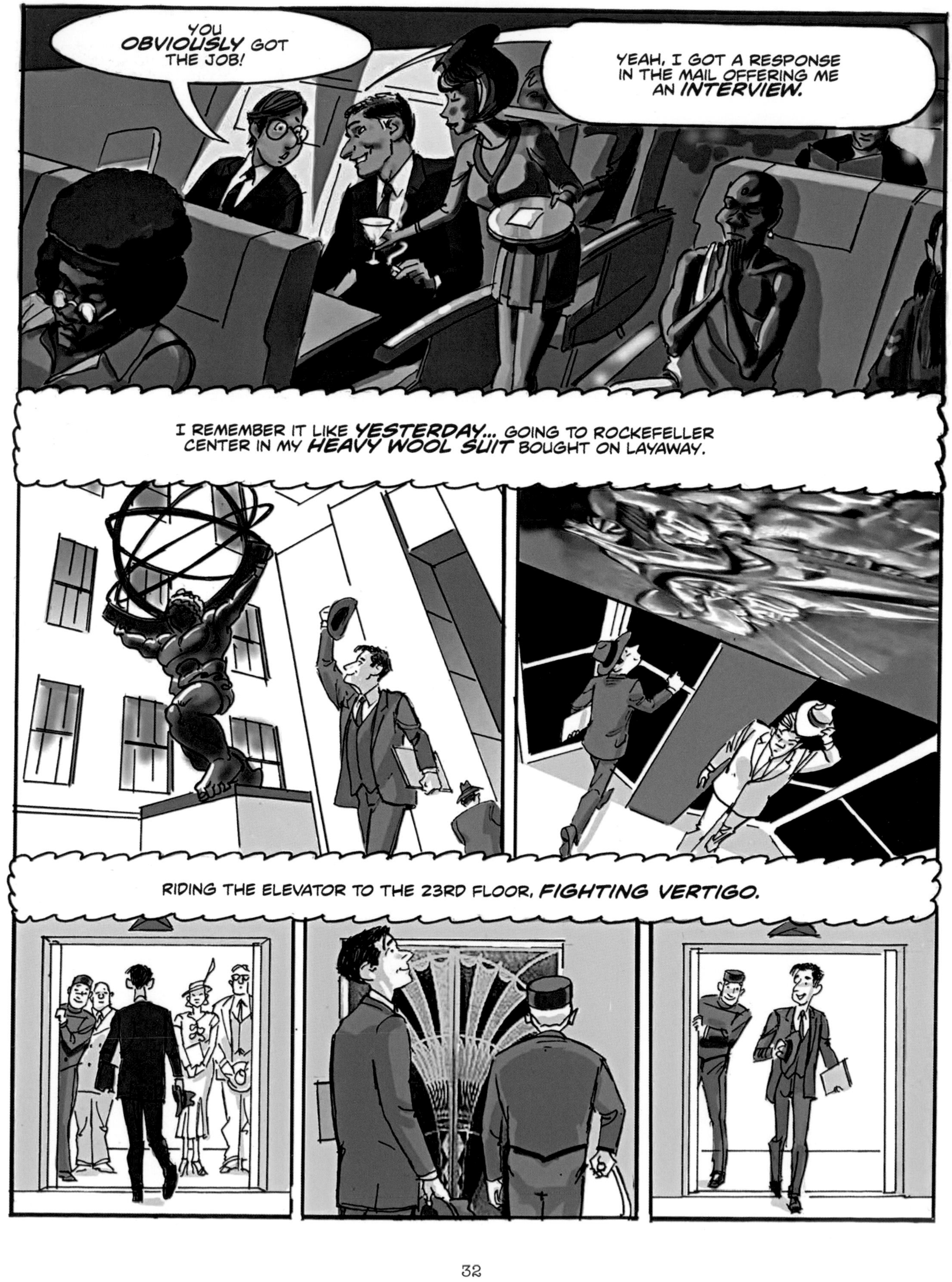
YOU OBVIOUSLY GOT THE JOB!
YEAH, I GOT A RESPONSE IN THE MAIL OFFERING ME AN INTERVIEW.
I REMEMBER IT LIKE YESTERDAY... GOING TO ROCKEFELLER CENTER IN MY HEAVY WOOL SUIT BOUGHT ON LAYAWAY.
RIDING THE ELEVATOR TO THE 23RD FLOOR, FIGHTING VERTIGO.

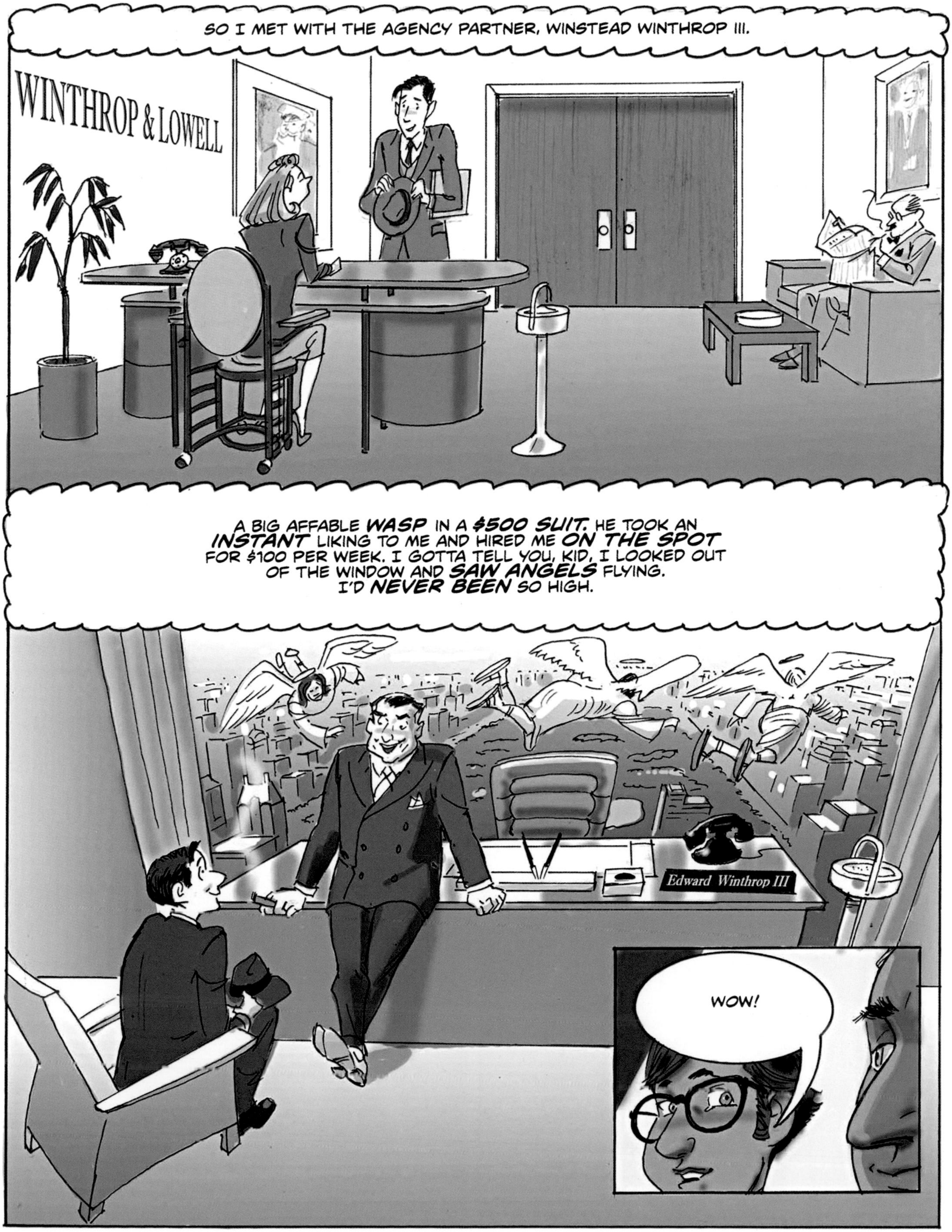
SO I MET WITH THE AGENCY PARTNER, WINSTEAD WINTHROP III.
WINTHROP & LOWELL
A BIG AFFABLE WASP IN A $500 SUIT. HE TOOK AN INSTANT LIKING TO ME AND HIRED ME ON THE SPOT FOR $100 PER WEEK. I GOTTA TELL YOU, KID, I LOOKED OUT OF THE WINDOW AND SAW ANGELS FLYING. I'D NEVER BEEN SO HIGH.
Edward Winthrop III
WOW!

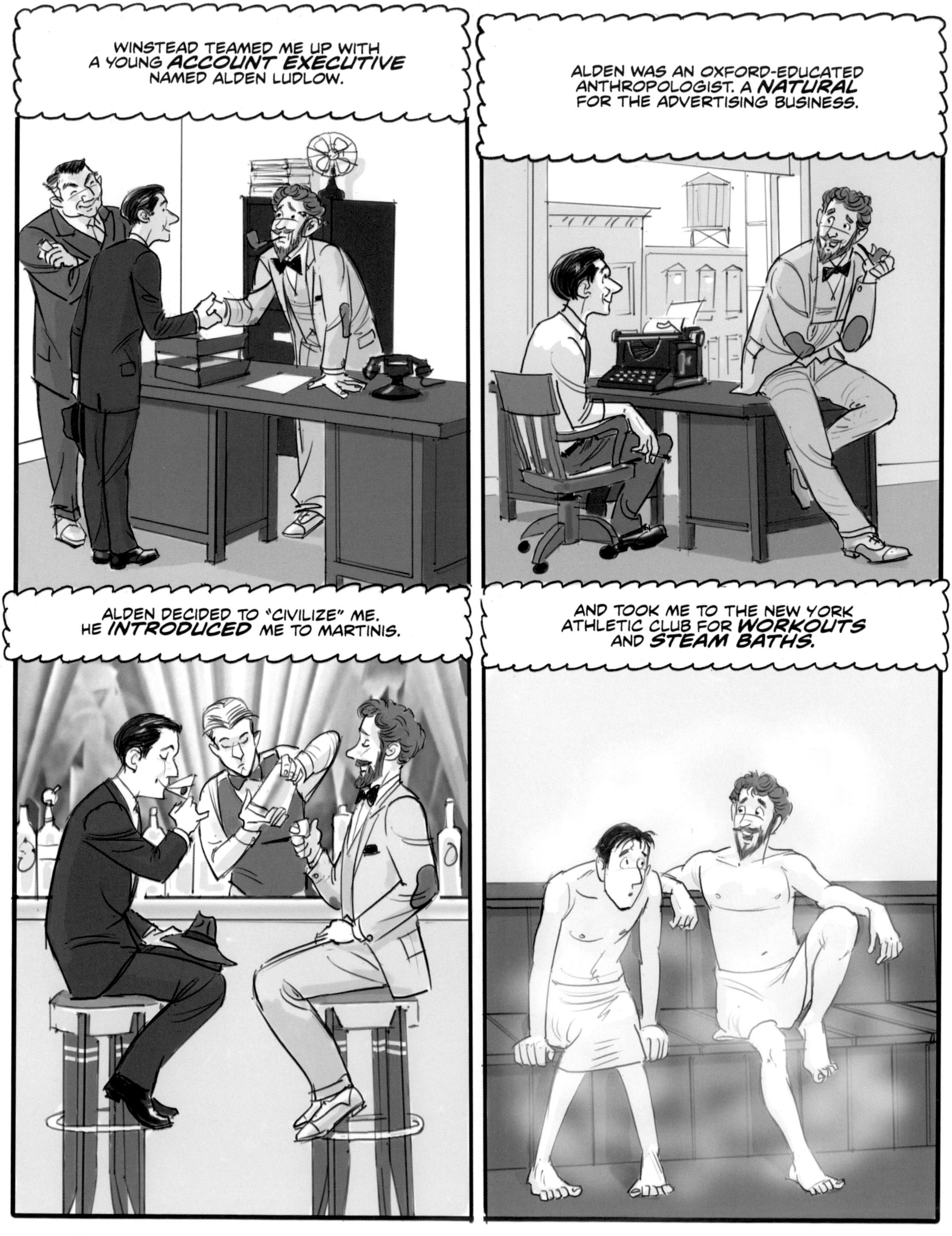
WINSTEAD TEAMED ME UP WITH A YOUNG ACCOUNT EXECUTIVE NAMED ALDEN LUDLOW.
ALDEN WAS AN OXFORD-EDUCATED ANTHROPOLOGIST. A NATURAL FOR THE ADVERTISING BUSINESS.
ALDEN DECIDED TO "CIVILIZE" ME. HE INTRODUCED ME TO MARTINIS.
AND TOOK ME TO THE NEW YORK ATHLETIC CLUB FOR WORKOUTS AND STEAM BATHS.

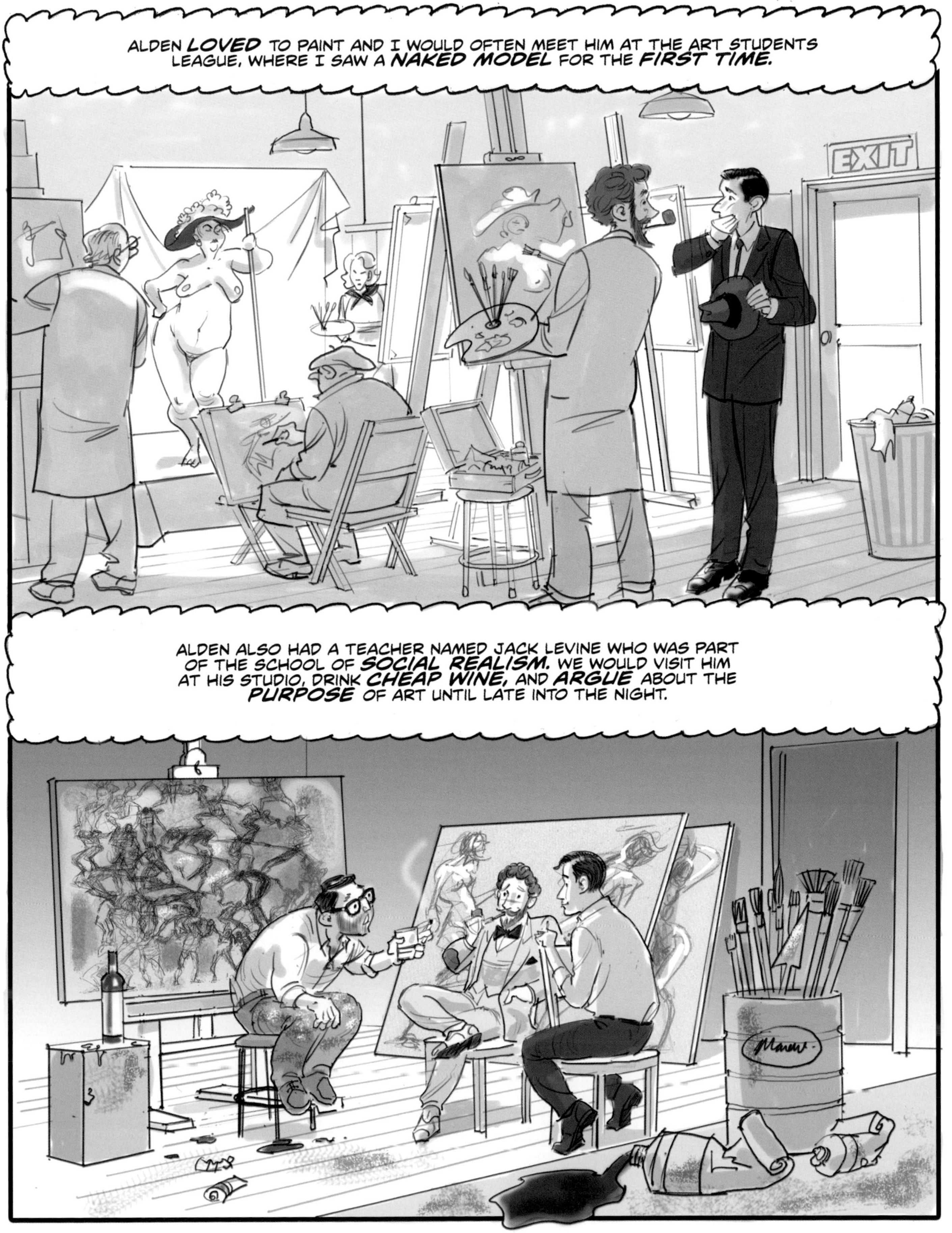
ALDEN LOVED TO PAINT AND I WOULD OFTEN MEET HIM AT THE ART STUDENTS LEAGUE, WHERE I SAW A NAKED MODEL FOR THE FIRST TIME.
EXIT
ALDEN ALSO HAD A TEACHER NAMED JACK LEVINE WHO WAS PART OF THE SCHOOL OF SOCIAL REALISM. WE WOULD VISIT HIM AT HIS STUDIO, DRINK CHEAP WINE, AND ARGUE ABOUT THE PURPOSE OF ART UNTIL LATE INTO THE NIGHT.

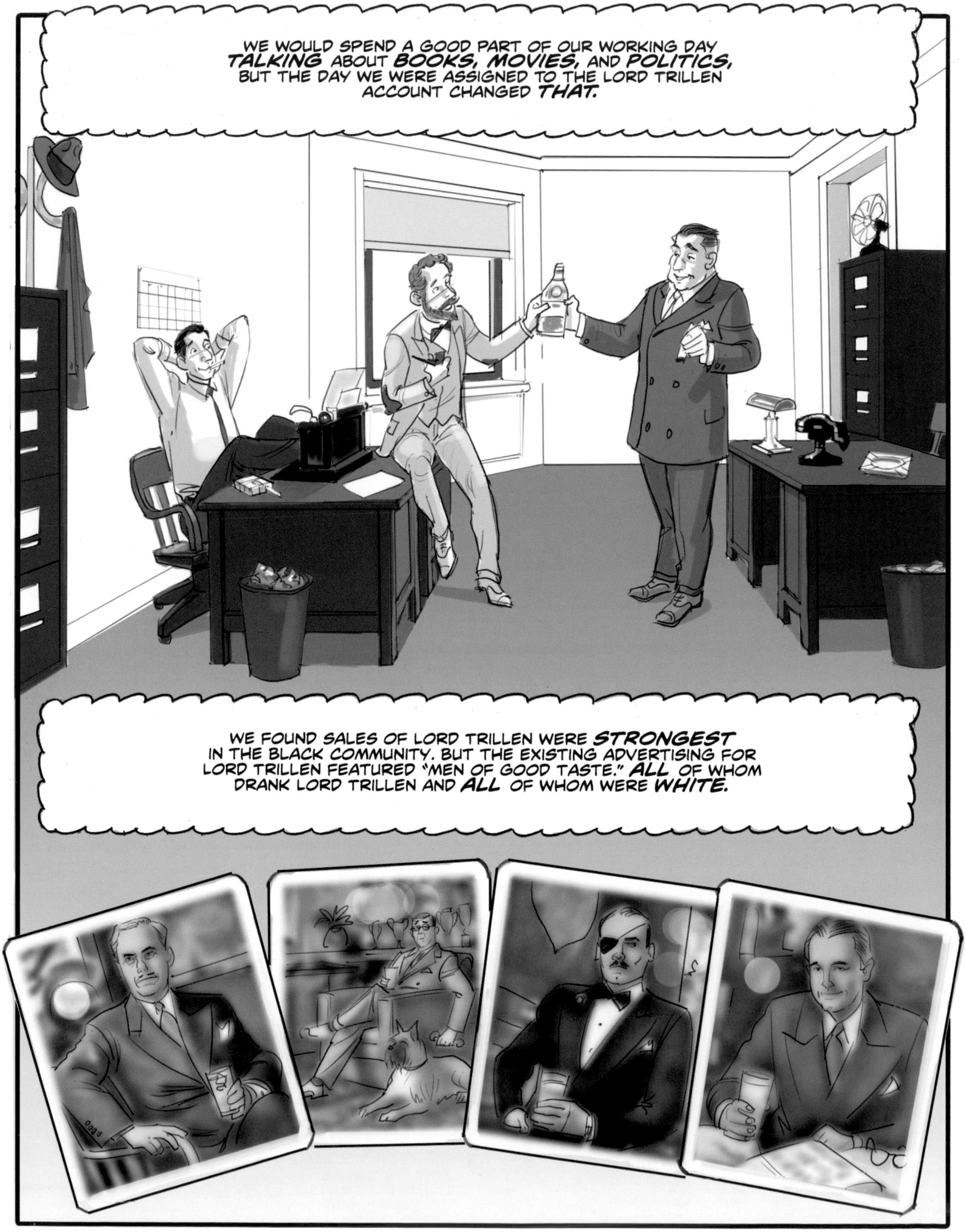
WE WOULD SPEND A GOOD PART OF OUR WORKING DAY *TALKING* ABOUT *BOOKS, MOVIES,* AND *POLITICS,* BUT THE DAY WE WERE ASSIGNED TO THE LORD TRILLEN ACCOUNT CHANGED *THAT.*
WE FOUND SALES OF LORD TRILLEN WERE *STRONGEST* IN THE BLACK COMMUNITY. BUT THE EXISTING ADVERTISING FOR LORD TRILLEN FEATURED "MEN OF GOOD TASTE." *ALL* OF WHOM DRANK LORD TRILLEN AND *ALL* OF WHOM WERE *WHITE.*

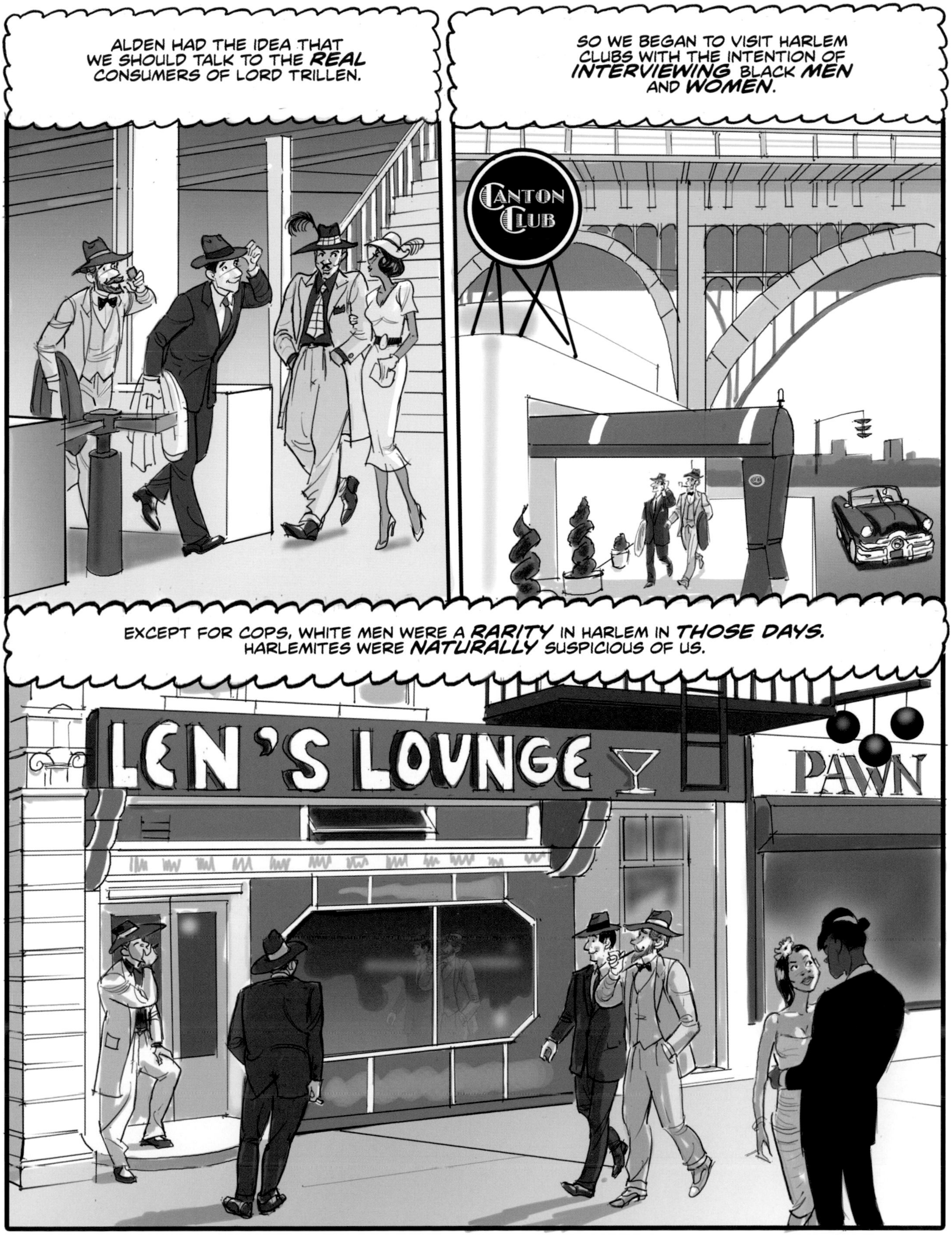
ALDEN HAD THE IDEA THAT WE SHOULD TALK TO THE REAL CONSUMERS OF LORD TRILLEN.
SO WE BEGAN TO VISIT HARLEM CLUBS WITH THE INTENTION OF INTERVIEWING BLACK MEN AND WOMEN.
CANTON CLUB
EXCEPT FOR COPS, WHITE MEN WERE A RARITY IN HARLEM IN THOSE DAYS. HARLEMITES WERE NATURALLY SUSPICIOUS OF US.
LEN'S LOUNGE
PAWN

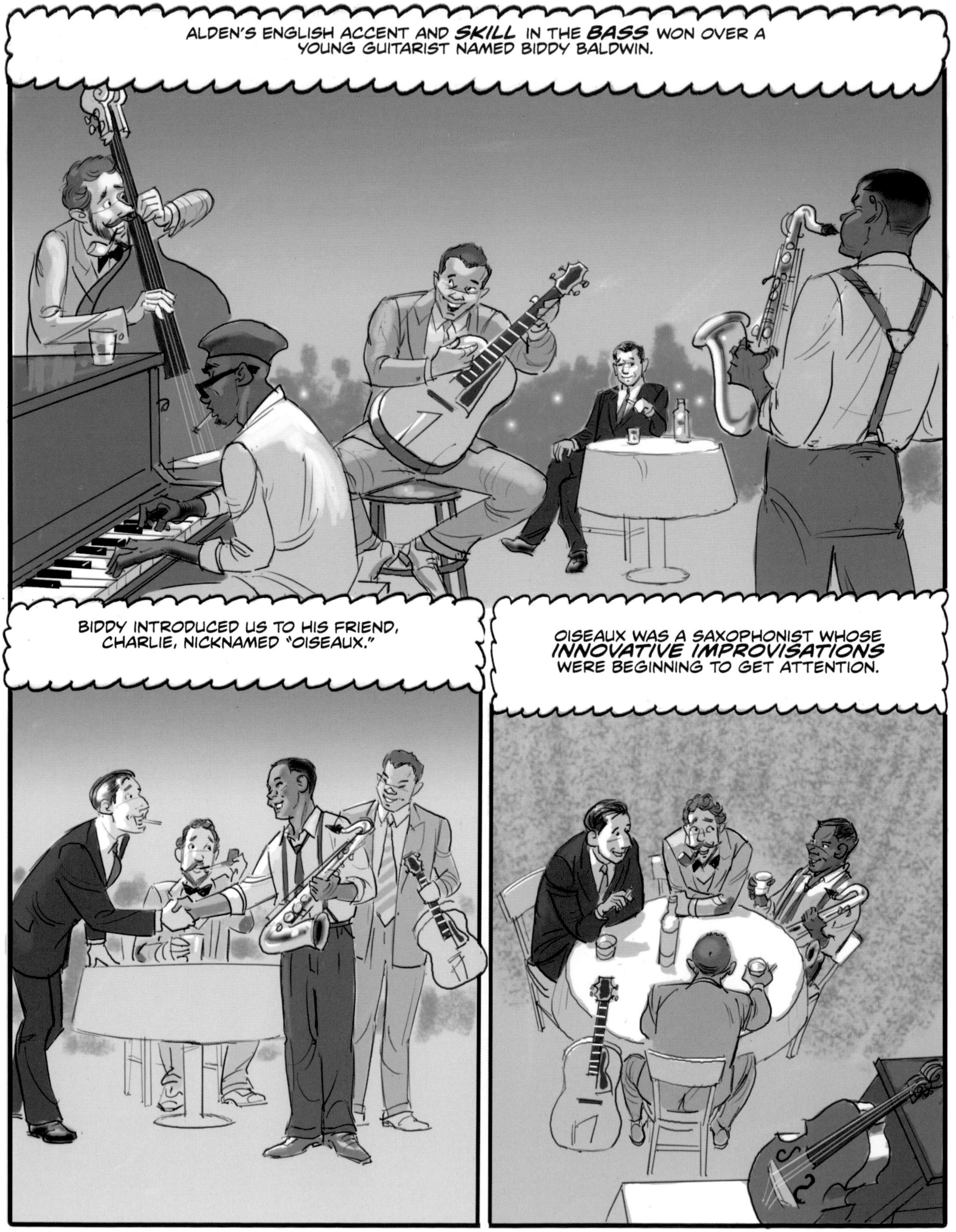

ALDEN'S ENGLISH ACCENT AND *SKILL* IN THE *BASS* WON OVER A YOUNG GUITARIST NAMED BIDDY BALDWIN.
BIDDY INTRODUCED US TO HIS FRIEND, CHARLIE, NICKNAMED "OISEAUX."
OISEAUX WAS A SAXOPHONIST WHOSE *INNOVATIVE IMPROVISATIONS* WERE BEGINNING TO GET ATTENTION.

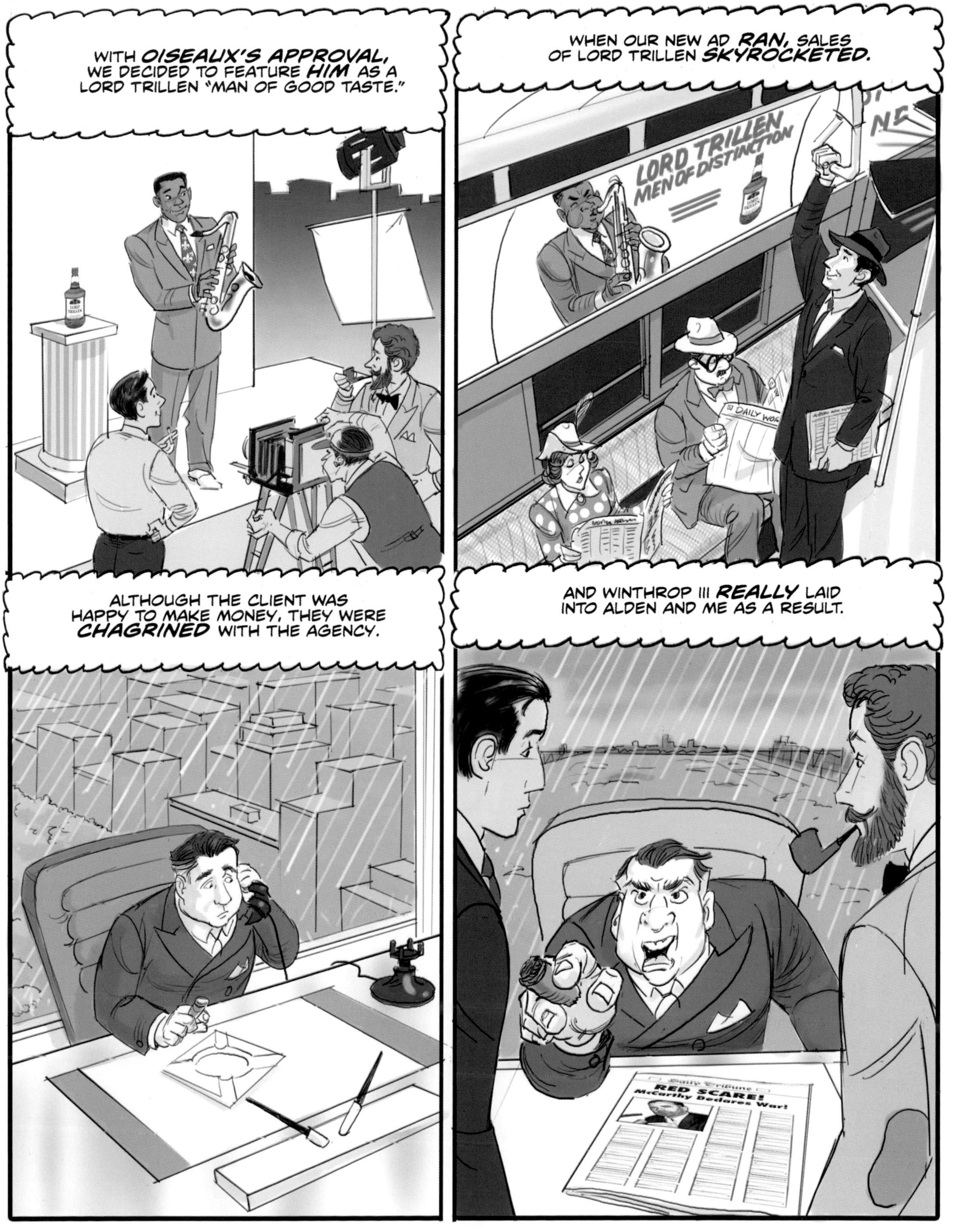
WITH OISEAUX'S APPROVAL, WE DECIDED TO FEATURE HIM AS A LORD TRILLEN "MAN OF GOOD TASTE."
WHEN OUR NEW AD RAN, SALES OF LORD TRILLEN SKYROCKETED.
LORD TRILLEN MEN OF DISTINCTION
ALTHOUGH THE CLIENT WAS HAPPY TO MAKE MONEY, THEY WERE CHAGRINED WITH THE AGENCY.
AND WINTHROP III REALLY LAID INTO ALDEN AND ME AS A RESULT.
RED SCARE! McCarthy Declares War!

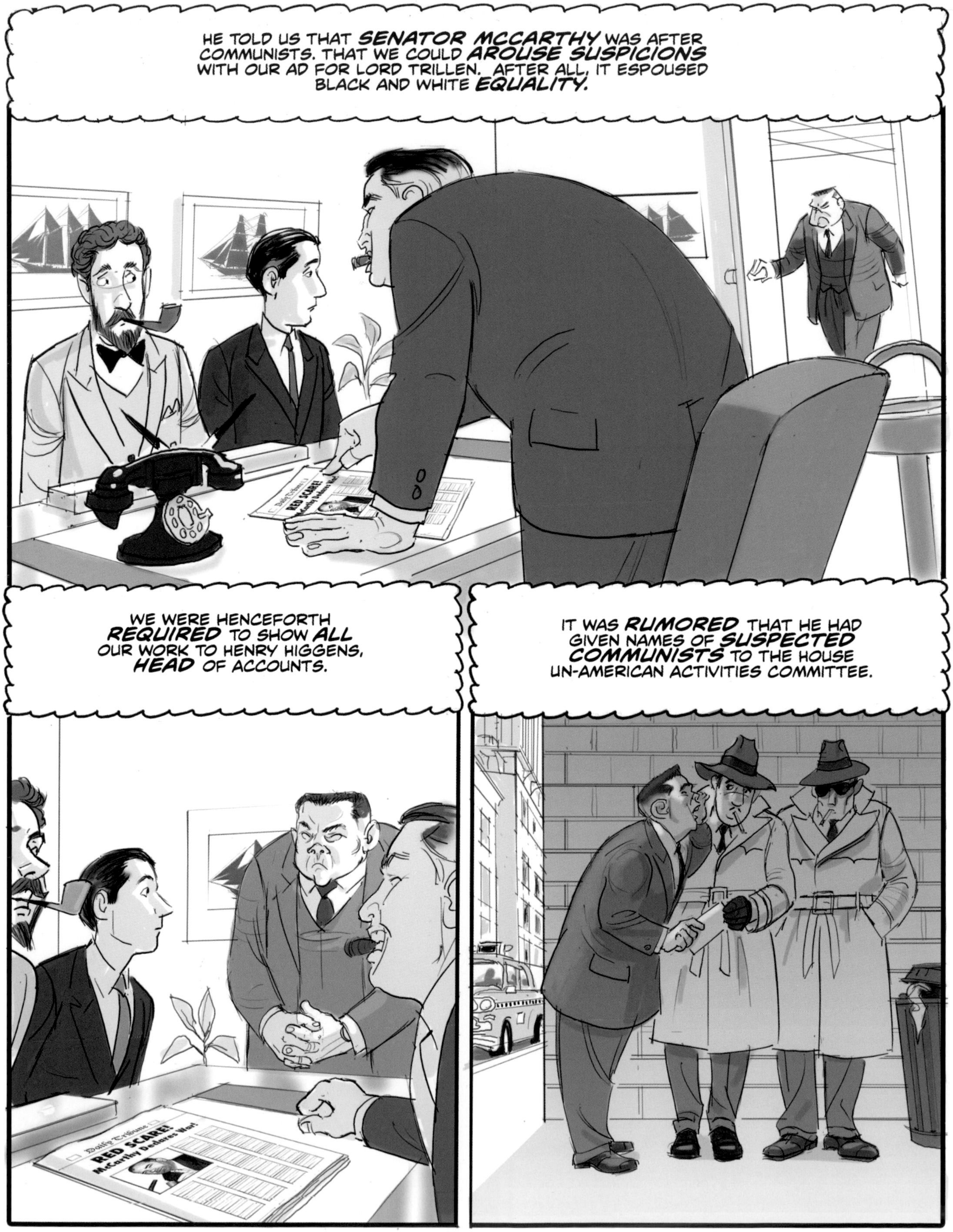
HE TOLD US THAT SENATOR MCCARTHY WAS AFTER COMMUNISTS. THAT WE COULD AROUSE SUSPICIONS WITH OUR AD FOR LORD TRILLEN. AFTER ALL, IT ESPOUSED BLACK AND WHITE EQUALITY.
WE WERE HENCEFORTH REQUIRED TO SHOW ALL OUR WORK TO HENRY HIGGENS, HEAD OF ACCOUNTS.
Daily Tribune
RED SCARE!
McCarthy Declares War!
IT WAS RUMORED THAT HE HAD GIVEN NAMES OF SUSPECTED COMMUNISTS TO THE HOUSE UN-AMERICAN ACTIVITIES COMMITTEE.

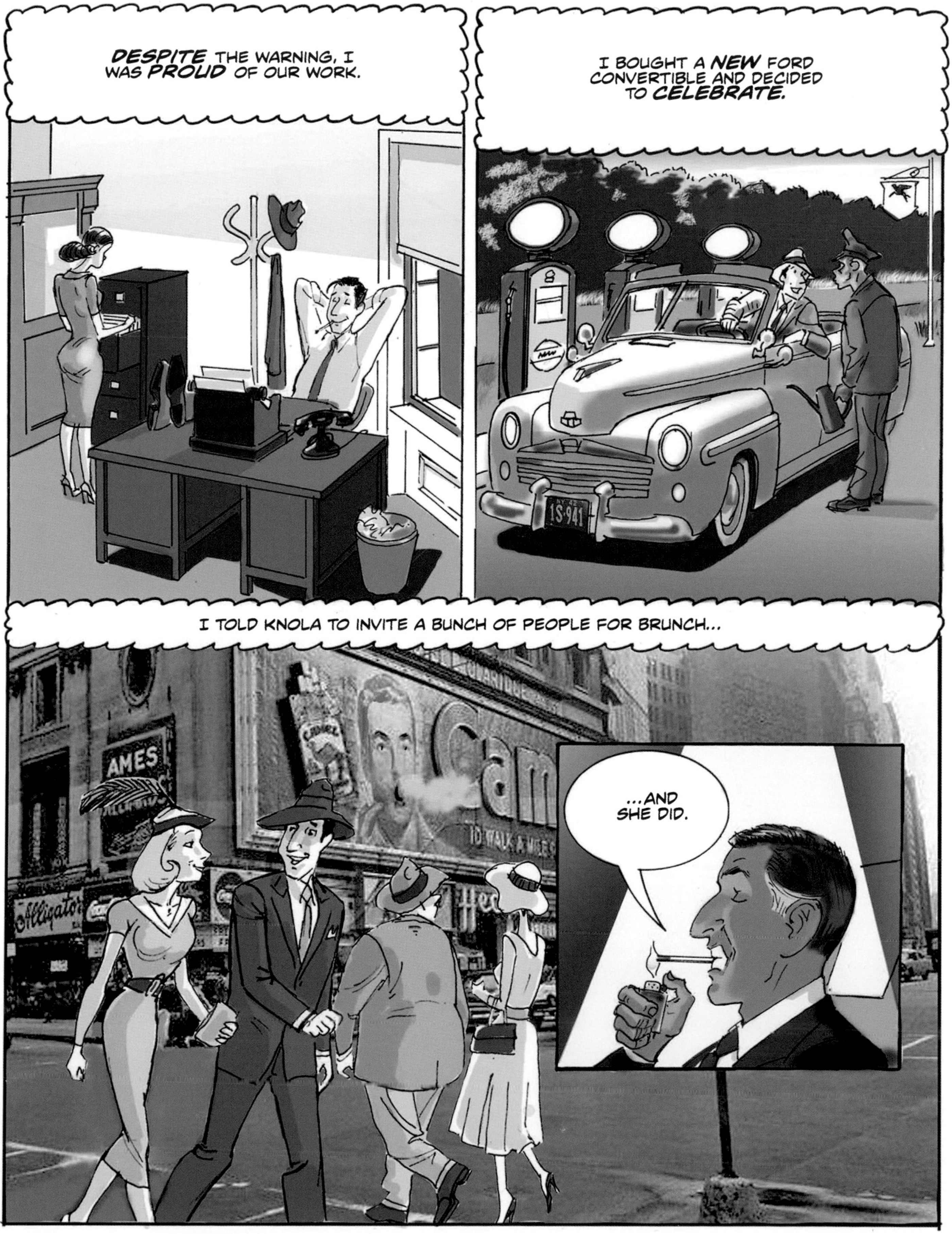
DESPITE THE WARNING, I WAS PROUD OF OUR WORK.
I BOUGHT A NEW FORD CONVERTIBLE AND DECIDED TO CELEBRATE.
I TOLD KNOLA TO INVITE A BUNCH OF PEOPLE FOR BRUNCH...
...AND SHE DID.

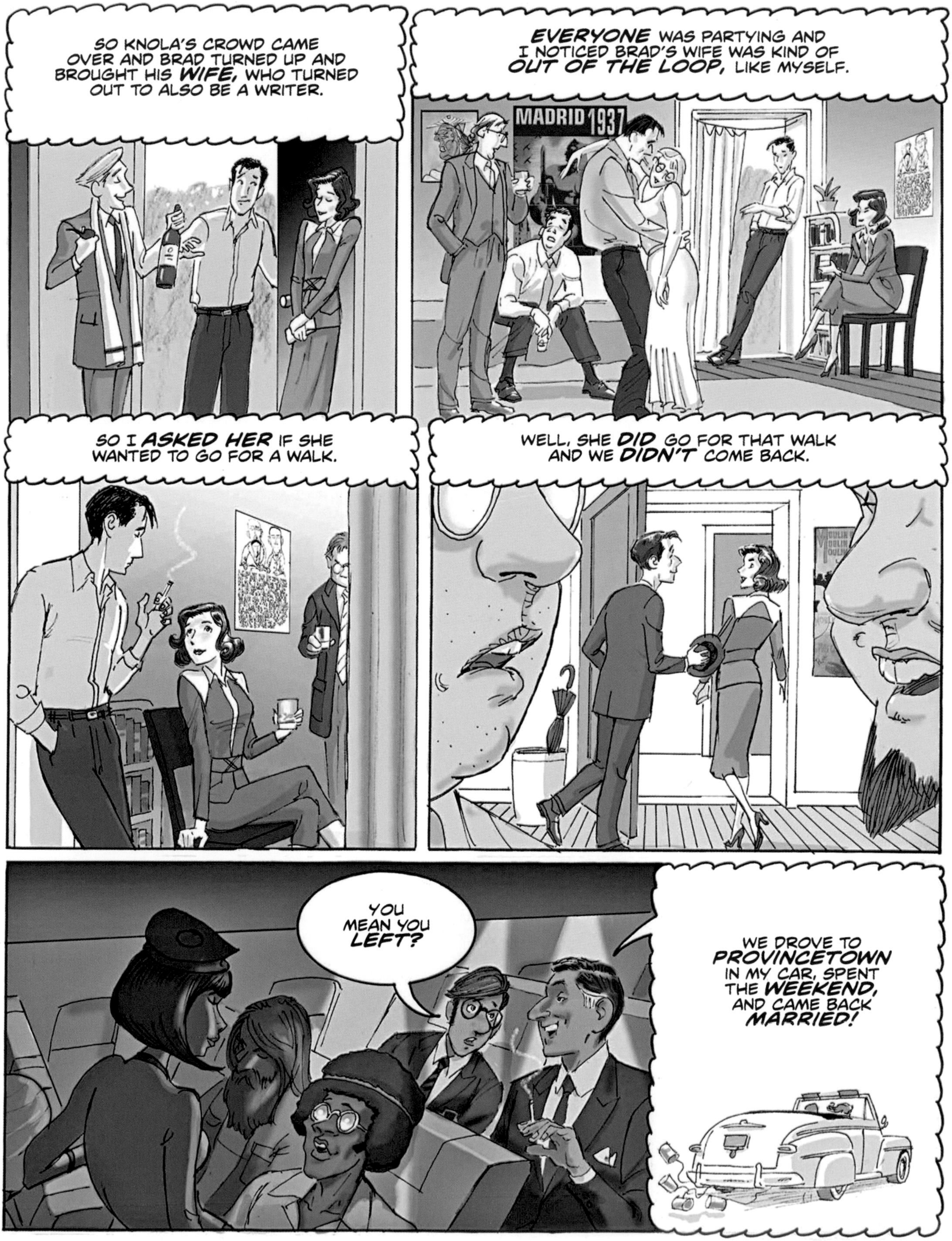

SO KNOLA'S CROWD CAME OVER AND BRAD TURNED UP AND BROUGHT HIS **WIFE,** WHO TURNED OUT TO ALSO BE A WRITER.
EVERYONE WAS PARTYING AND I NOTICED BRAD'S WIFE WAS KIND OF **OUT OF THE LOOP,** LIKE MYSELF.
MADRID 1937
SO I **ASKED HER** IF SHE WANTED TO GO FOR A WALK.
WELL, SHE **DID** GO FOR THAT WALK AND WE **DIDN'T** COME BACK.
YOU MEAN YOU **LEFT?**
WE DROVE TO **PROVINCETOWN** IN MY CAR, SPENT THE **WEEKEND,** AND CAME BACK **MARRIED!**

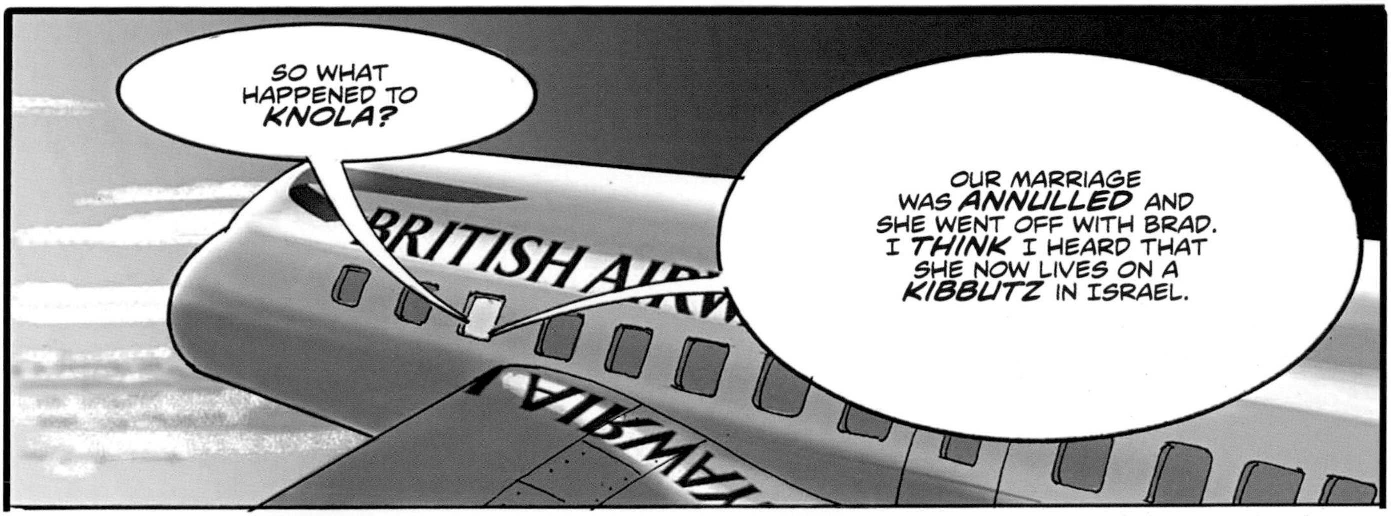
SO WHAT HAPPENED TO KNOLA?
OUR MARRIAGE WAS ANNULLED AND SHE WENT OFF WITH BRAD. I THINK I HEARD THAT SHE NOW LIVES ON A KIBBUTZ IN ISRAEL.
BRITISH AIRW

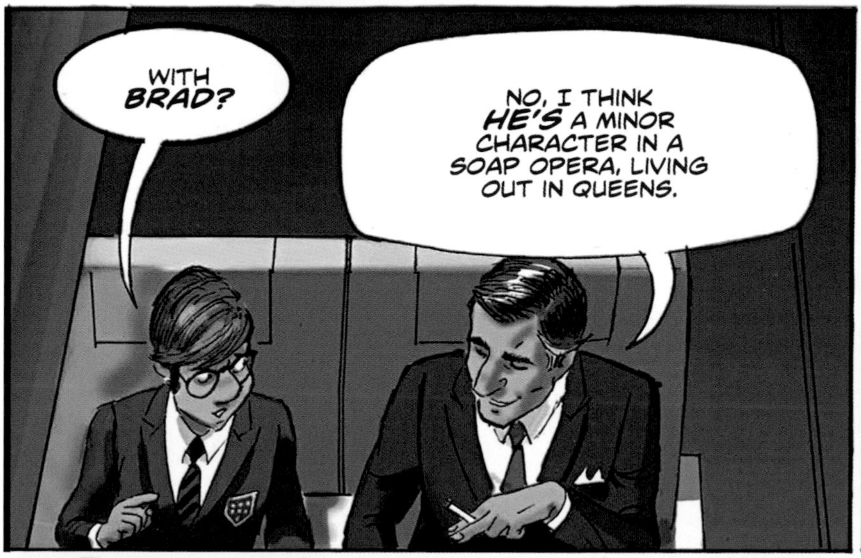
WITH BRAD?
NO, I THINK HE'S A MINOR CHARACTER IN A SOAP OPERA, LIVING OUT IN QUEENS.

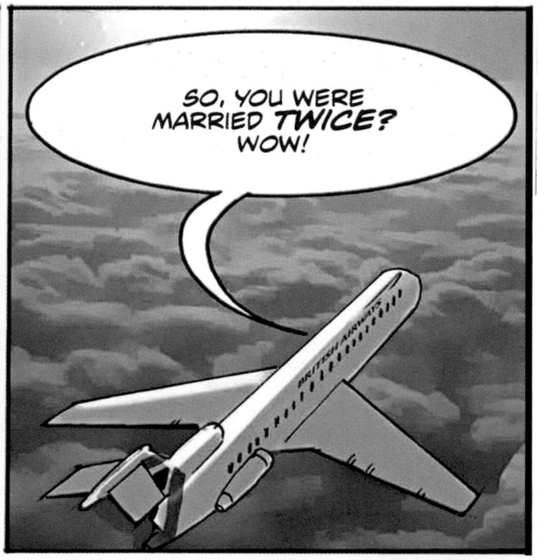
SO, YOU WERE MARRIED TWICE? WOW!

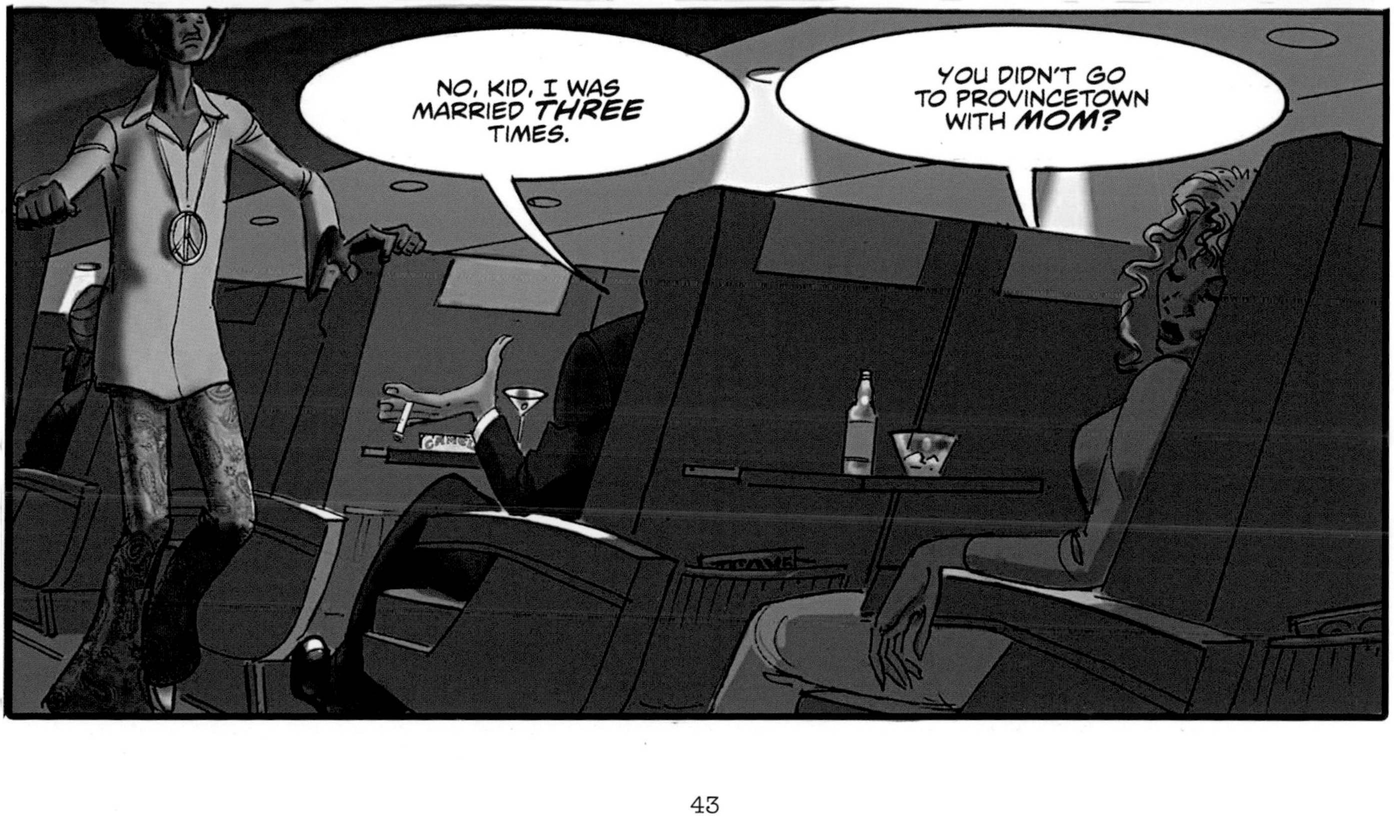
NO, KID, I WAS MARRIED THREE TIMES.
YOU DIDN'T GO TO PROVINCETOWN WITH MOM?

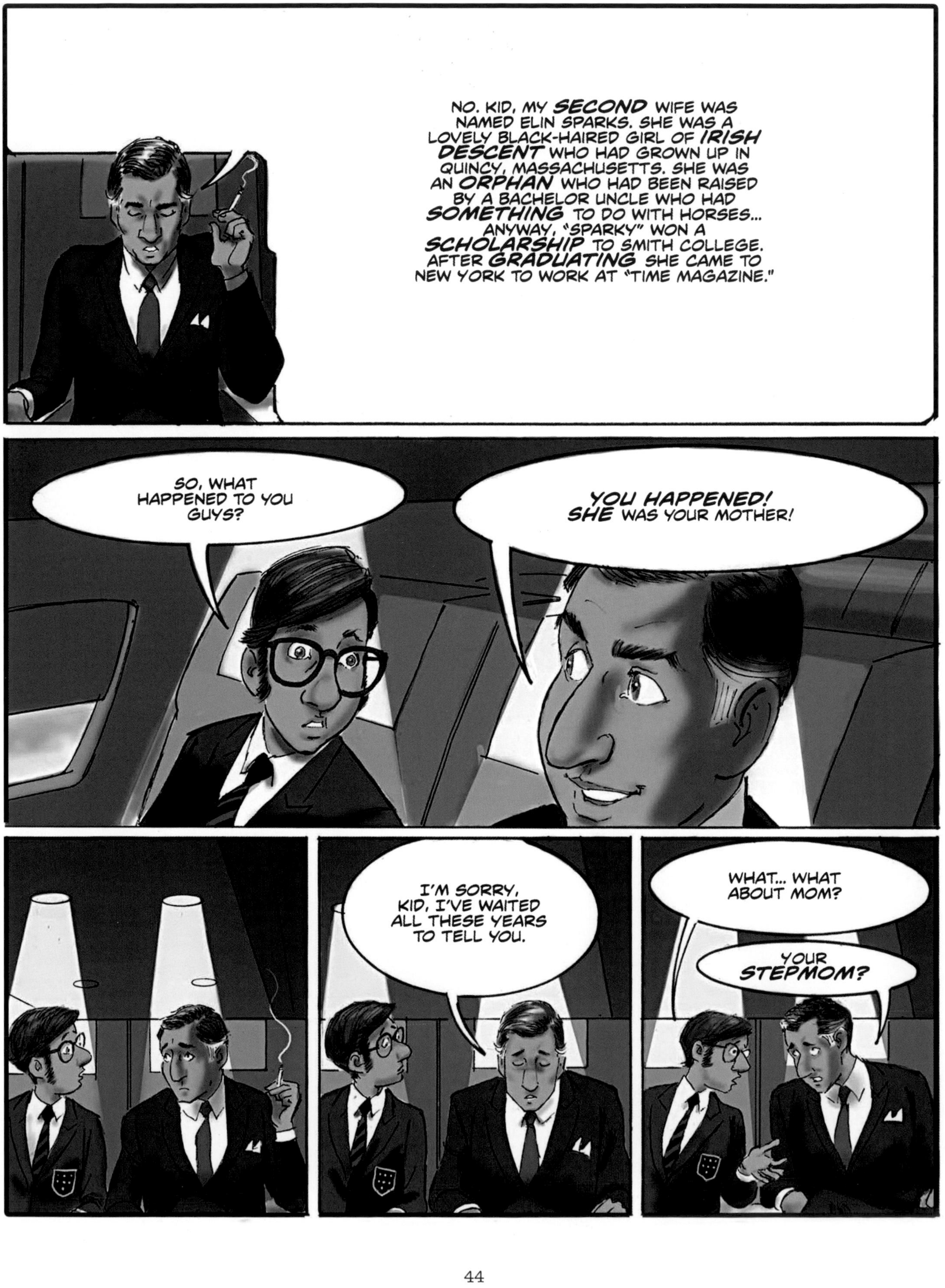
NO. KID, MY SECOND WIFE WAS NAMED ELIN SPARKS. SHE WAS A LOVELY BLACK-HAIRED GIRL OF IRISH DESCENT WHO HAD GROWN UP IN QUINCY, MASSACHUSETTS. SHE WAS AN ORPHAN WHO HAD BEEN RAISED BY A BACHELOR UNCLE WHO HAD SOMETHING TO DO WITH HORSES... ANYWAY, "SPARKY" WON A SCHOLARSHIP TO SMITH COLLEGE. AFTER GRADUATING SHE CAME TO NEW YORK TO WORK AT "TIME MAGAZINE."
SO, WHAT HAPPENED TO YOU GUYS?
YOU HAPPENED! SHE WAS YOUR MOTHER!
I'M SORRY, KID, I'VE WAITED ALL THESE YEARS TO TELL YOU.
WHAT... WHAT ABOUT MOM?
YOUR STEPMOM?

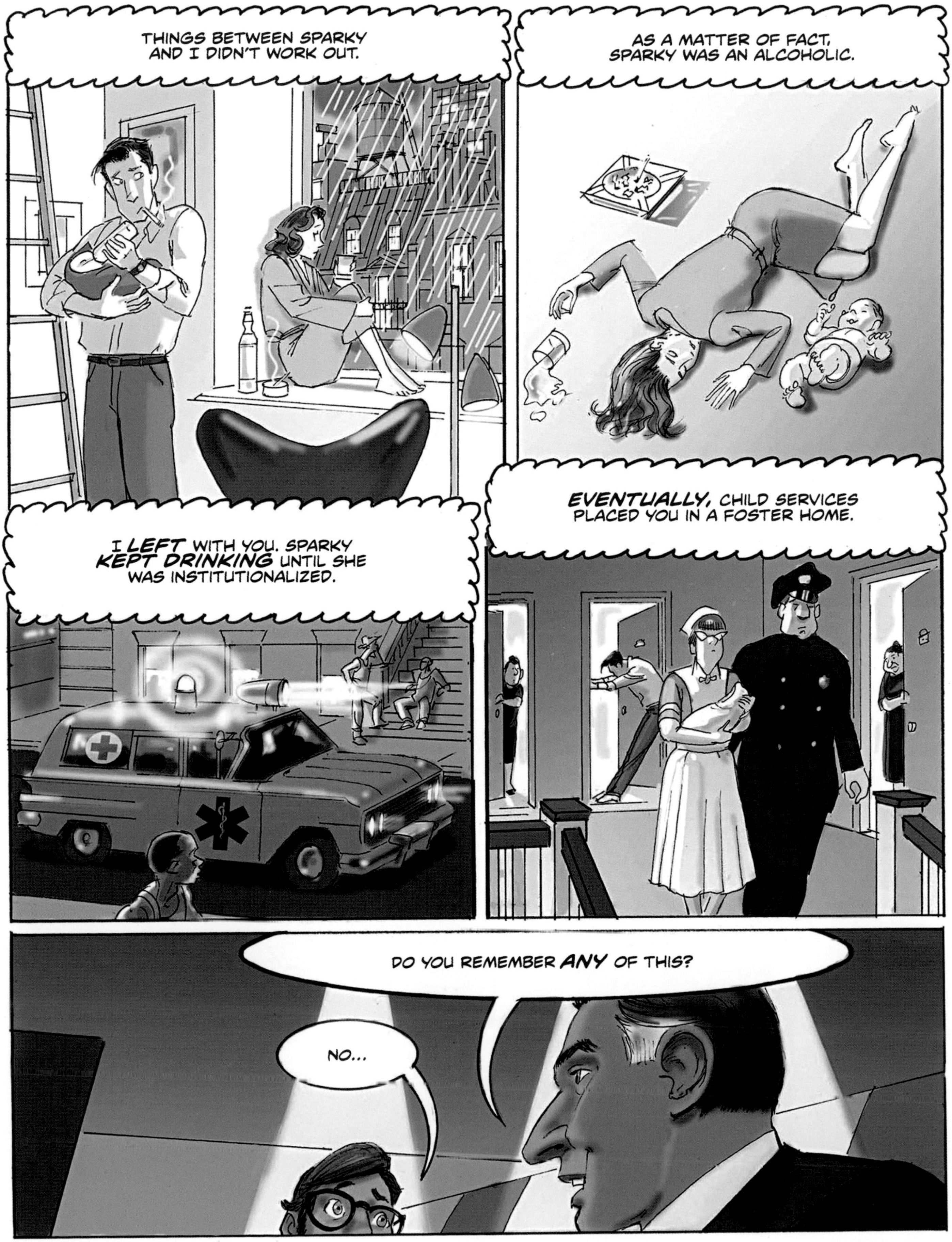
THINGS BETWEEN SPARKY AND I DIDN'T WORK OUT.
AS A MATTER OF FACT, SPARKY WAS AN ALCOHOLIC.
I LEFT WITH YOU. SPARKY KEPT DRINKING UNTIL SHE WAS INSTITUTIONALIZED.
EVENTUALLY, CHILD SERVICES PLACED YOU IN A FOSTER HOME.
DO YOU REMEMBER ANY OF THIS?
NO...

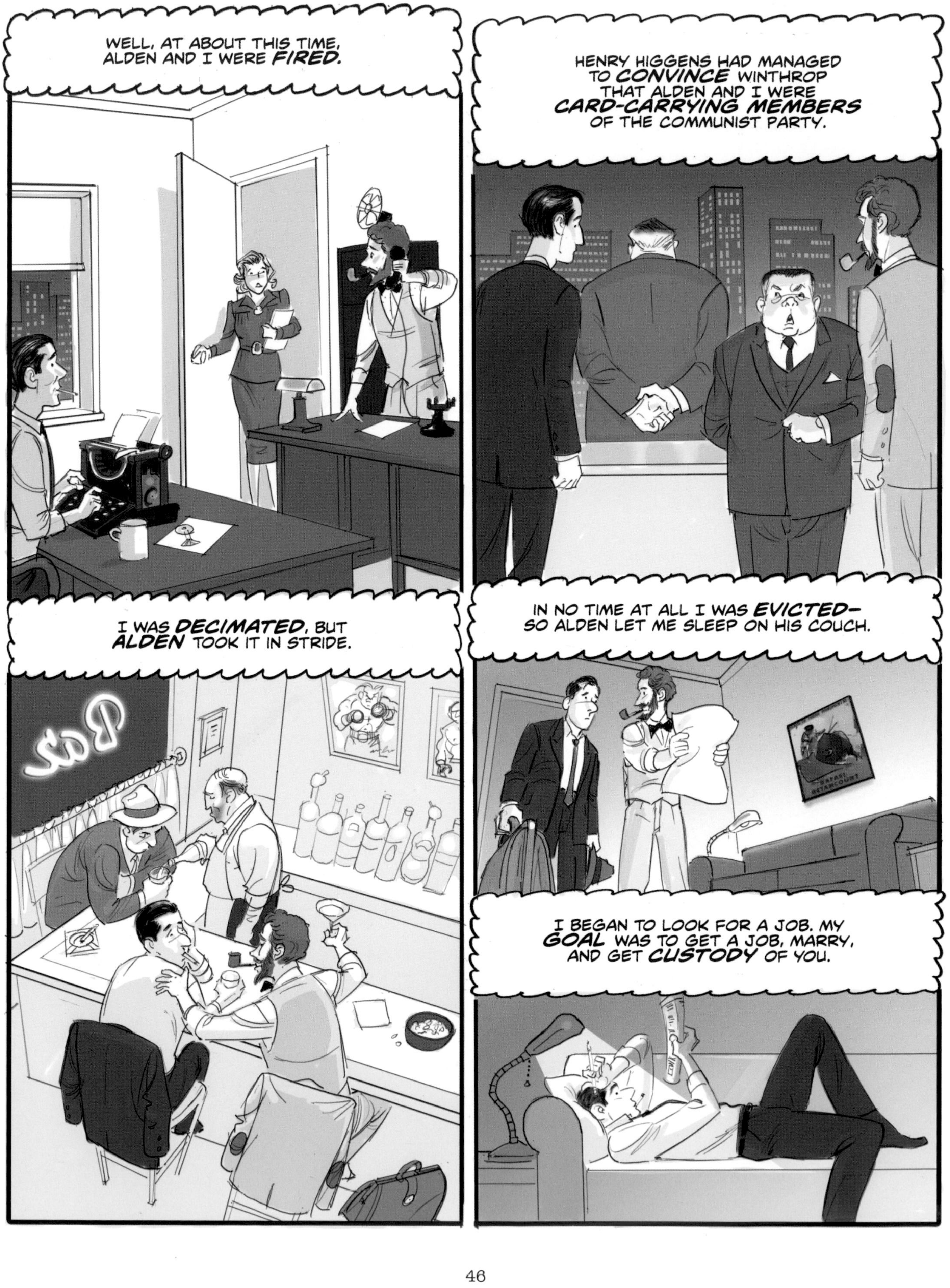
WELL, AT ABOUT THIS TIME, ALDEN AND I WERE FIRED.
HENRY HIGGENS HAD MANAGED TO CONVINCE WINTHROP THAT ALDEN AND I WERE CARD-CARRYING MEMBERS OF THE COMMUNIST PARTY.
I WAS DECIMATED, BUT ALDEN TOOK IT IN STRIDE.
IN NO TIME AT ALL I WAS EVICTED– SO ALDEN LET ME SLEEP ON HIS COUCH.
I BEGAN TO LOOK FOR A JOB. MY GOAL WAS TO GET A JOB, MARRY, AND GET CUSTODY OF YOU.

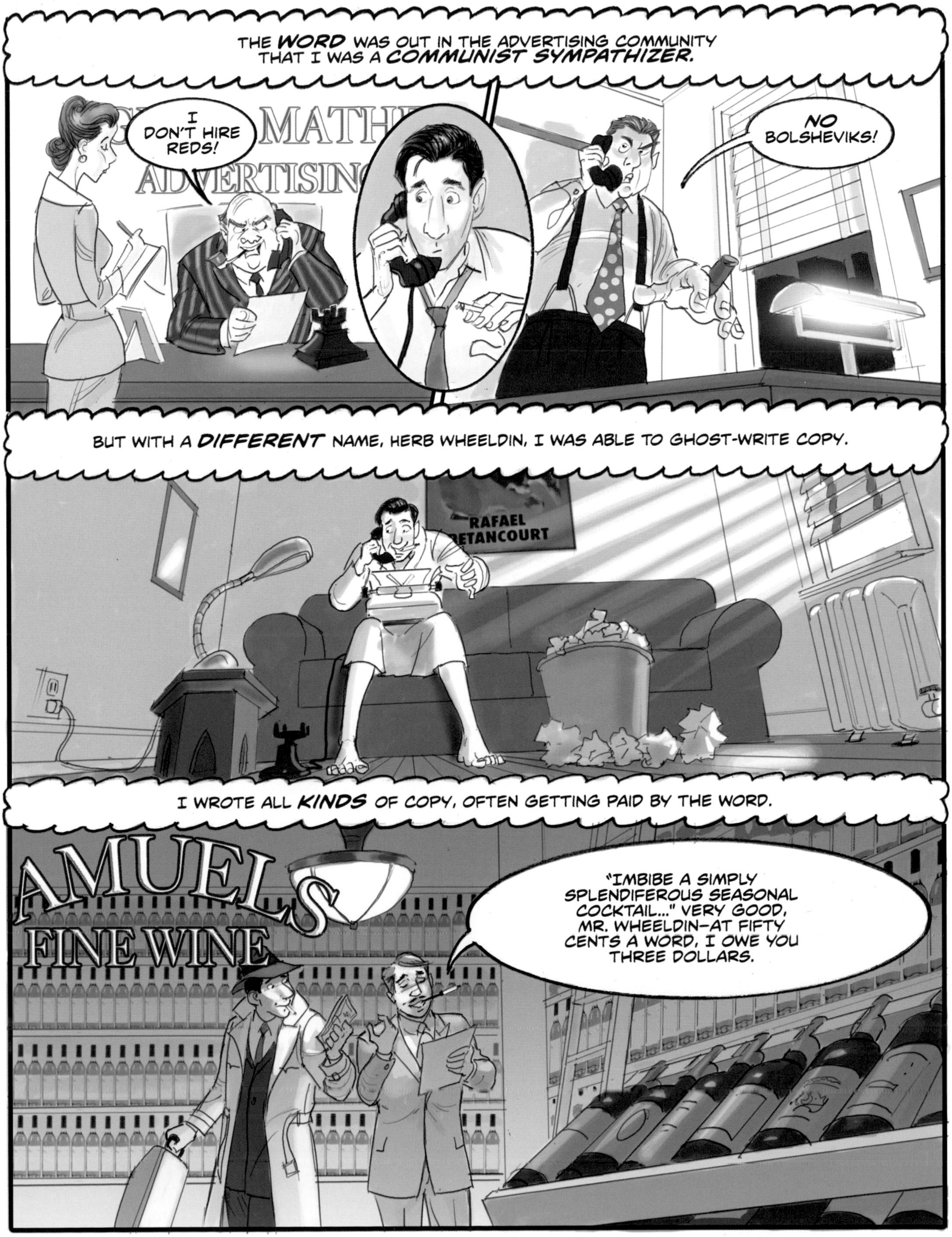
THE WORD WAS OUT IN THE ADVERTISING COMMUNITY THAT I WAS A COMMUNIST SYMPATHIZER.
MATH
ADVERTISING
I DON'T HIRE REDS!
NO BOLSHEVIKS!
BUT WITH A DIFFERENT NAME, HERB WHEELDIN, I WAS ABLE TO GHOST-WRITE COPY.
RAFAEL
BETANCOURT
I WROTE ALL KINDS OF COPY, OFTEN GETTING PAID BY THE WORD.
AMUELS
FINE WINE
"IMBIBE A SIMPLY SPLENDIFEROUS SEASONAL COCKTAIL..." VERY GOOD, MR. WHEELDIN—AT FIFTY CENTS A WORD, I OWE YOU THREE DOLLARS.

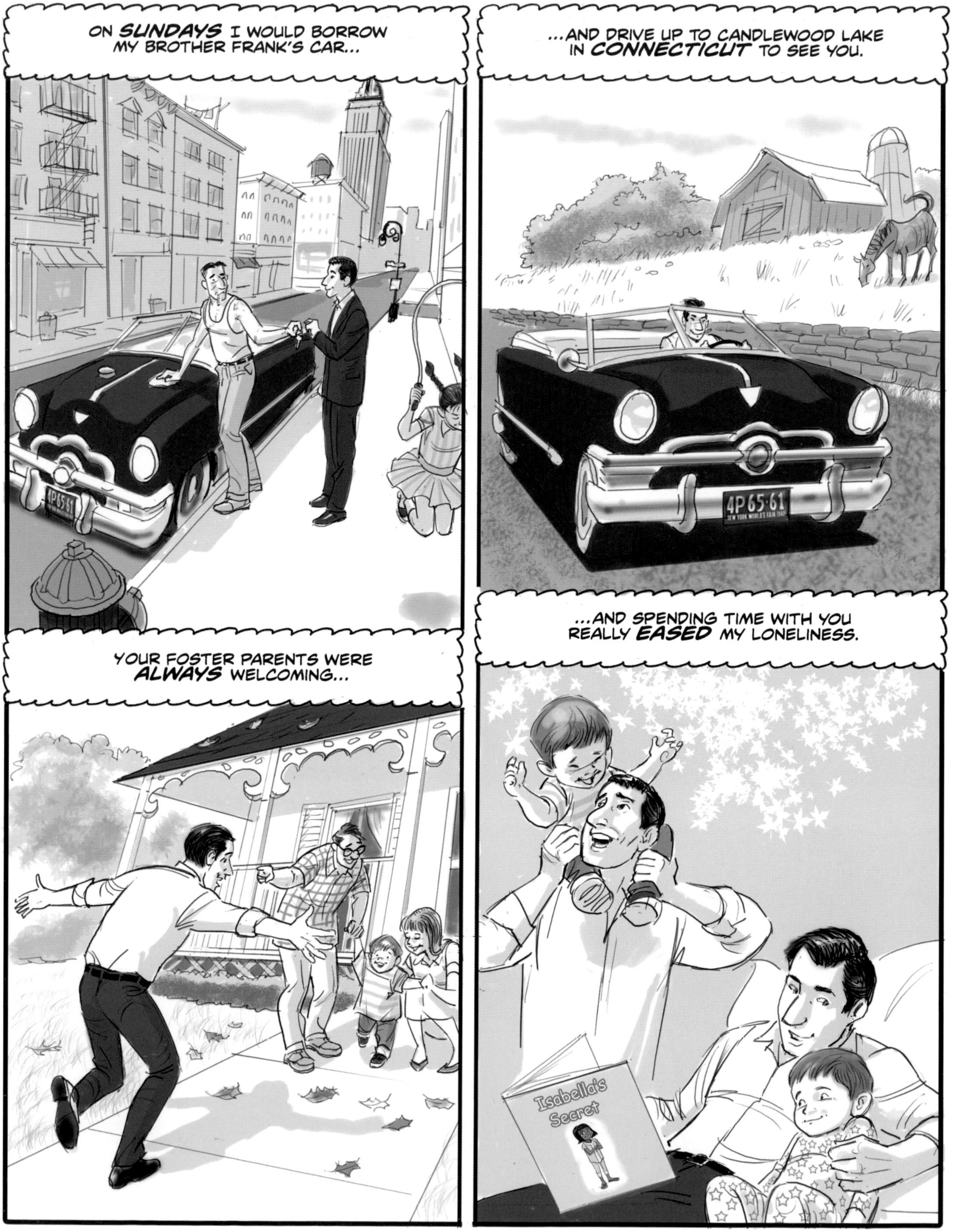
ON SUNDAYS I WOULD BORROW MY BROTHER FRANK'S CAR...
...AND DRIVE UP TO CANDLEWOOD LAKE IN CONNECTICUT TO SEE YOU.
4P 65·61
YOUR FOSTER PARENTS WERE ALWAYS WELCOMING...
...AND SPENDING TIME WITH YOU REALLY EASED MY LONELINESS.
Isabella's Secret

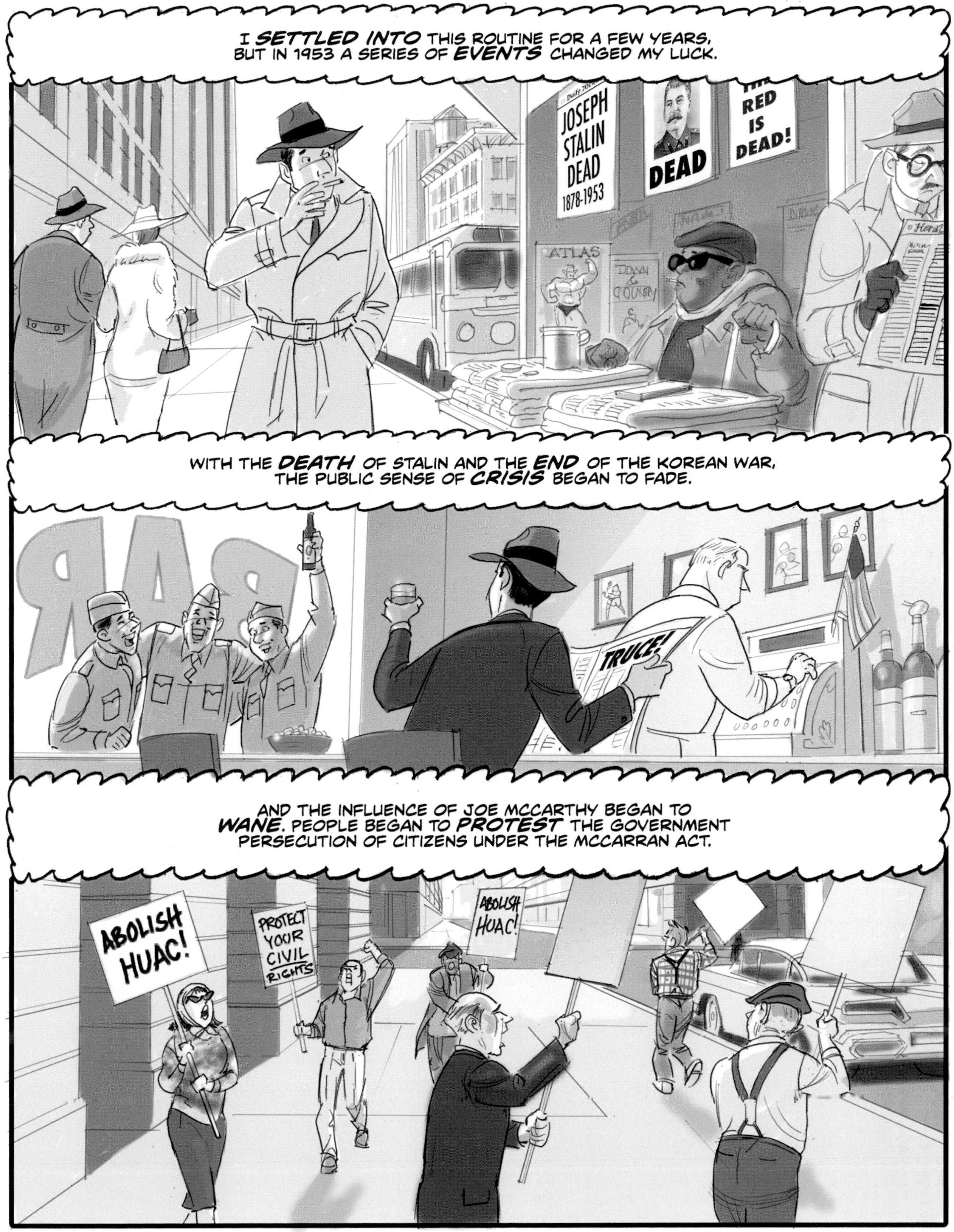
I SETTLED INTO THIS ROUTINE FOR A FEW YEARS, BUT IN 1953 A SERIES OF EVENTS CHANGED MY LUCK.
JOSEPH STALIN DEAD 1878-1953
DEAD
RED IS DEAD!
ATLAS
TOWN & COUNTRY
WITH THE DEATH OF STALIN AND THE END OF THE KOREAN WAR, THE PUBLIC SENSE OF CRISIS BEGAN TO FADE.
TRUCE!
AND THE INFLUENCE OF JOE MCCARTHY BEGAN TO WANE. PEOPLE BEGAN TO PROTEST THE GOVERNMENT PERSECUTION OF CITIZENS UNDER THE MCCARRAN ACT.
ABOLISH HUAC!
PROTECT YOUR CIVIL RIGHTS
ABOLISH HUAC!

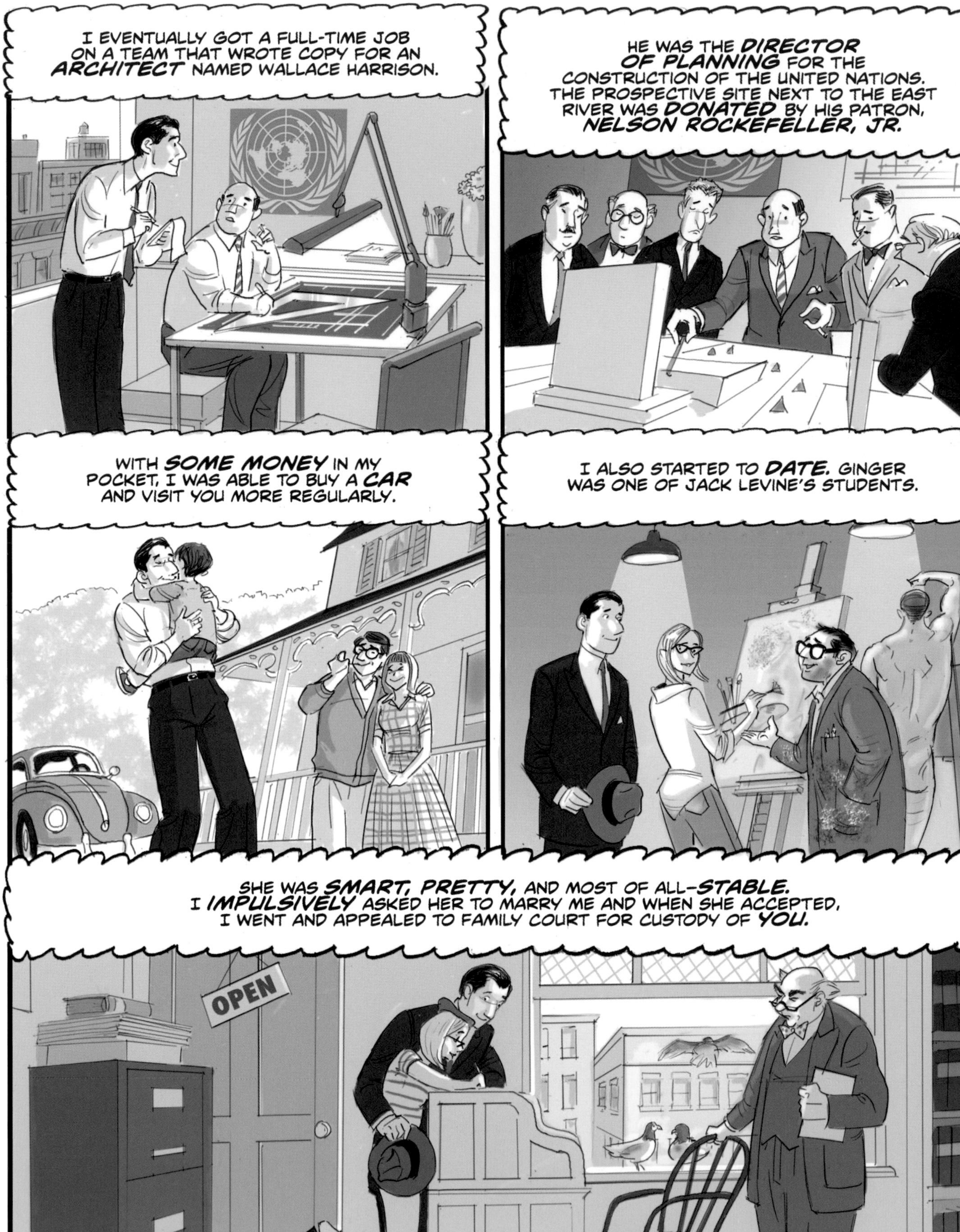
I EVENTUALLY GOT A FULL-TIME JOB ON A TEAM THAT WROTE COPY FOR AN ARCHITECT NAMED WALLACE HARRISON.
HE WAS THE DIRECTOR OF PLANNING FOR THE CONSTRUCTION OF THE UNITED NATIONS. THE PROSPECTIVE SITE NEXT TO THE EAST RIVER WAS DONATED BY HIS PATRON, NELSON ROCKEFELLER, JR.
WITH SOME MONEY IN MY POCKET, I WAS ABLE TO BUY A CAR AND VISIT YOU MORE REGULARLY.
I ALSO STARTED TO DATE. GINGER WAS ONE OF JACK LEVINE'S STUDENTS.
SHE WAS SMART, PRETTY, AND MOST OF ALL–STABLE. I IMPULSIVELY ASKED HER TO MARRY ME AND WHEN SHE ACCEPTED, I WENT AND APPEALED TO FAMILY COURT FOR CUSTODY OF YOU.
OPEN

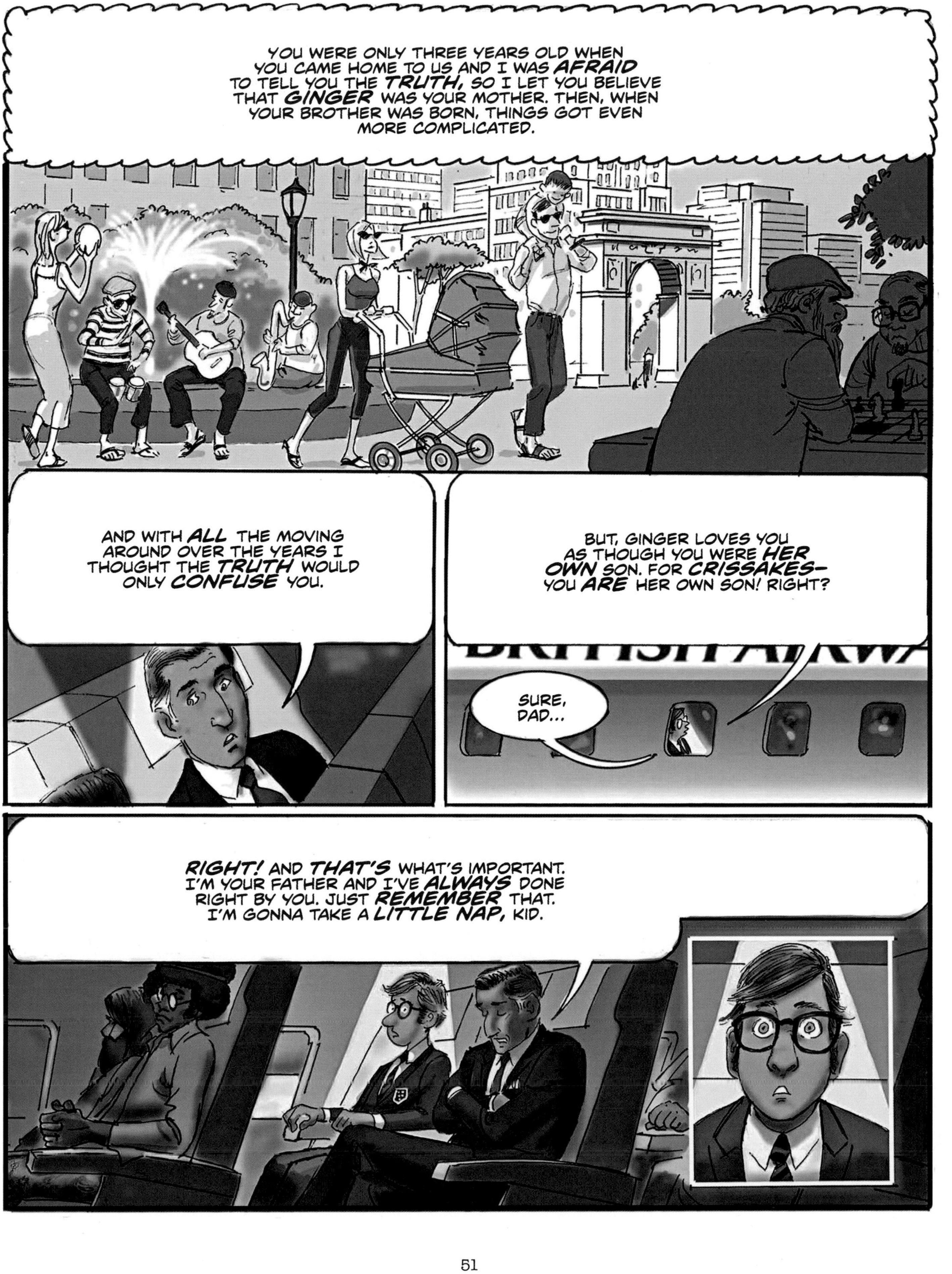
YOU WERE ONLY THREE YEARS OLD WHEN YOU CAME HOME TO US AND I WAS AFRAID TO TELL YOU THE TRUTH, SO I LET YOU BELIEVE THAT GINGER WAS YOUR MOTHER. THEN, WHEN YOUR BROTHER WAS BORN, THINGS GOT EVEN MORE COMPLICATED.
AND WITH ALL THE MOVING AROUND OVER THE YEARS I THOUGHT THE TRUTH WOULD ONLY CONFUSE YOU.
BUT, GINGER LOVES YOU AS THOUGH YOU WERE HER OWN SON. FOR CRISSAKES- YOU ARE HER OWN SON! RIGHT?
SURE, DAD...
RIGHT! AND THAT'S WHAT'S IMPORTANT. I'M YOUR FATHER AND I'VE ALWAYS DONE RIGHT BY YOU. JUST REMEMBER THAT. I'M GONNA TAKE A LITTLE NAP, KID.

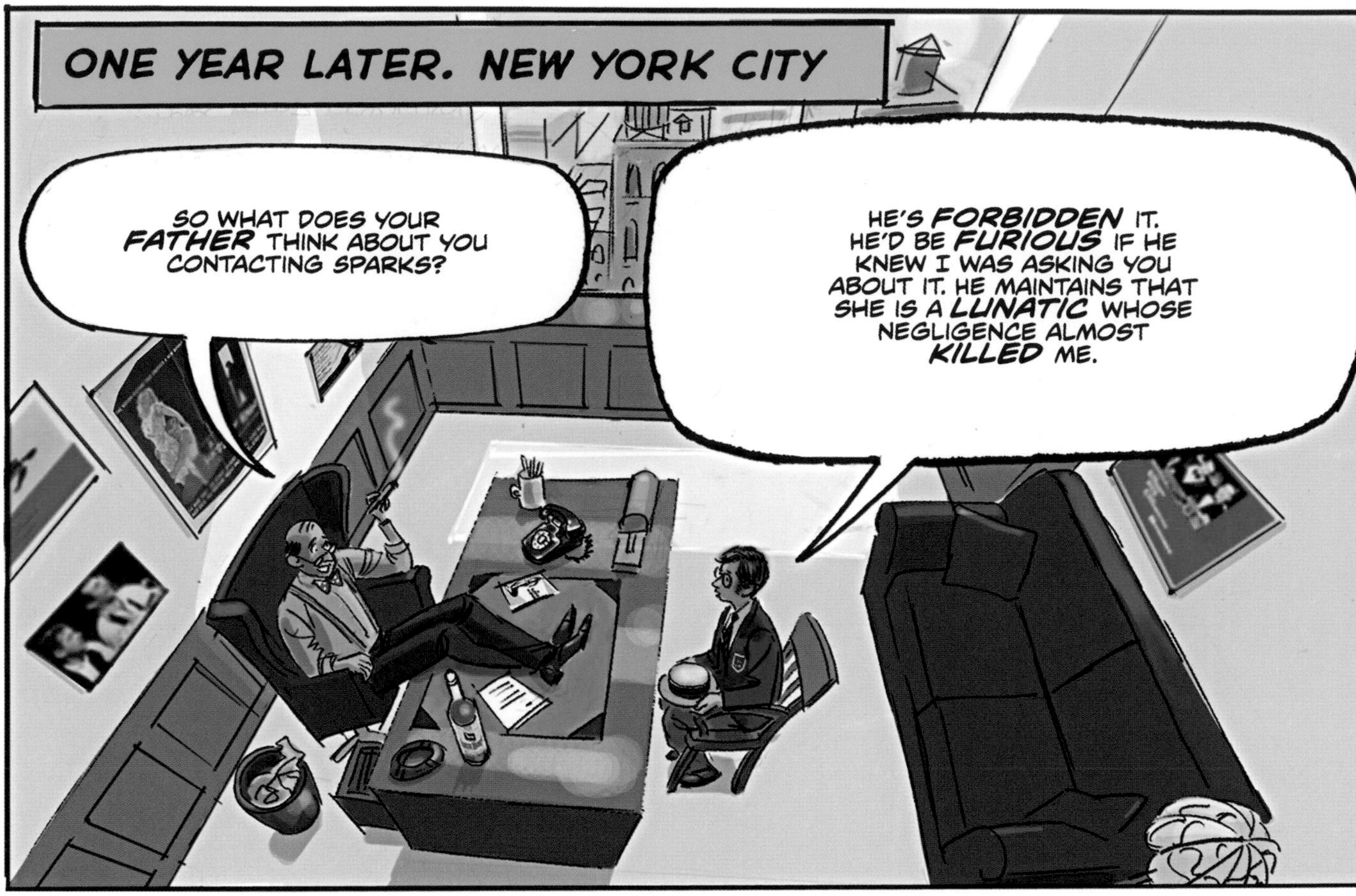
ONE YEAR LATER. NEW YORK CITY
SO WHAT DOES YOUR FATHER THINK ABOUT YOU CONTACTING SPARKS?
HE'S FORBIDDEN IT. HE'D BE FURIOUS IF HE KNEW I WAS ASKING YOU ABOUT IT. HE MAINTAINS THAT SHE IS A LUNATIC WHOSE NEGLIGENCE ALMOST KILLED ME.

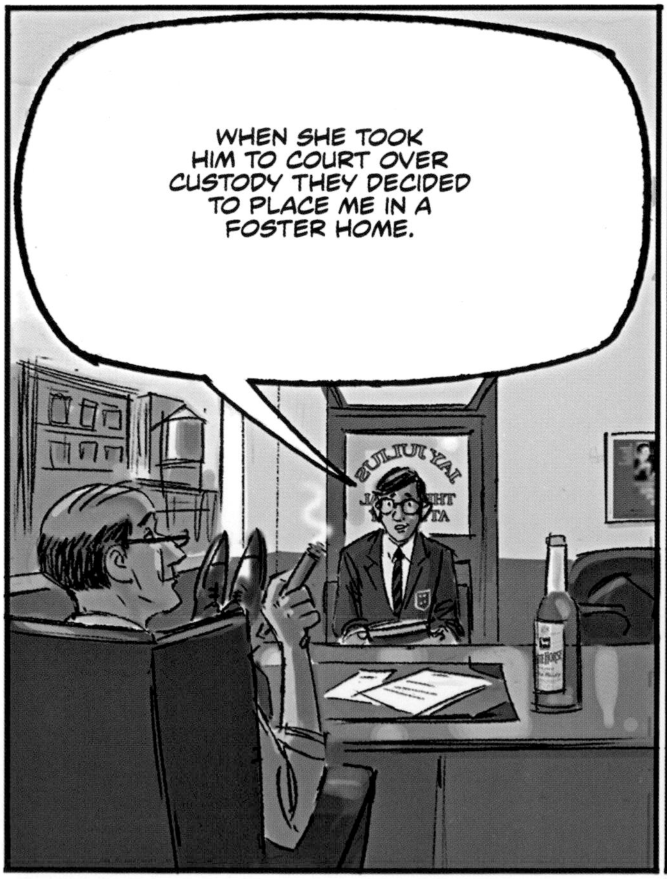
WHEN SHE TOOK HIM TO COURT OVER CUSTODY THEY DECIDED TO PLACE ME IN A FOSTER HOME.

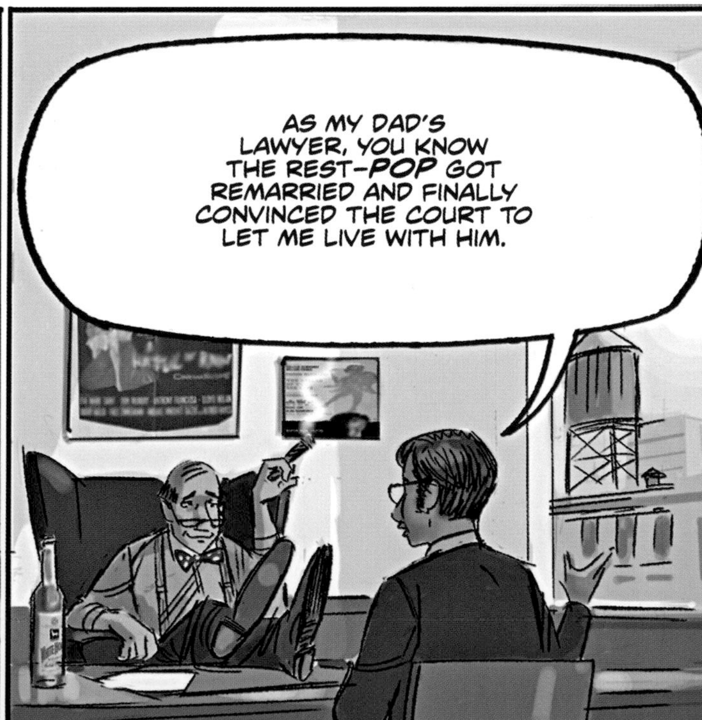
AS MY DAD'S LAWYER, YOU KNOW THE REST–POP GOT REMARRIED AND FINALLY CONVINCED THE COURT TO LET ME LIVE WITH HIM.

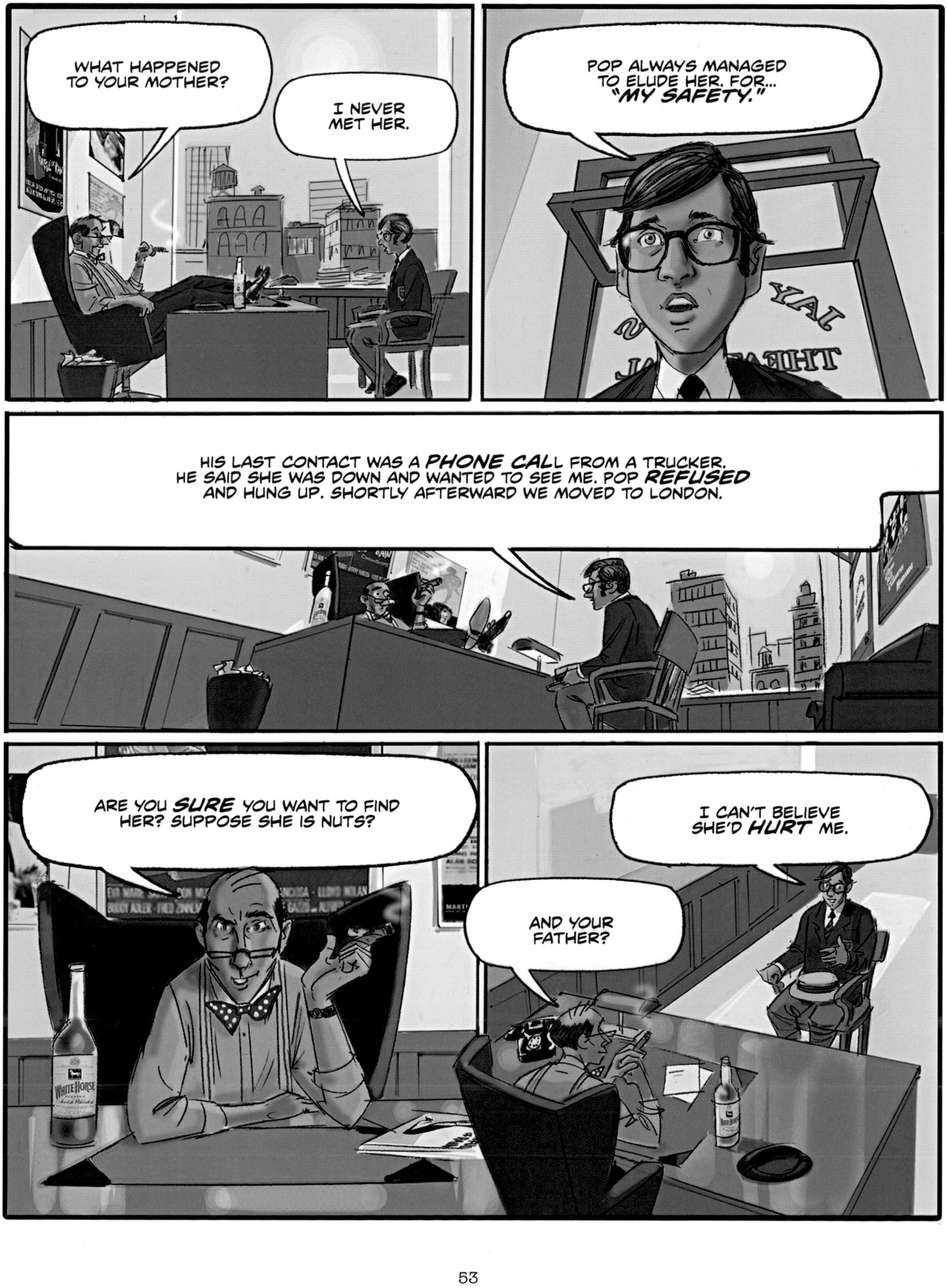
WHAT HAPPENED TO YOUR MOTHER?
I NEVER MET HER.
POP ALWAYS MANAGED TO ELUDE HER. FOR... "MY SAFETY."
HIS LAST CONTACT WAS A PHONE CALL FROM A TRUCKER. HE SAID SHE WAS DOWN AND WANTED TO SEE ME. POP REFUSED AND HUNG UP. SHORTLY AFTERWARD WE MOVED TO LONDON.
ARE YOU SURE YOU WANT TO FIND HER? SUPPOSE SHE IS NUTS?
I CAN'T BELIEVE SHE'D HURT ME.
AND YOUR FATHER?

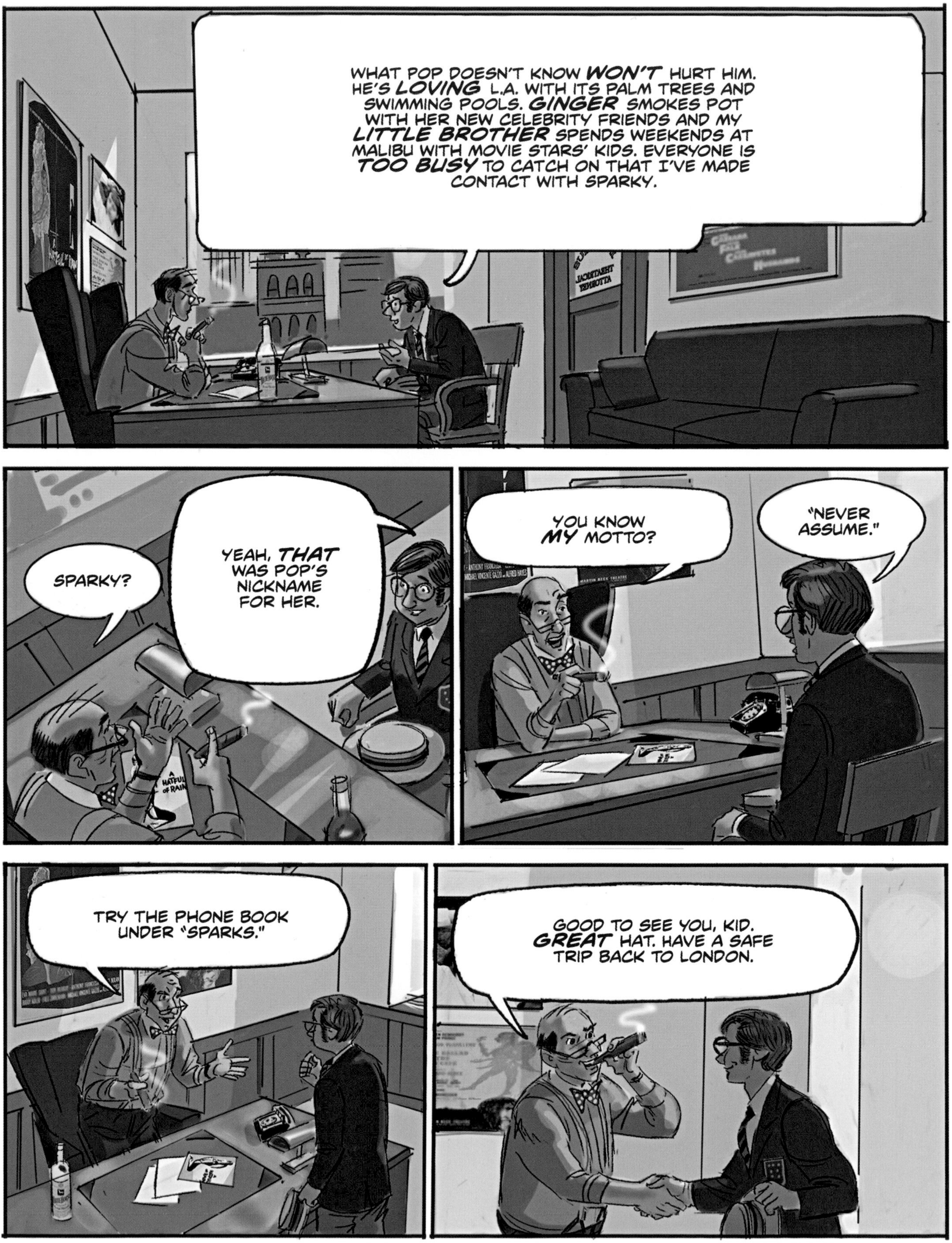

WHAT POP DOESN'T KNOW WON'T HURT HIM. HE'S LOVING L.A. WITH ITS PALM TREES AND SWIMMING POOLS. GINGER SMOKES POT WITH HER NEW CELEBRITY FRIENDS AND MY LITTLE BROTHER SPENDS WEEKENDS AT MALIBU WITH MOVIE STARS' KIDS. EVERYONE IS TOO BUSY TO CATCH ON THAT I'VE MADE CONTACT WITH SPARKY.
SPARKY?
YEAH, THAT WAS POP'S NICKNAME FOR HER.
YOU KNOW MY MOTTO?
"NEVER ASSUME."
TRY THE PHONE BOOK UNDER "SPARKS."
GOOD TO SEE YOU, KID. GREAT HAT. HAVE A SAFE TRIP BACK TO LONDON.

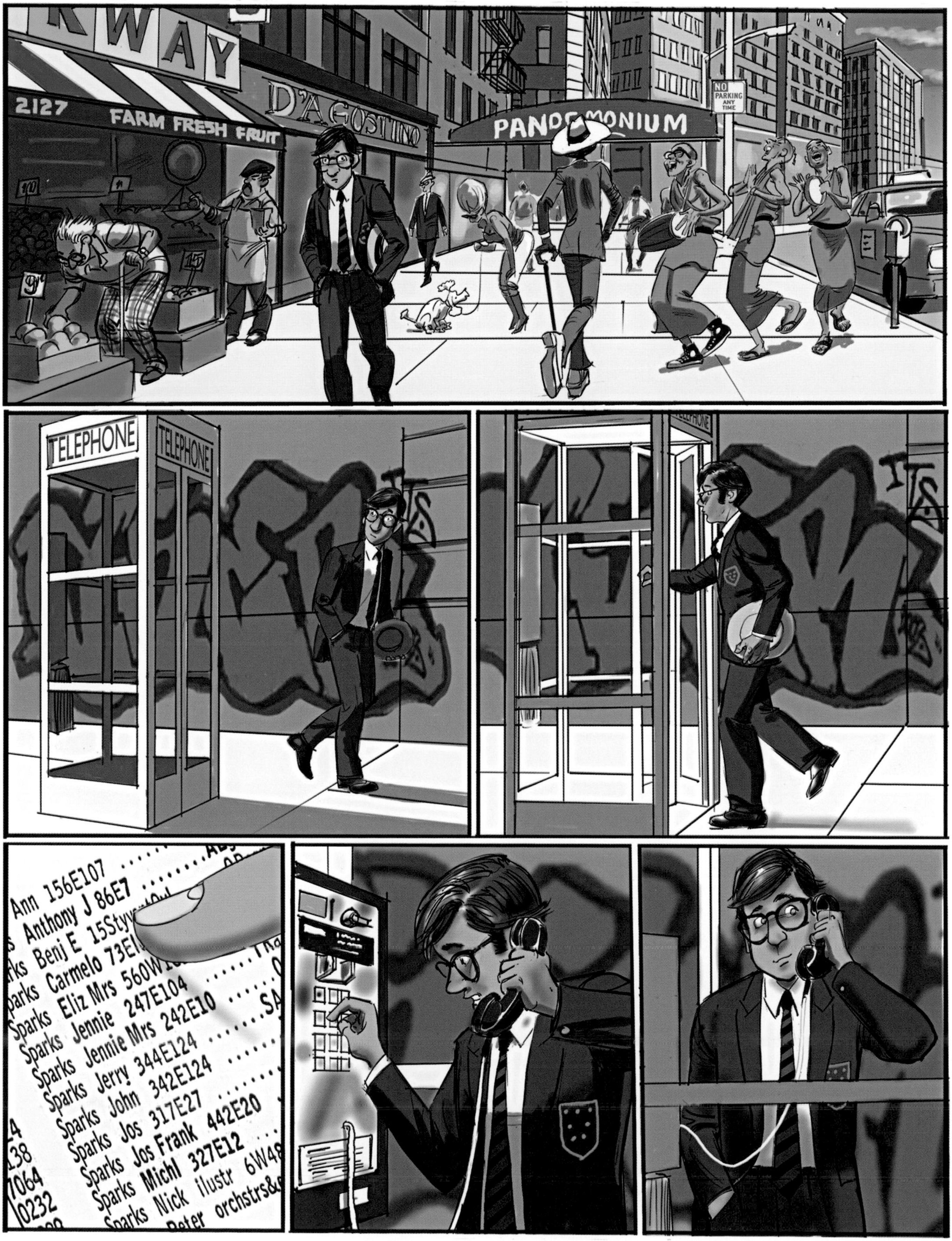

2127
FARM FRESH FRUIT
D'AGOSTINO
NO PARKING ANY TIME
TELEPHONE
TELEPHONE
Ann 156E107
Anthony J 86E7
Sparks Eliz Mrs 560W
Sparks Jennie 247E104
Sparks Jennie Mrs 242E10
Sparks Jerry 344E124
Sparks John 342E124
Sparks Jos 317E27
Sparks Jos Frank 442E20
Sparks Michl 327E12
Sparks Nick ilustr 6W48

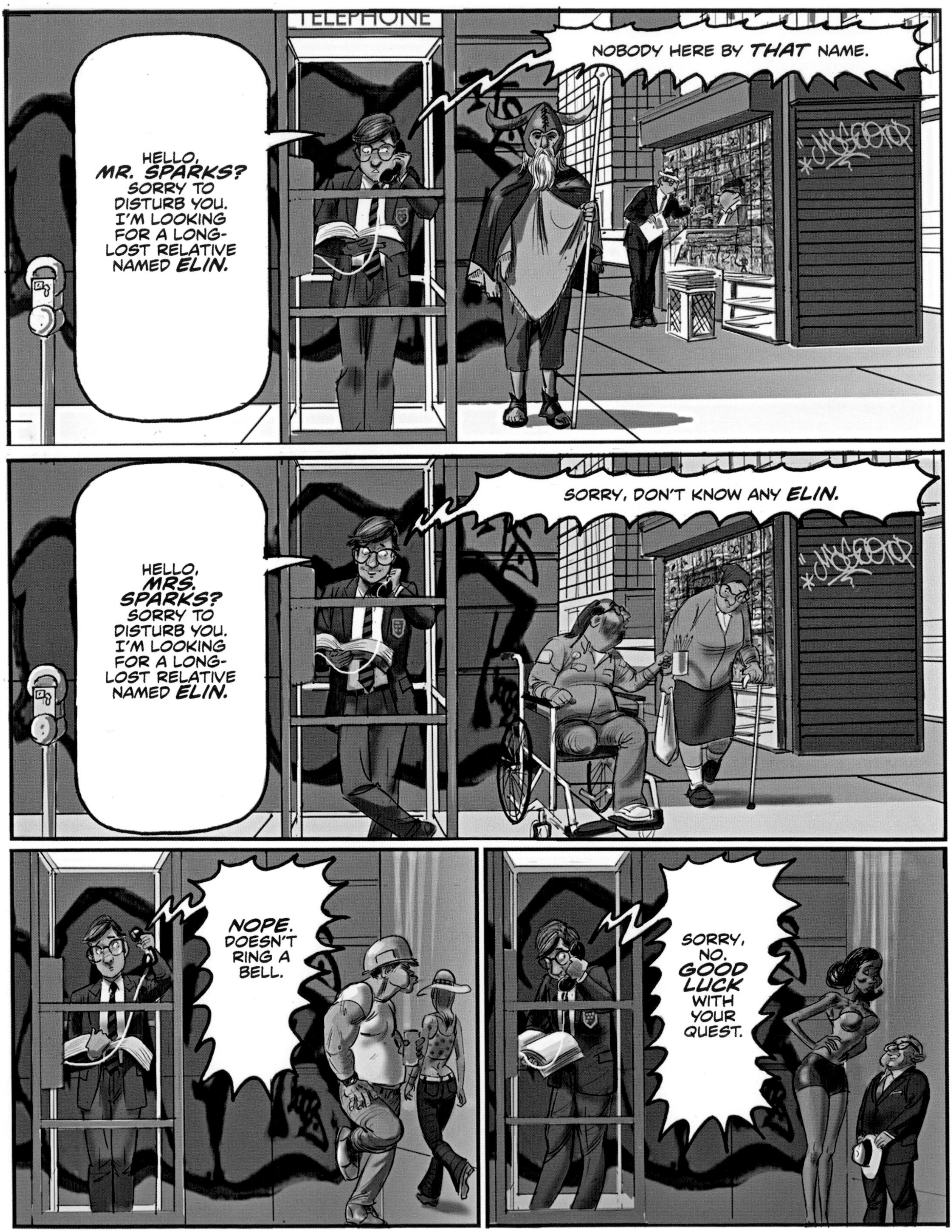
HELLO, MR. SPARKS? SORRY TO DISTURB YOU. I'M LOOKING FOR A LONG-LOST RELATIVE NAMED ELIN.
NOBODY HERE BY THAT NAME.
TELEPHONE
HELLO, MRS. SPARKS? SORRY TO DISTURB YOU. I'M LOOKING FOR A LONG-LOST RELATIVE NAMED ELIN.
SORRY, DON'T KNOW ANY ELIN.
NOPE. DOESN'T RING A BELL.
SORRY, NO. GOOD LUCK WITH YOUR QUEST.

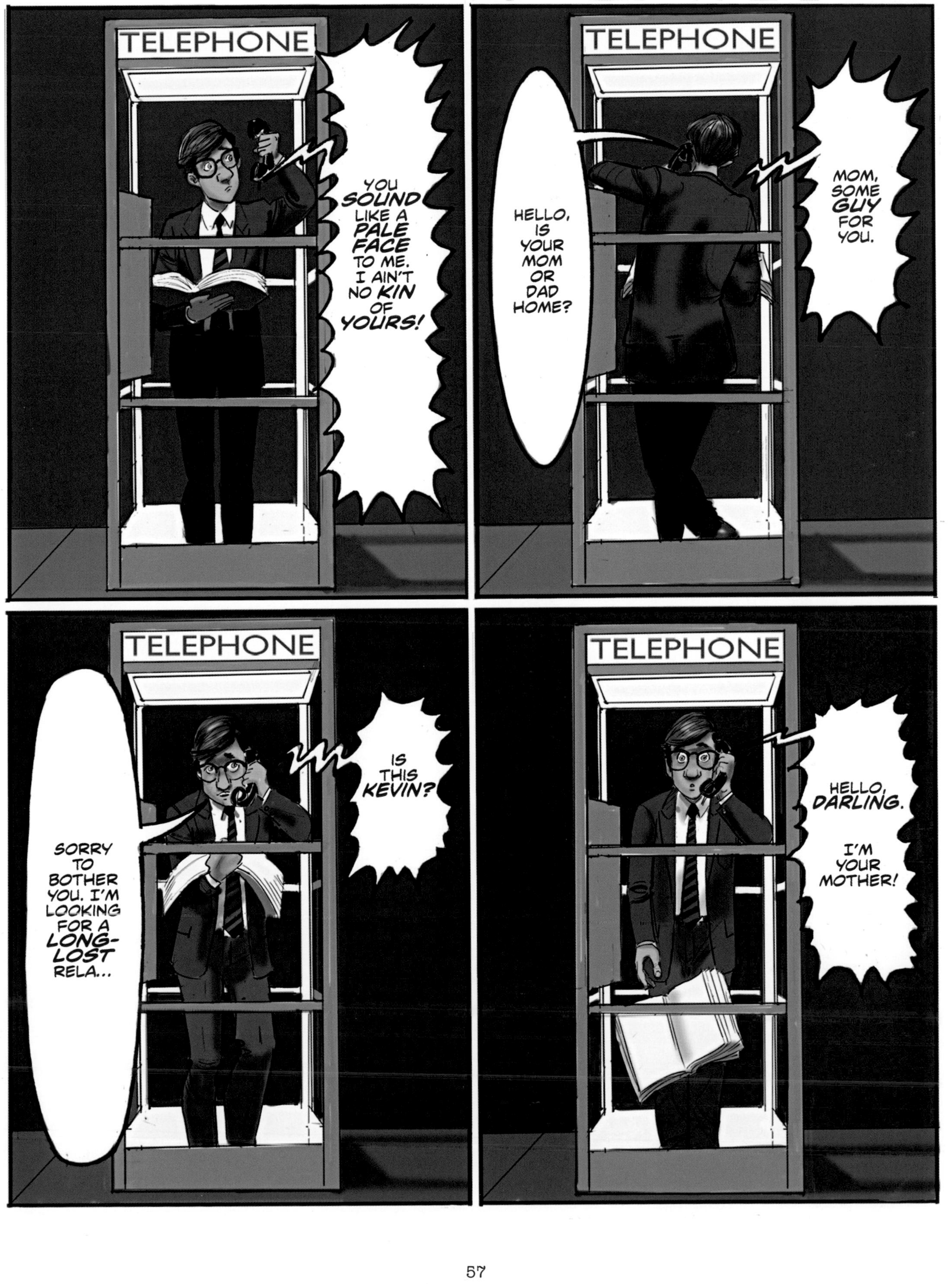
TELEPHONE
YOU SOUND LIKE A PALE FACE TO ME. I AIN'T NO KIN OF YOURS!
TELEPHONE
HELLO, IS YOUR MOM OR DAD HOME?
MOM, SOME GUY FOR YOU.
TELEPHONE
IS THIS KEVIN?
SORRY TO BOTHER YOU. I'M LOOKING FOR A LONG-LOST RELA...
TELEPHONE
HELLO, DARLING.
I'M YOUR MOTHER!

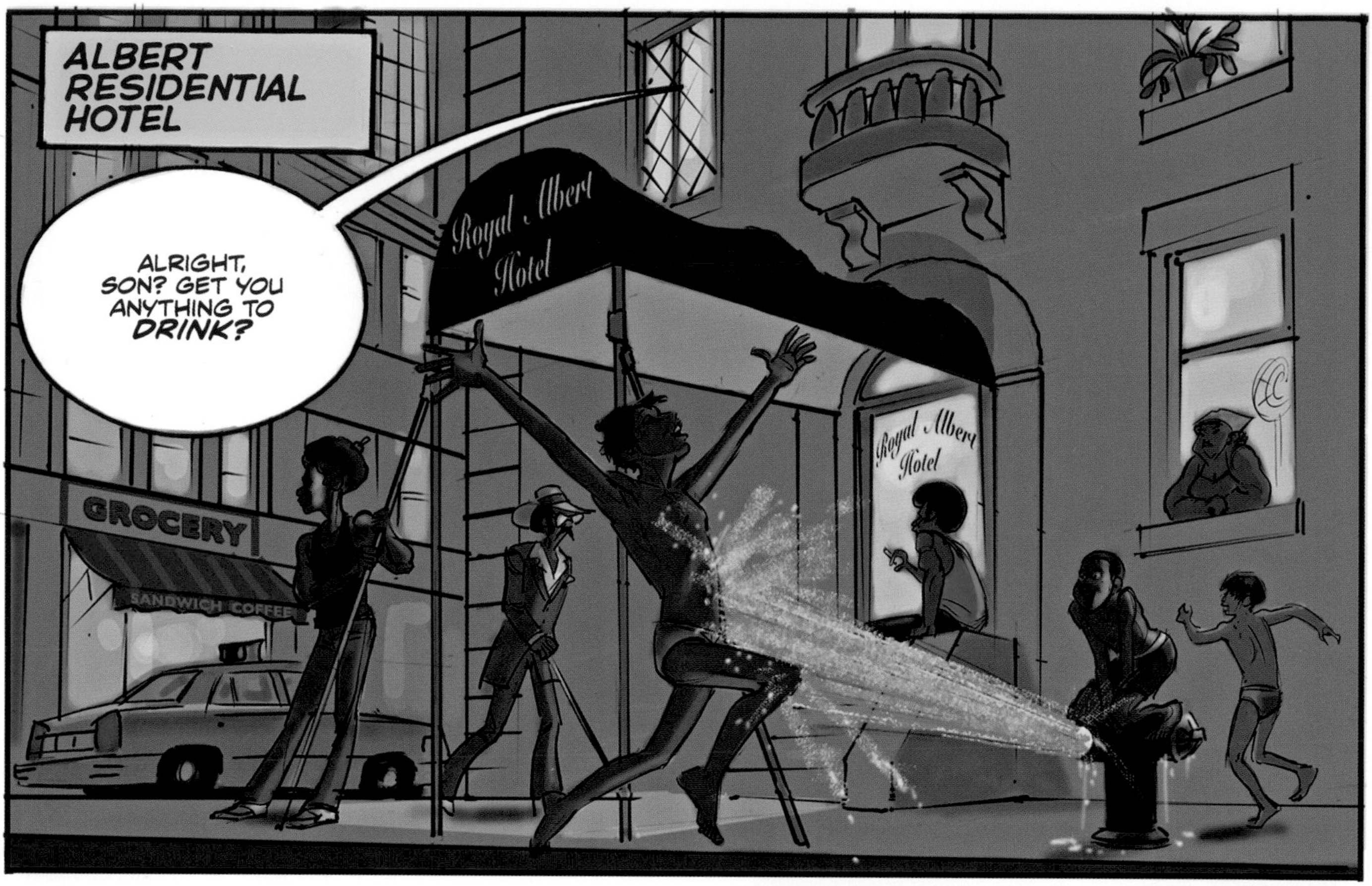
ALBERT RESIDENTIAL HOTEL
ALRIGHT, SON? GET YOU ANYTHING TO DRINK?
Royal Albert Hotel
GROCERY
SANDWICH COFFEE
Royal Albert Hotel

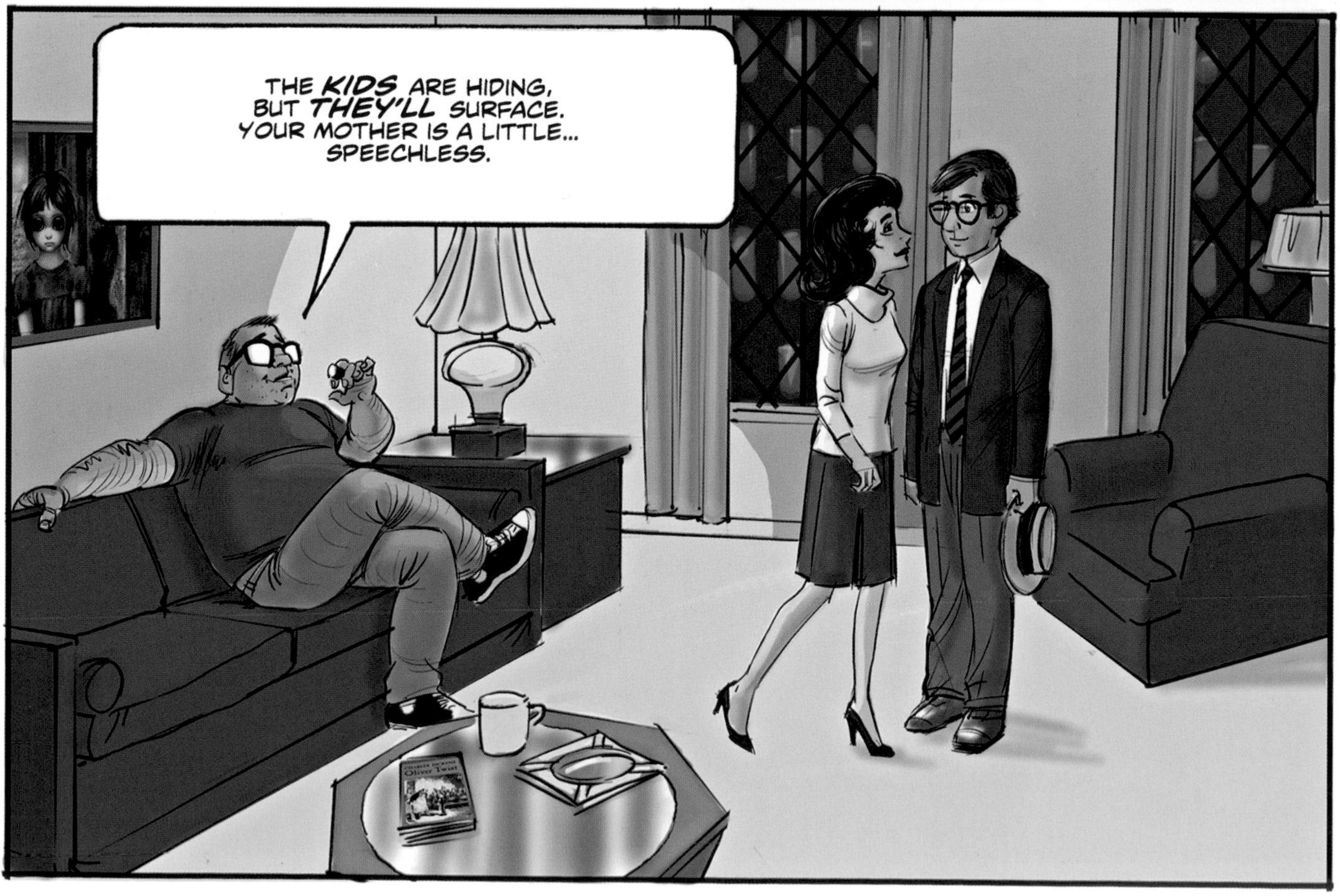
THE KIDS ARE HIDING, BUT THEY'LL SURFACE. YOUR MOTHER IS A LITTLE... SPEECHLESS.
Oliver Twist

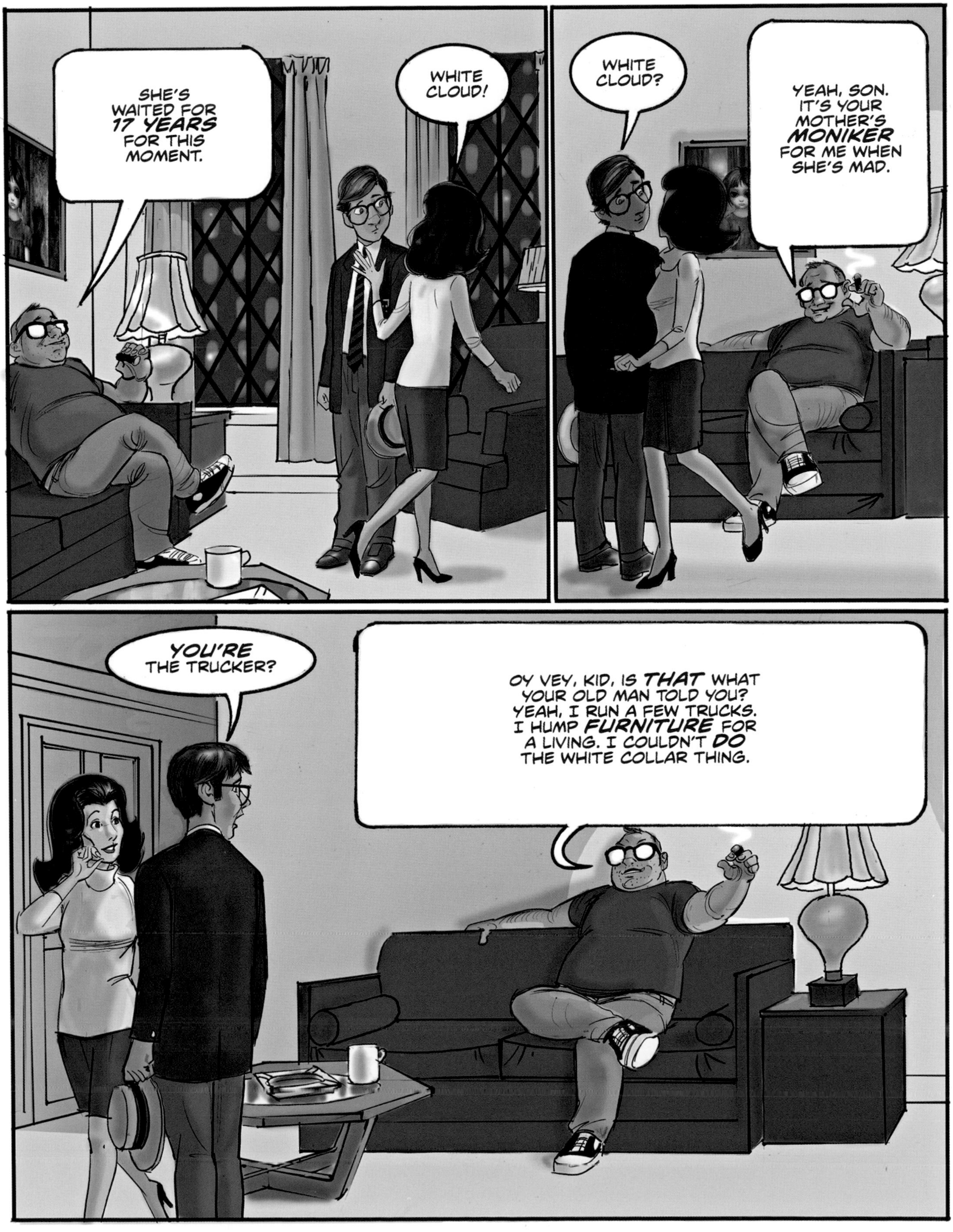
SHE'S WAITED FOR *17 YEARS* FOR THIS MOMENT.
WHITE CLOUD!
WHITE CLOUD?
YEAH, SON. IT'S YOUR MOTHER'S *MONIKER* FOR ME WHEN SHE'S MAD.
YOU'RE THE TRUCKER?
OY VEY, KID, IS *THAT* WHAT YOUR OLD MAN TOLD YOU? YEAH, I RUN A FEW TRUCKS. I HUMP *FURNITURE* FOR A LIVING. I COULDN'T *DO* THE WHITE COLLAR THING.

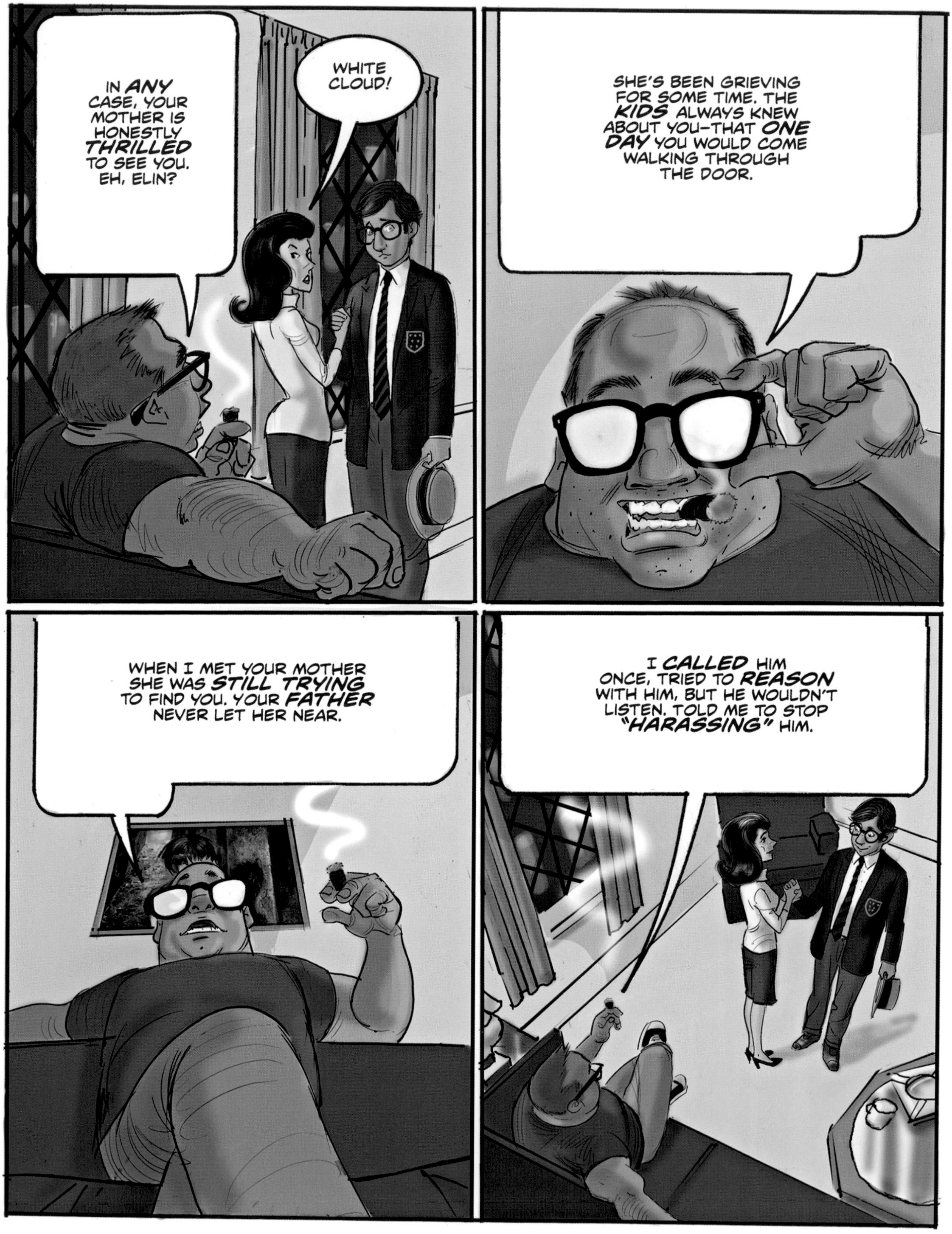
IN ANY CASE, YOUR MOTHER IS HONESTLY THRILLED TO SEE YOU. EH, ELIN?
WHITE CLOUD!
SHE'S BEEN GRIEVING FOR SOME TIME. THE KIDS ALWAYS KNEW ABOUT YOU–THAT ONE DAY YOU WOULD COME WALKING THROUGH THE DOOR.
WHEN I MET YOUR MOTHER SHE WAS STILL TRYING TO FIND YOU. YOUR FATHER NEVER LET HER NEAR.
I CALLED HIM ONCE, TRIED TO REASON WITH HIM, BUT HE WOULDN'T LISTEN. TOLD ME TO STOP "HARASSING" HIM.

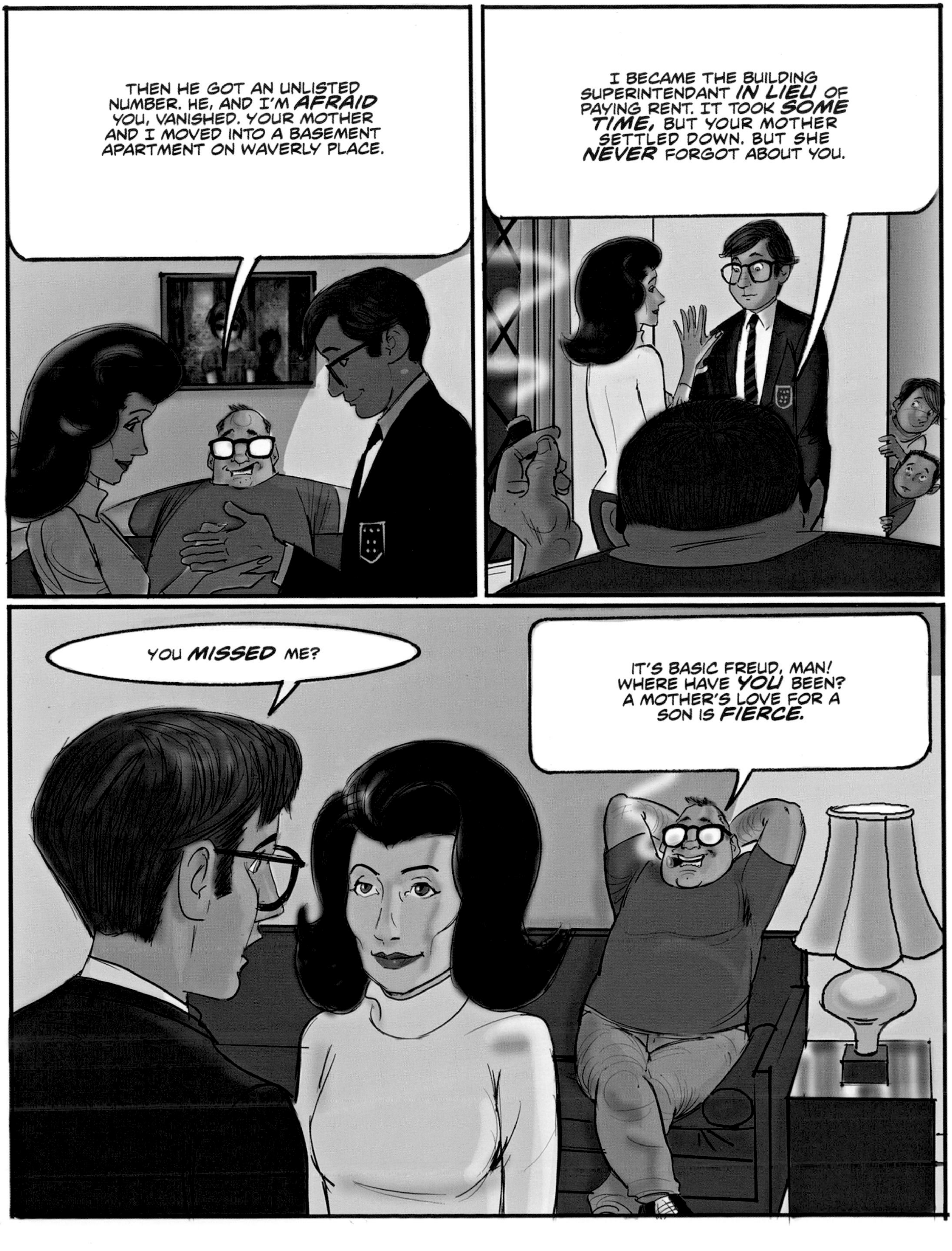
THEN HE GOT AN UNLISTED NUMBER. HE, AND I'M **AFRAID** YOU, VANISHED. YOUR MOTHER AND I MOVED INTO A BASEMENT APARTMENT ON WAVERLY PLACE.
I BECAME THE BUILDING SUPERINTENDANT **IN LIEU** OF PAYING RENT. IT TOOK **SOME TIME,** BUT YOUR MOTHER SETTLED DOWN. BUT SHE **NEVER** FORGOT ABOUT YOU.
YOU **MISSED** ME?
IT'S BASIC FREUD, MAN! WHERE HAVE **YOU** BEEN? A MOTHER'S LOVE FOR A SON IS **FIERCE.**

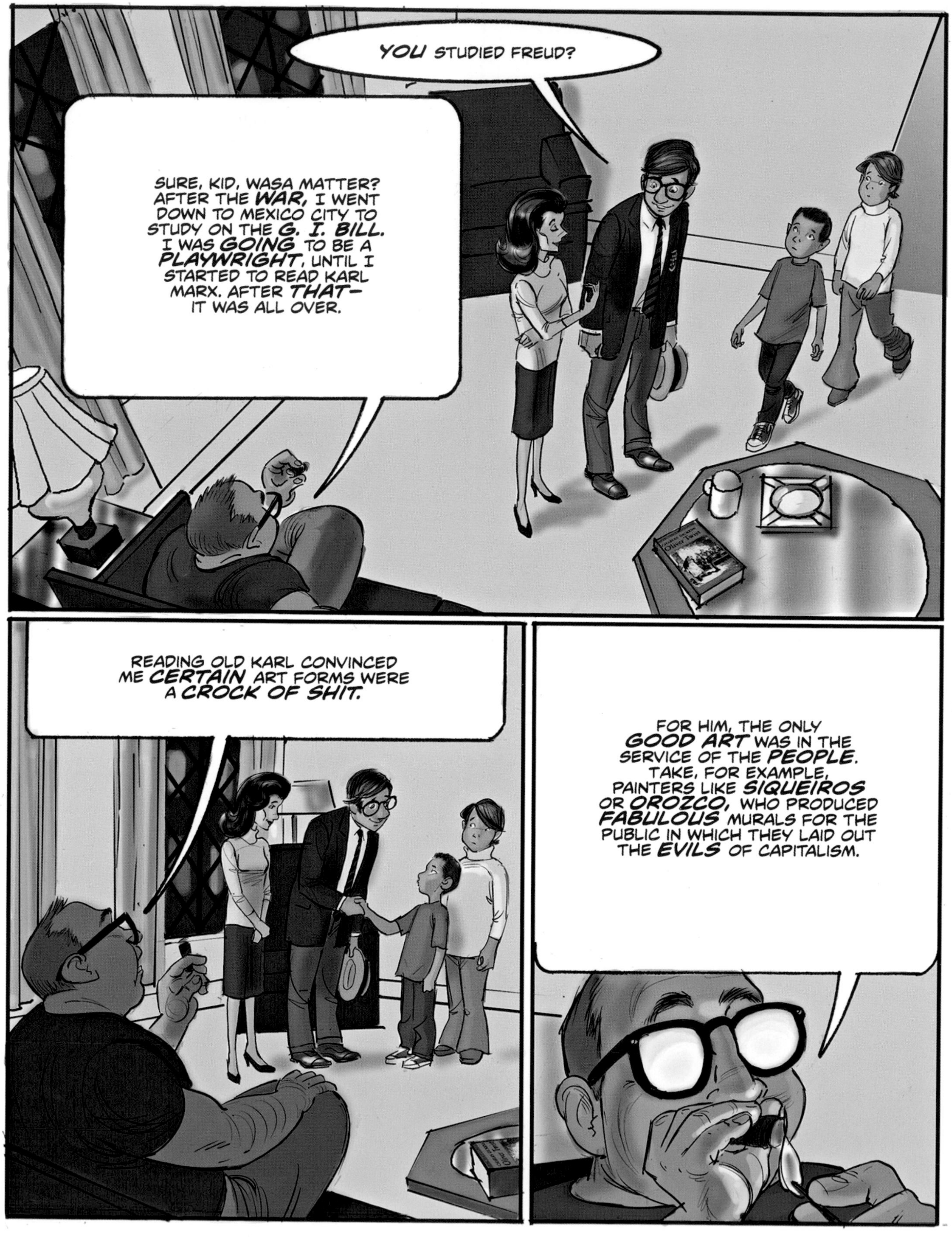
YOU STUDIED FREUD?
SURE, KID, WASA MATTER? AFTER THE WAR, I WENT DOWN TO MEXICO CITY TO STUDY ON THE G. I. BILL. I WAS GOING TO BE A PLAYWRIGHT, UNTIL I STARTED TO READ KARL MARX. AFTER THAT– IT WAS ALL OVER.
Oliver Twist
READING OLD KARL CONVINCED ME CERTAIN ART FORMS WERE A CROCK OF SHIT.
FOR HIM, THE ONLY GOOD ART WAS IN THE SERVICE OF THE PEOPLE. TAKE, FOR EXAMPLE, PAINTERS LIKE SIQUEIROS OR OROZCO, WHO PRODUCED FABULOUS MURALS FOR THE PUBLIC IN WHICH THEY LAID OUT THE EVILS OF CAPITALISM.

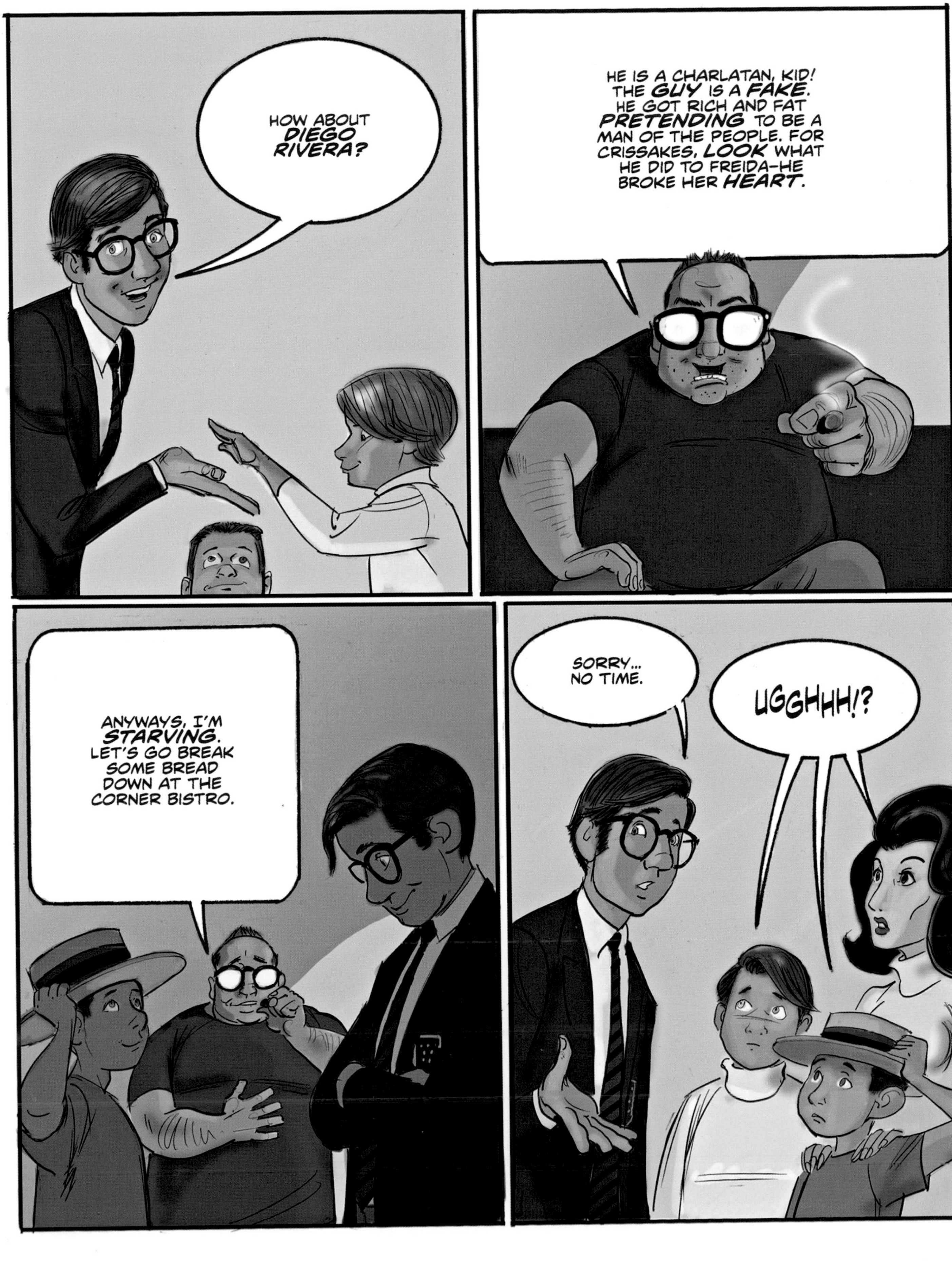
HOW ABOUT DIEGO RIVERA?
HE IS A CHARLATAN, KID! THE GUY IS A FAKE. HE GOT RICH AND FAT PRETENDING TO BE A MAN OF THE PEOPLE. FOR CRISSAKES, LOOK WHAT HE DID TO FREIDA–HE BROKE HER HEART.
ANYWAYS, I'M STARVING. LET'S GO BREAK SOME BREAD DOWN AT THE CORNER BISTRO.
SORRY... NO TIME.
UGGHHH!?

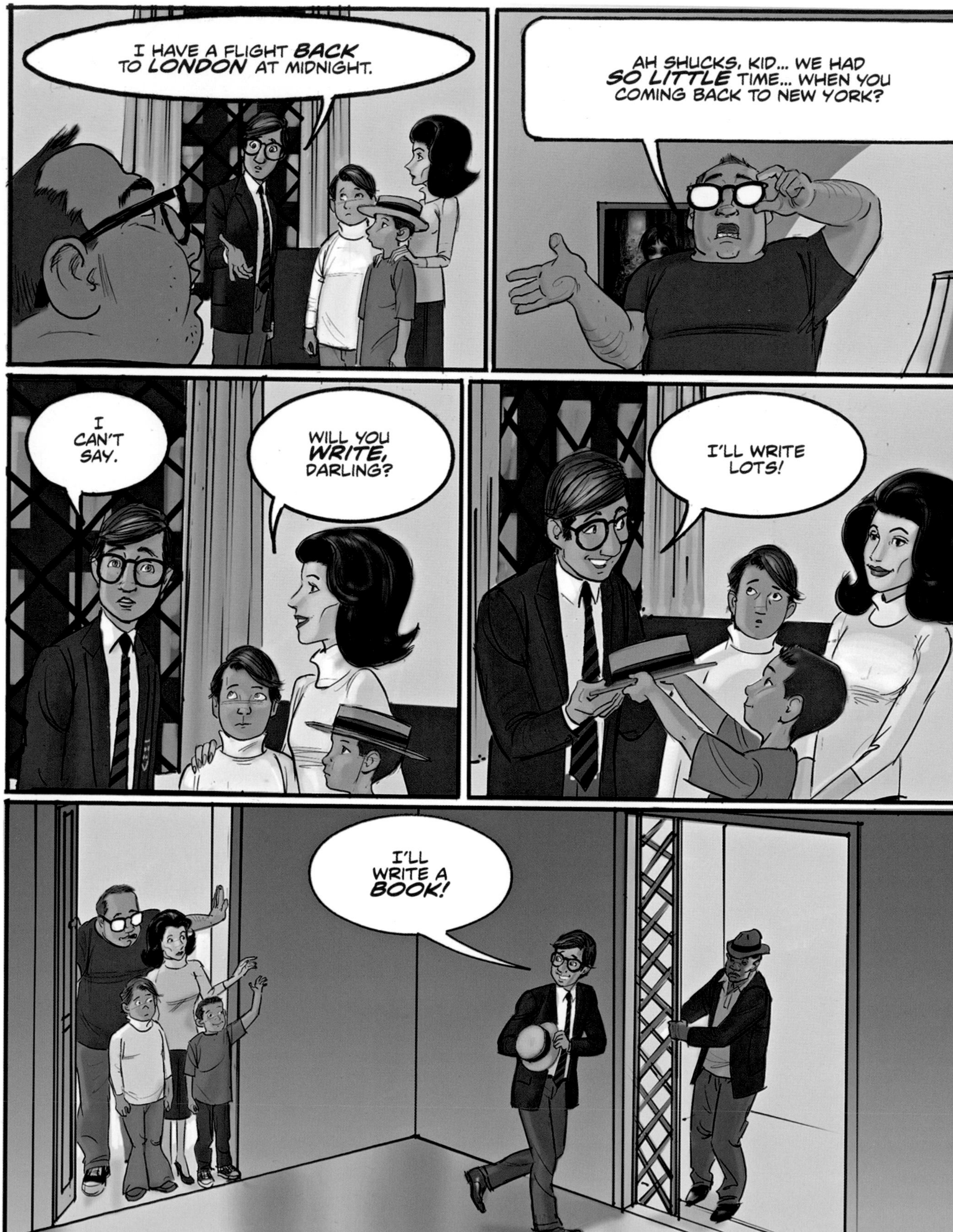
I HAVE A FLIGHT BACK TO LONDON AT MIDNIGHT.
AH SHUCKS, KID... WE HAD SO LITTLE TIME... WHEN YOU COMING BACK TO NEW YORK?
I CAN'T SAY.
WILL YOU WRITE, DARLING?
I'LL WRITE LOTS!
I'LL WRITE A BOOK!

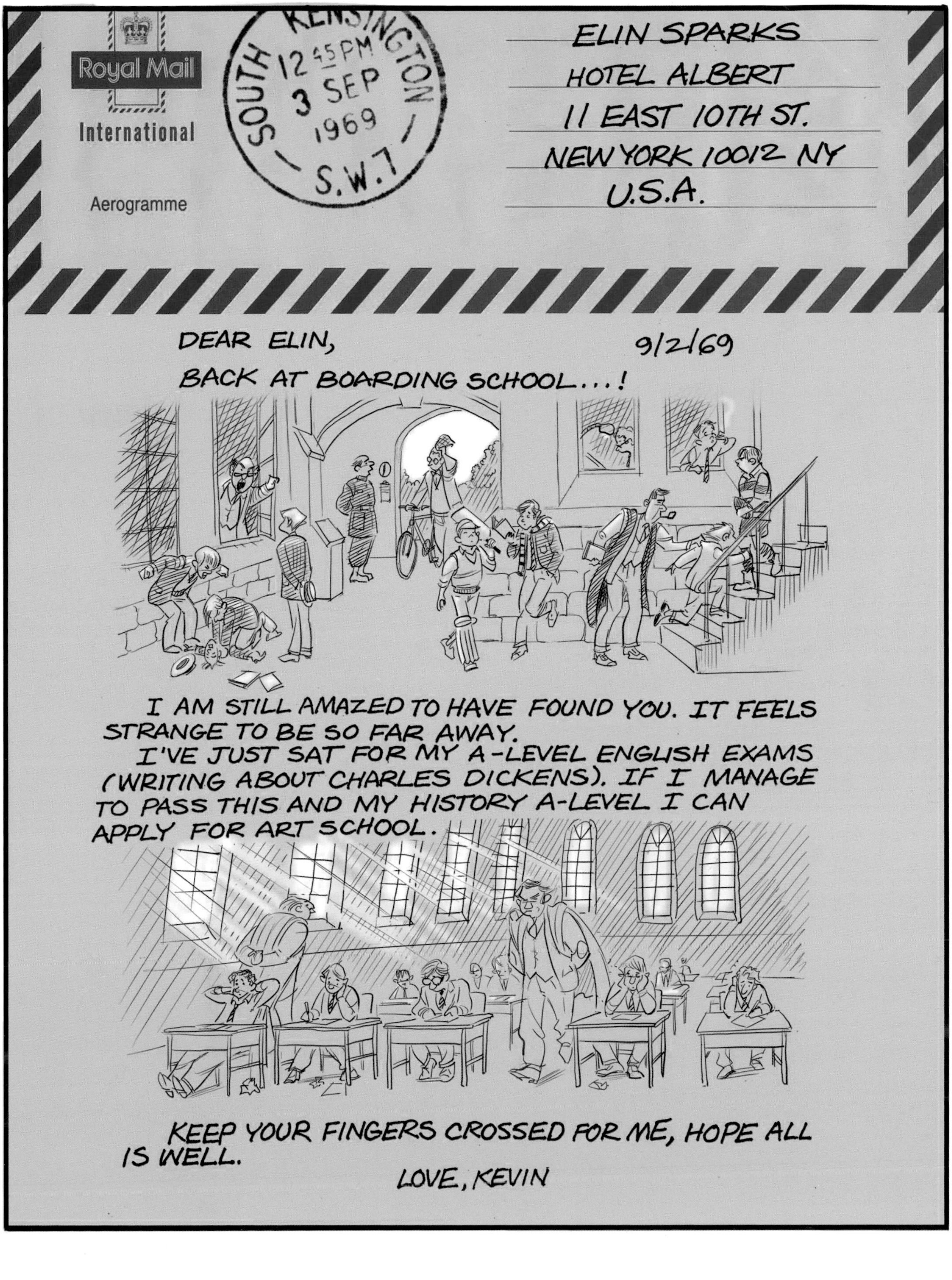
Royal Mail
International
Aerogramme
SOUTH KENSINGTON
12 45 PM
3 SEP
1969
S.W.7
ELIN SPARKS
HOTEL ALBERT
11 EAST 10TH ST.
NEW YORK 10012 NY
U.S.A.
DEAR ELIN,
9/2/69
BACK AT BOARDING SCHOOL...!
I AM STILL AMAZED TO HAVE FOUND YOU. IT FEELS STRANGE TO BE SO FAR AWAY.
I'VE JUST SAT FOR MY A-LEVEL ENGLISH EXAMS (WRITING ABOUT CHARLES DICKENS). IF I MANAGE TO PASS THIS AND MY HISTORY A-LEVEL I CAN APPLY FOR ART SCHOOL.
KEEP YOUR FINGERS CROSSED FOR ME, HOPE ALL IS WELL.
LOVE, KEVIN

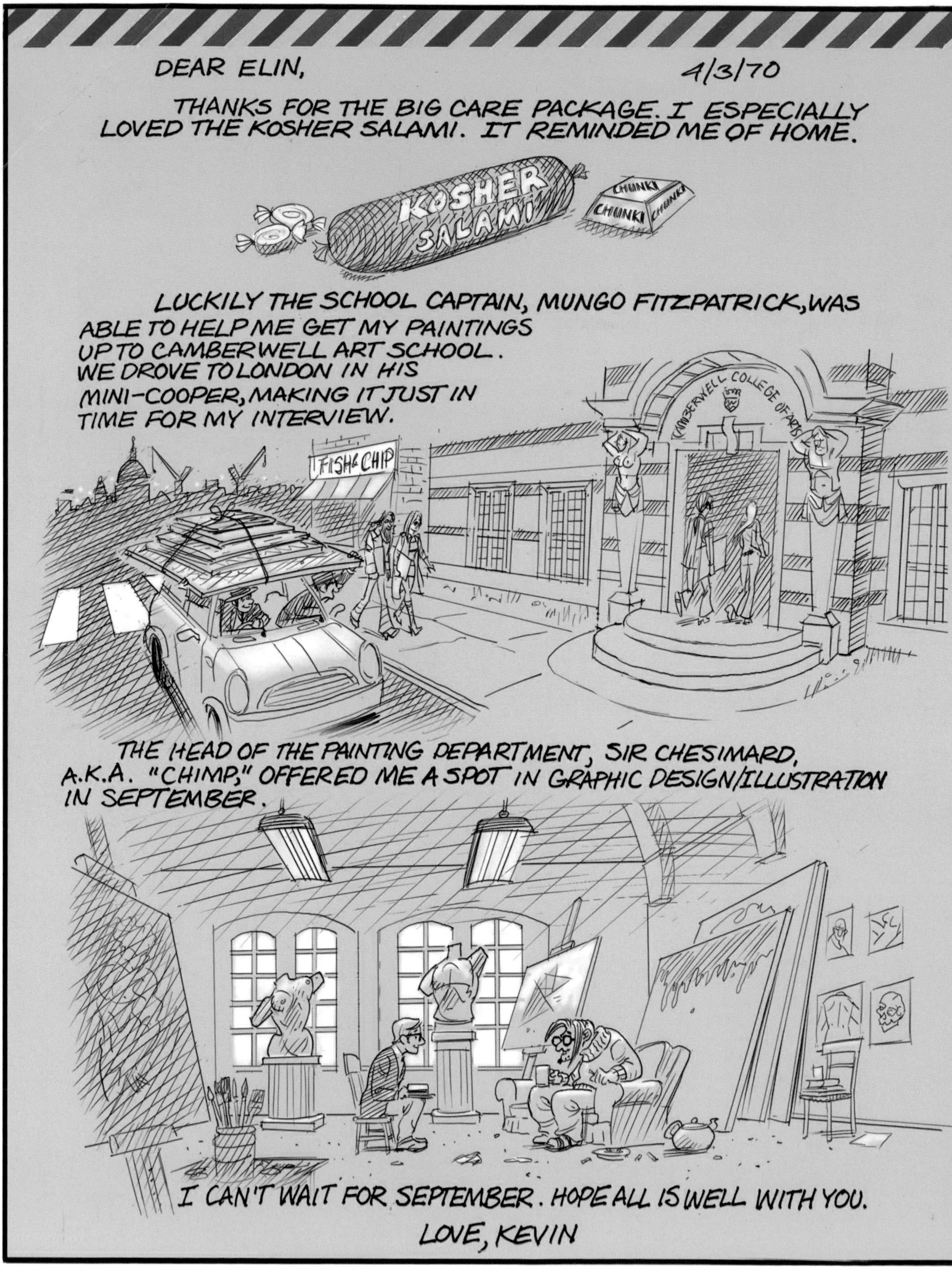
DEAR ELIN,
4/3/70
THANKS FOR THE BIG CARE PACKAGE. I ESPECIALLY LOVED THE KOSHER SALAMI. IT REMINDED ME OF HOME.
KOSHER SALAMI
CHUNKI
LUCKILY THE SCHOOL CAPTAIN, MUNGO FITZPATRICK, WAS ABLE TO HELP ME GET MY PAINTINGS UP TO CAMBERWELL ART SCHOOL. WE DROVE TO LONDON IN HIS MINI-COOPER, MAKING IT JUST IN TIME FOR MY INTERVIEW.
FISH & CHIP
CAMBERWELL COLLEGE OF ARTS
THE HEAD OF THE PAINTING DEPARTMENT, SIR CHESIMARD, A.K.A. "CHIMP," OFFERED ME A SPOT IN GRAPHIC DESIGN/ILLUSTRATION IN SEPTEMBER.
I CAN'T WAIT FOR SEPTEMBER. HOPE ALL IS WELL WITH YOU.
LOVE, KEVIN

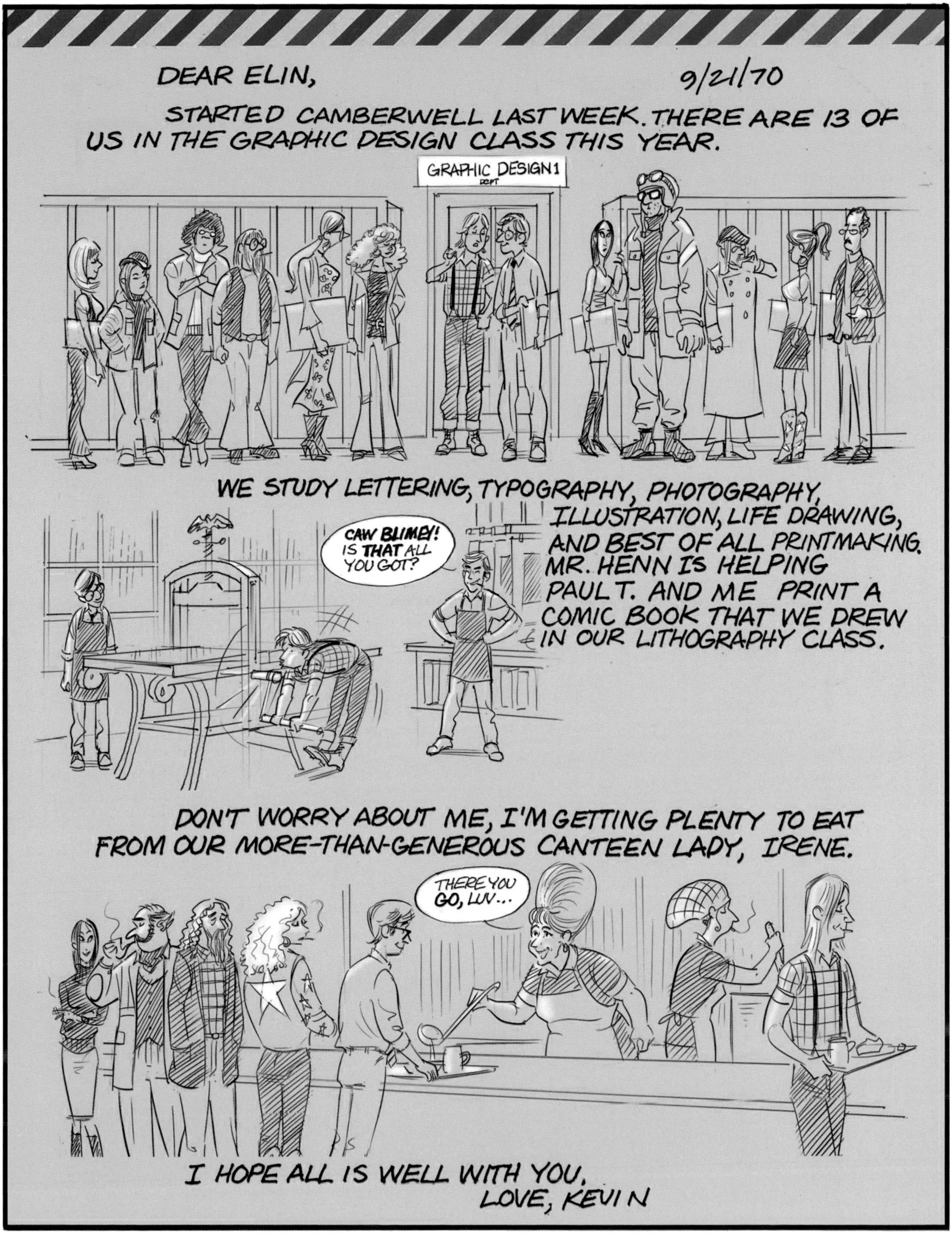
DEAR ELIN,
9/21/70
STARTED CAMBERWELL LAST WEEK. THERE ARE 13 OF US IN THE GRAPHIC DESIGN CLASS THIS YEAR.
GRAPHIC DESIGN 1 DEPT
WE STUDY LETTERING, TYPOGRAPHY, PHOTOGRAPHY, ILLUSTRATION, LIFE DRAWING, AND BEST OF ALL PRINTMAKING.
CAW BLIMEY! IS THAT ALL YOU GOT?
MR. HENN IS HELPING PAUL T. AND ME PRINT A COMIC BOOK THAT WE DREW IN OUR LITHOGRAPHY CLASS.
DON'T WORRY ABOUT ME, I'M GETTING PLENTY TO EAT FROM OUR MORE-THAN-GENEROUS CANTEEN LADY, IRENE.
THERE YOU GO, LUV...
I HOPE ALL IS WELL WITH YOU,
LOVE, KEVIN

DEAR ELIN, 12/3/70

PAUL T. AND I HAVE STARTED BARTERING PORTRAITS FOR BEER. IT BEGAN AT THE "PIG AND WHISTLE" WHEN TWO BROTHERS, RONALD AND REGINALD, WERE CHATTING WITH US OVER A PINT. WHEN THEY FOUND OUT WE WERE ART STUDENTS THEY CHALLENGED US TO DRAW THEM.

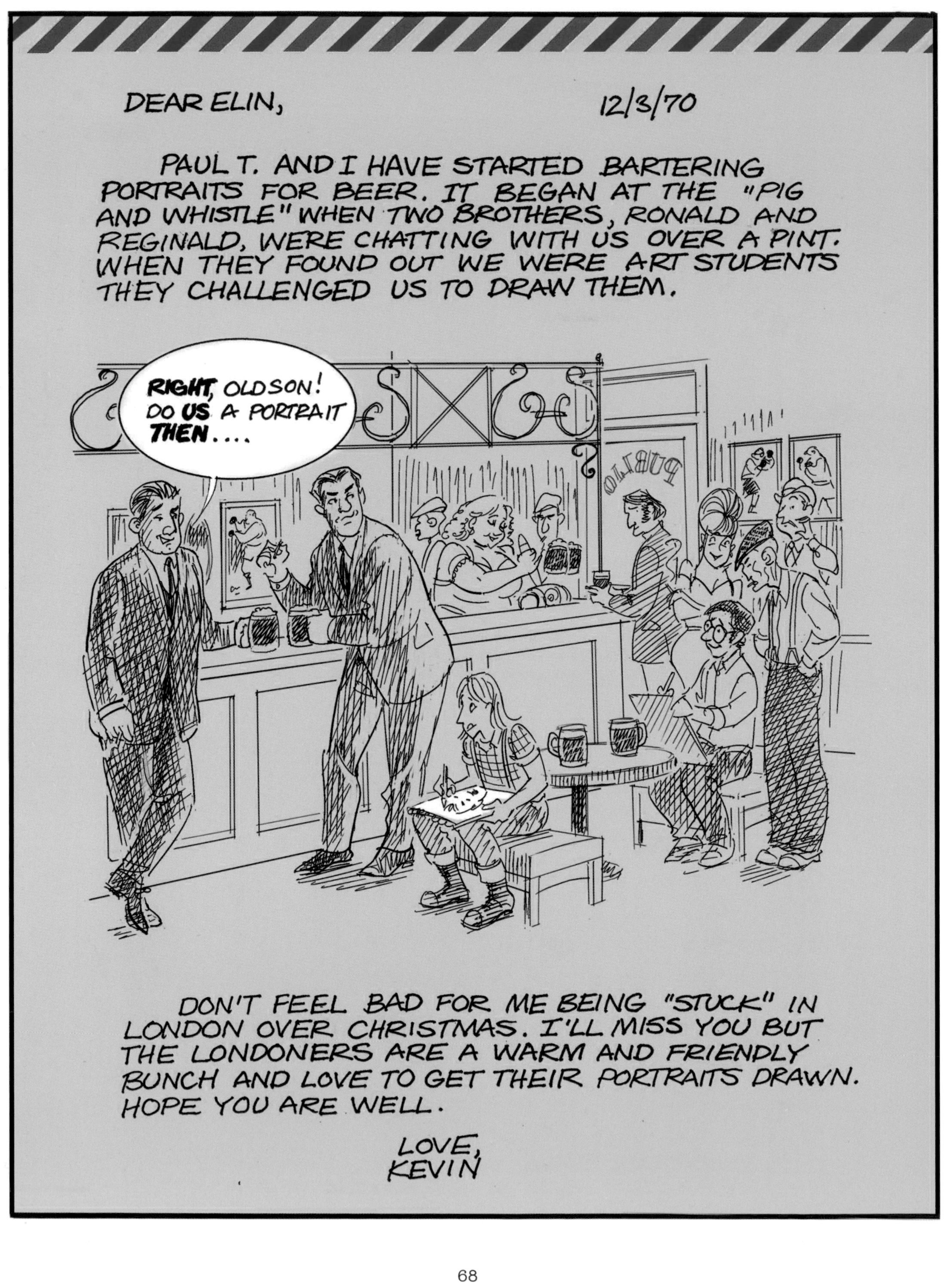
RIGHT, OLD SON! DO **US** A PORTRAIT **THEN**....

DON'T FEEL BAD FOR ME BEING "STUCK" IN LONDON OVER CHRISTMAS. I'LL MISS YOU BUT THE LONDONERS ARE A WARM AND FRIENDLY BUNCH AND LOVE TO GET THEIR PORTRAITS DRAWN. HOPE YOU ARE WELL.

LOVE,
KEVIN

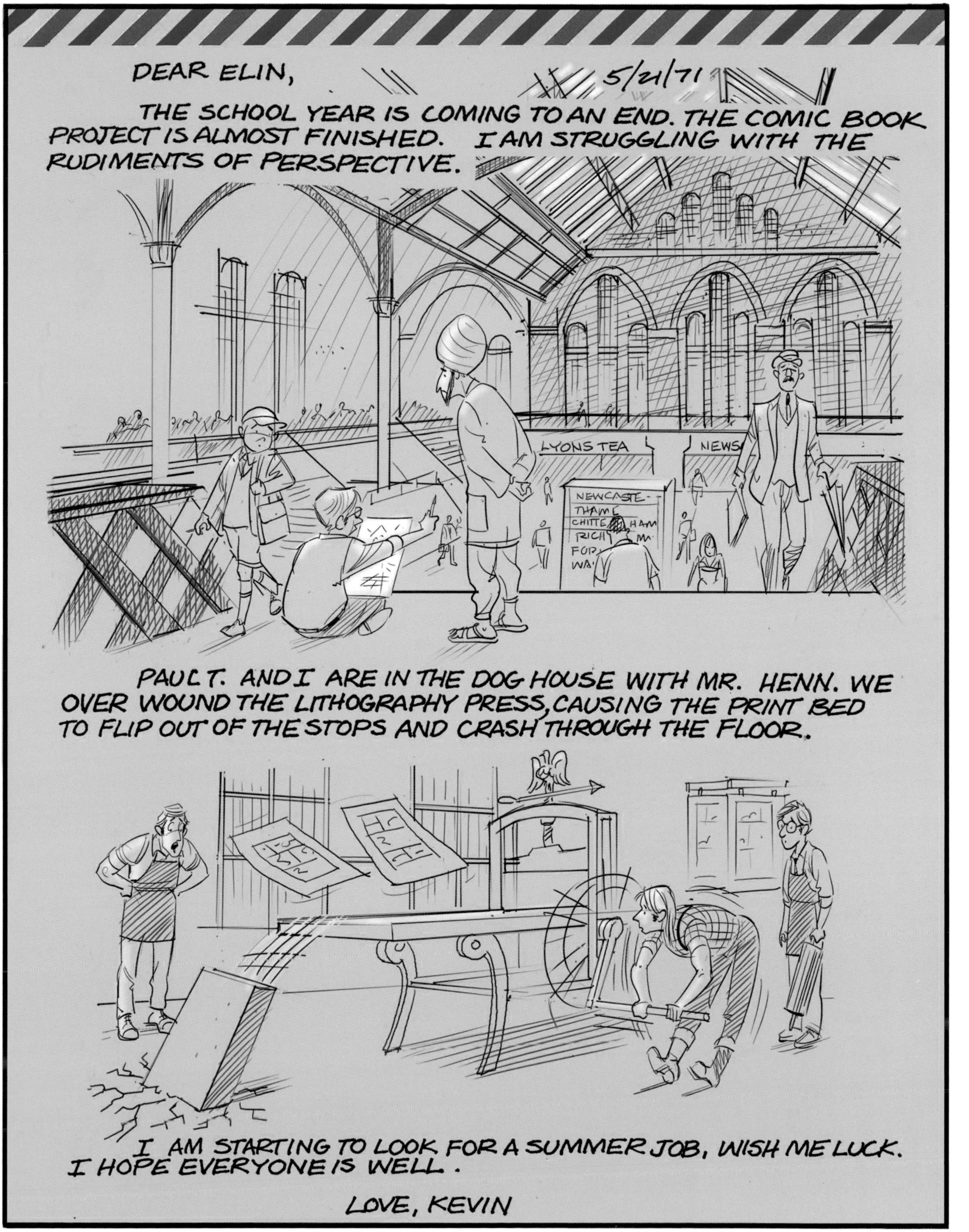
DEAR ELIN,
5/21/71
THE SCHOOL YEAR IS COMING TO AN END. THE COMIC BOOK PROJECT IS ALMOST FINISHED. I AM STRUGGLING WITH THE RUDIMENTS OF PERSPECTIVE.
LYONS TEA
PAUL T. AND I ARE IN THE DOG HOUSE WITH MR. HENN. WE OVER WOUND THE LITHOGRAPHY PRESS, CAUSING THE PRINT BED TO FLIP OUT OF THE STOPS AND CRASH THROUGH THE FLOOR.
I AM STARTING TO LOOK FOR A SUMMER JOB, WISH ME LUCK. I HOPE EVERYONE IS WELL.
LOVE, KEVIN

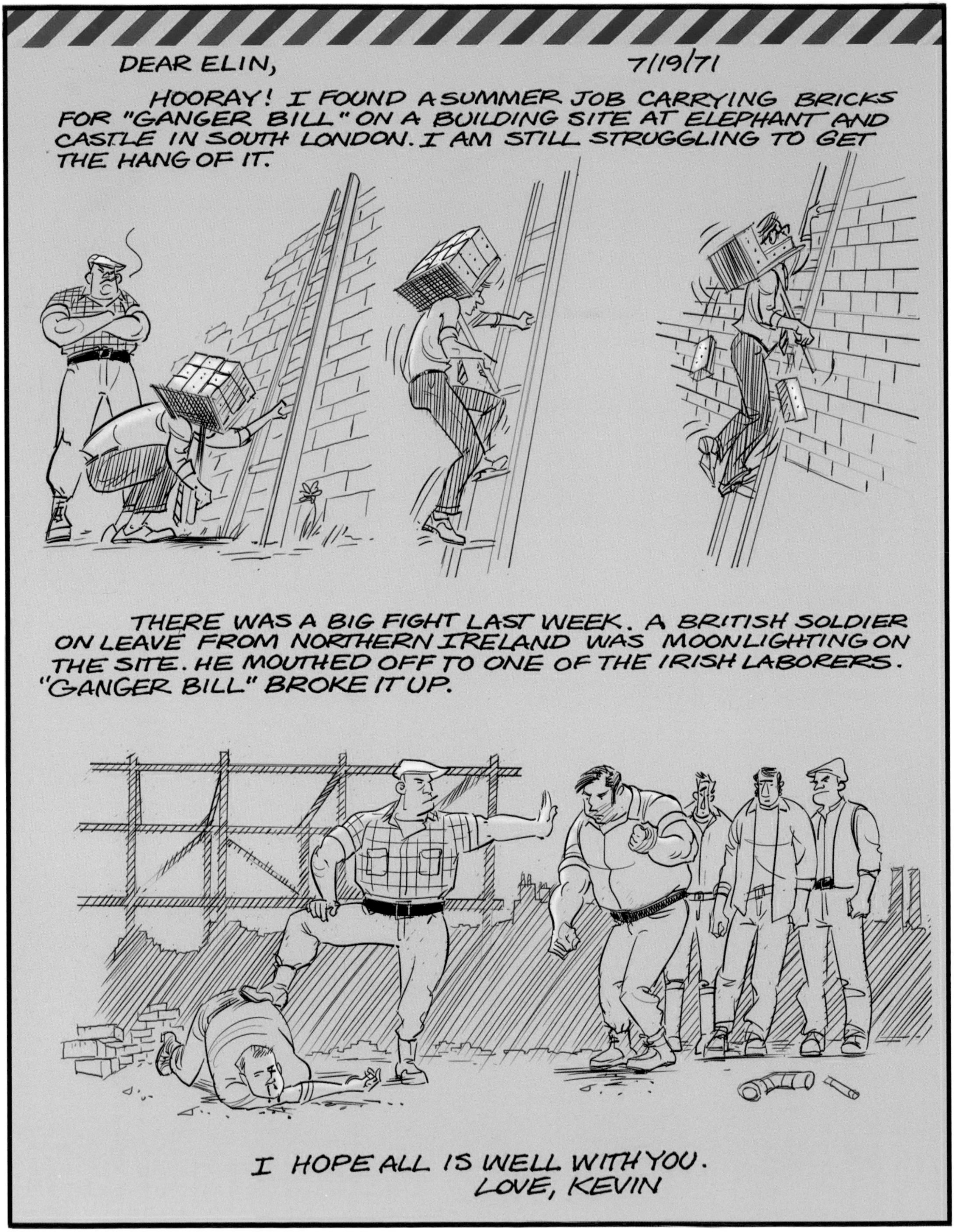
DEAR ELIN,
7/19/71
HOORAY! I FOUND A SUMMER JOB CARRYING BRICKS FOR "GANGER BILL" ON A BUILDING SITE AT ELEPHANT AND CASTLE IN SOUTH LONDON. I AM STILL STRUGGLING TO GET THE HANG OF IT.
THERE WAS A BIG FIGHT LAST WEEK. A BRITISH SOLDIER ON LEAVE FROM NORTHERN IRELAND WAS MOONLIGHTING ON THE SITE. HE MOUTHED OFF TO ONE OF THE IRISH LABORERS. "GANGER BILL" BROKE IT UP.
I HOPE ALL IS WELL WITH YOU.
LOVE, KEVIN

DEAR ELIN, 8/10/71

PAUL T. AND I GOT LUCKY LAST WEEK. WE RAN INTO SOME SKINHEADS ON THE WAY HOME FROM THE PUB.

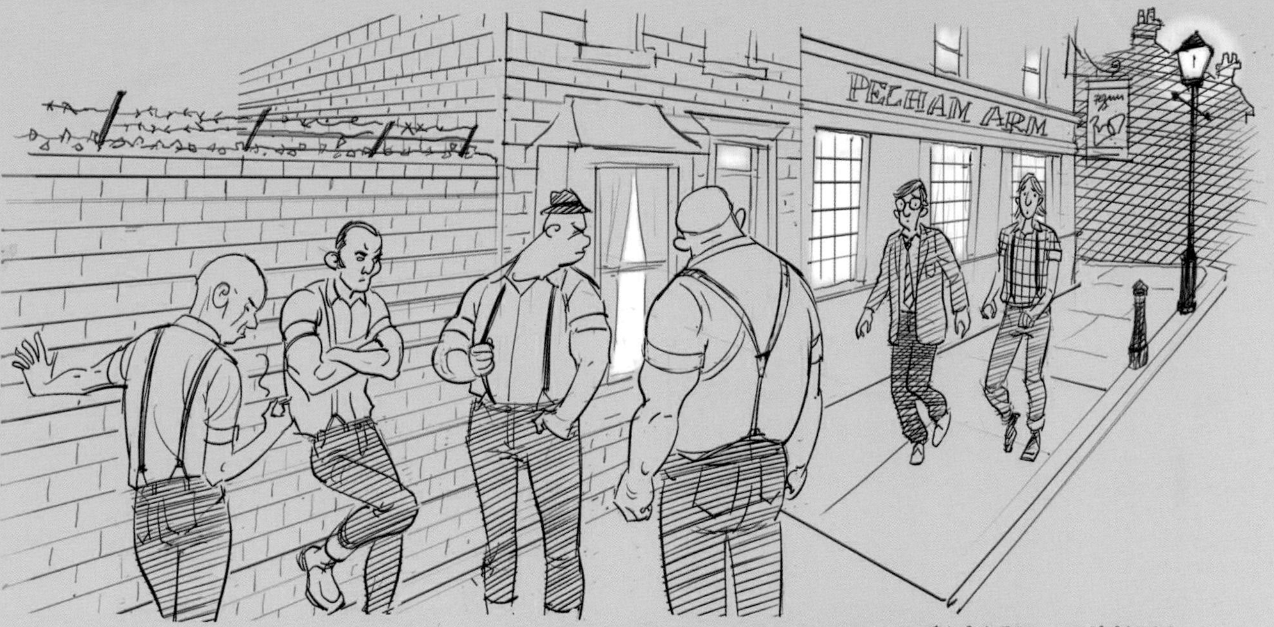
PELHAM ARM

WE WERE JUST ABOUT TO BE PUMMELLED WHEN REGINALD AND RONALD PULLED UP IN THEIR JAGUAR.

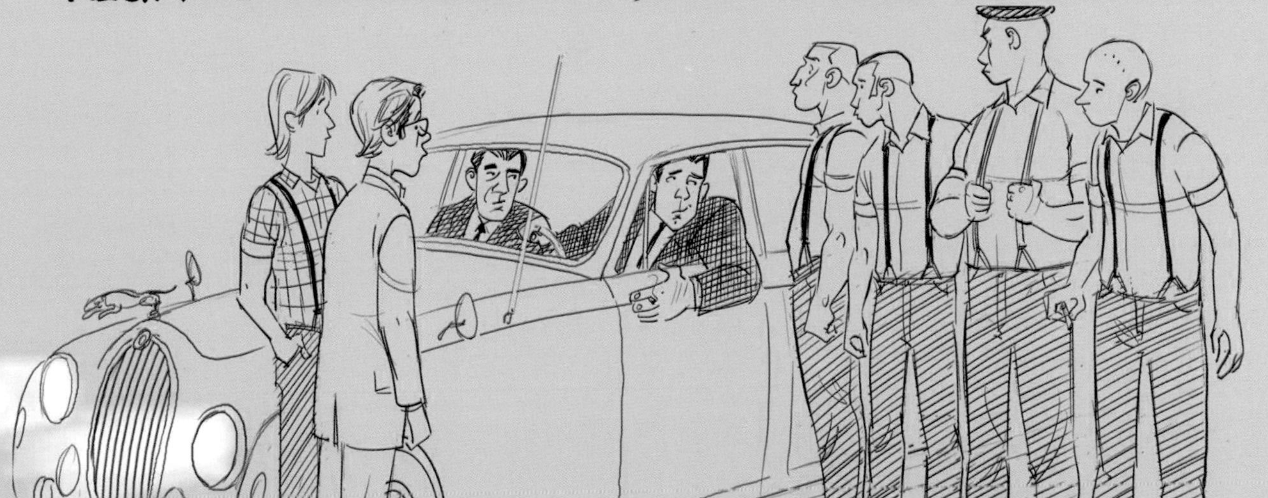
KRAY2

THEY TOLD US THAT WE SHOULD LET EVERYONE KNOW THAT WE WERE FRIENDS OF THE KRAY BROTHERS. WHICH WE DID AND NO TROUBLES SINCE. HOPE ALL IS WELL WITH YOU.

LOVE, KEVIN

P.S. SAVED ENOUGH MONEY, GOING TO SICILY NEXT WEEK.

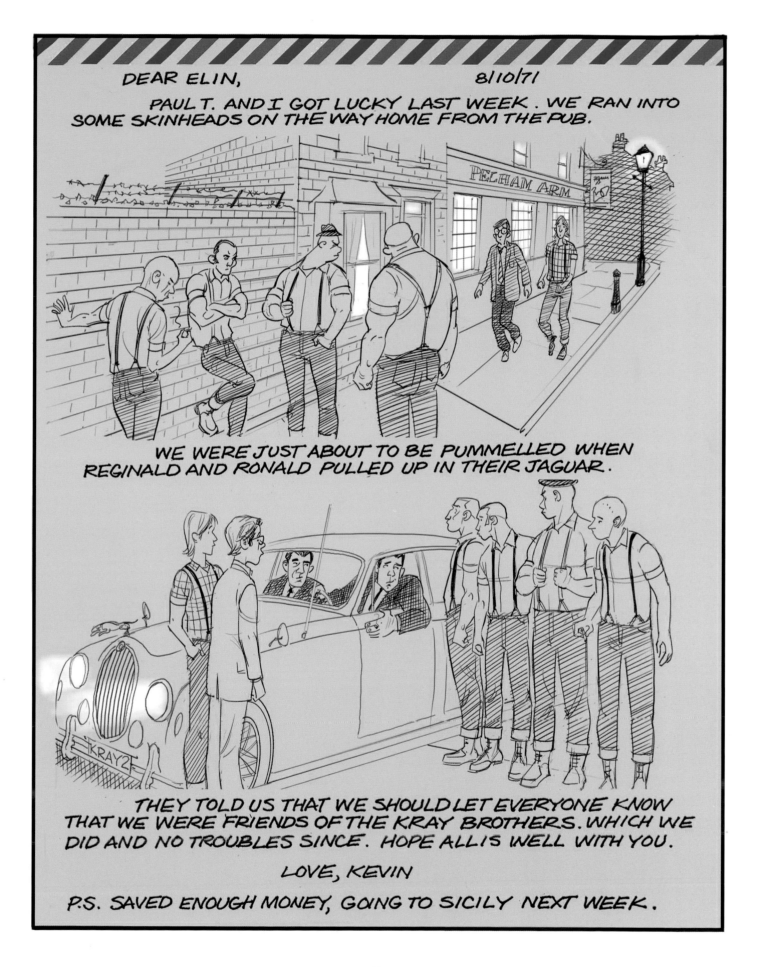

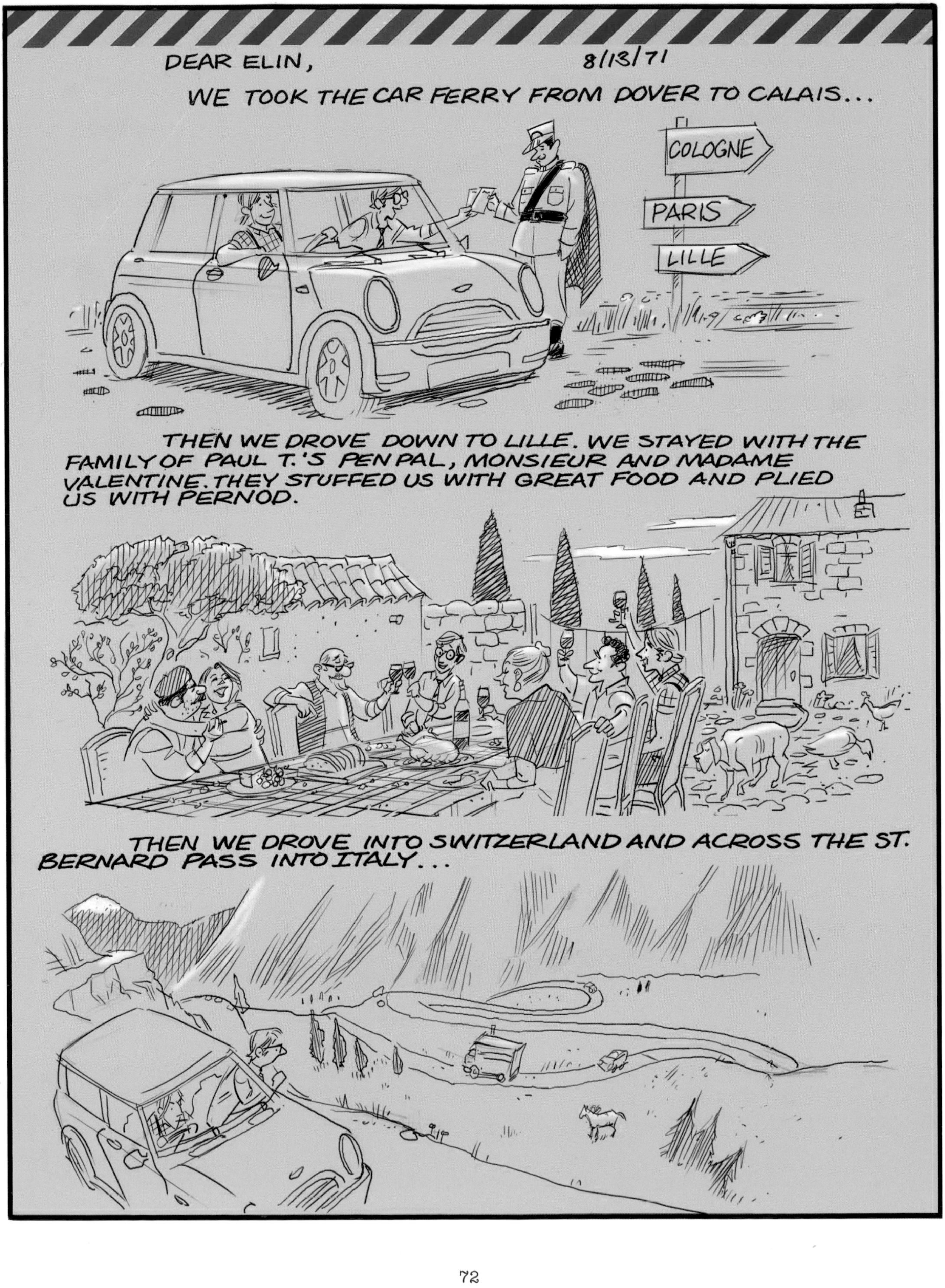
DEAR ELIN,
8/13/71
WE TOOK THE CAR FERRY FROM DOVER TO CALAIS...
COLOGNE
PARIS
LILLE
THEN WE DROVE DOWN TO LILLE. WE STAYED WITH THE FAMILY OF PAUL T.'S PEN PAL, MONSIEUR AND MADAME VALENTINE. THEY STUFFED US WITH GREAT FOOD AND PLIED US WITH PERNOD.
THEN WE DROVE INTO SWITZERLAND AND ACROSS THE ST. BERNARD PASS INTO ITALY...

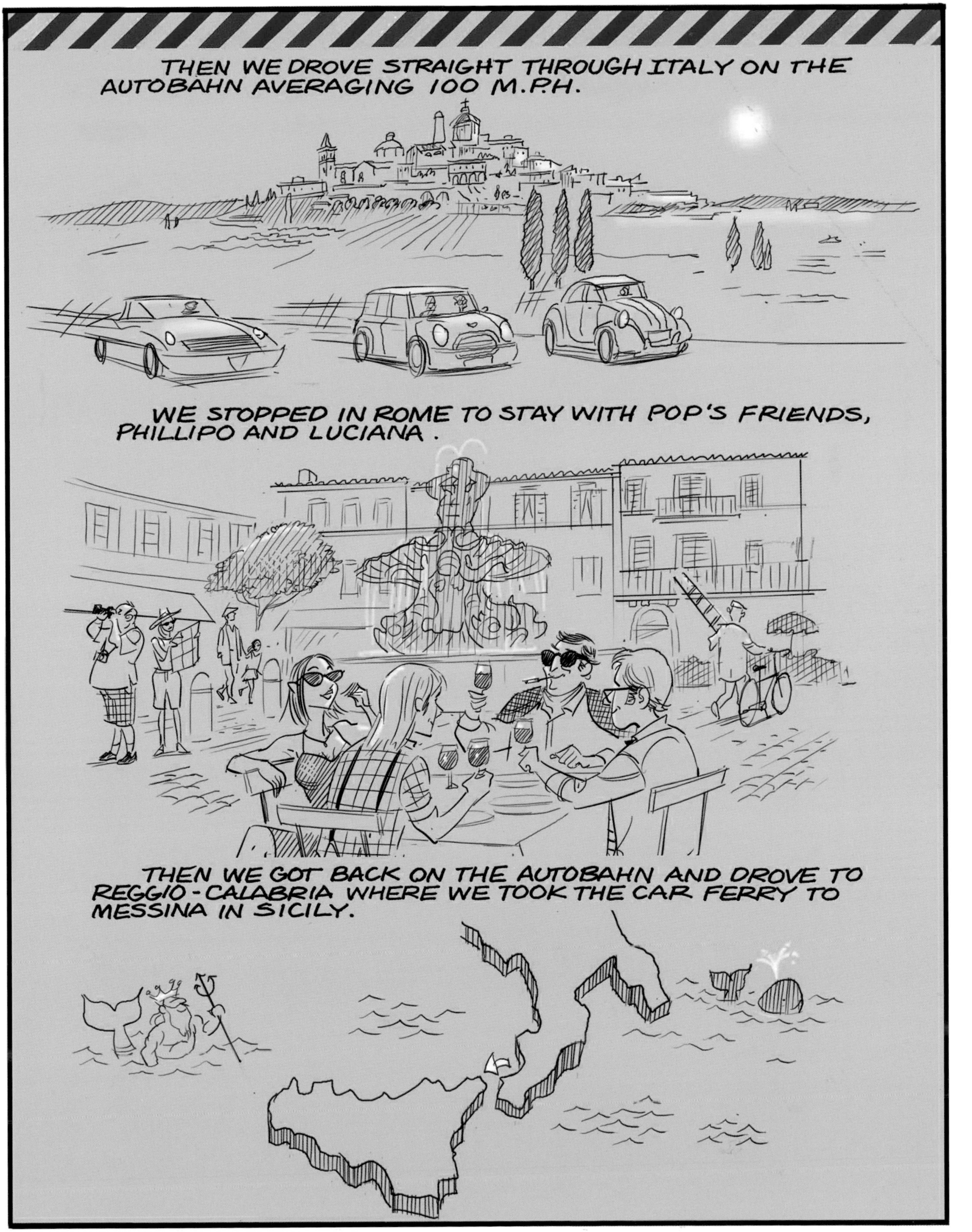
THEN WE DROVE STRAIGHT THROUGH ITALY ON THE AUTOBAHN AVERAGING 100 M.P.H.
WE STOPPED IN ROME TO STAY WITH POP'S FRIENDS, PHILLIPO AND LUCIANA.
THEN WE GOT BACK ON THE AUTOBAHN AND DROVE TO REGGIO-CALABRIA WHERE WE TOOK THE CAR FERRY TO MESSINA IN SICILY.

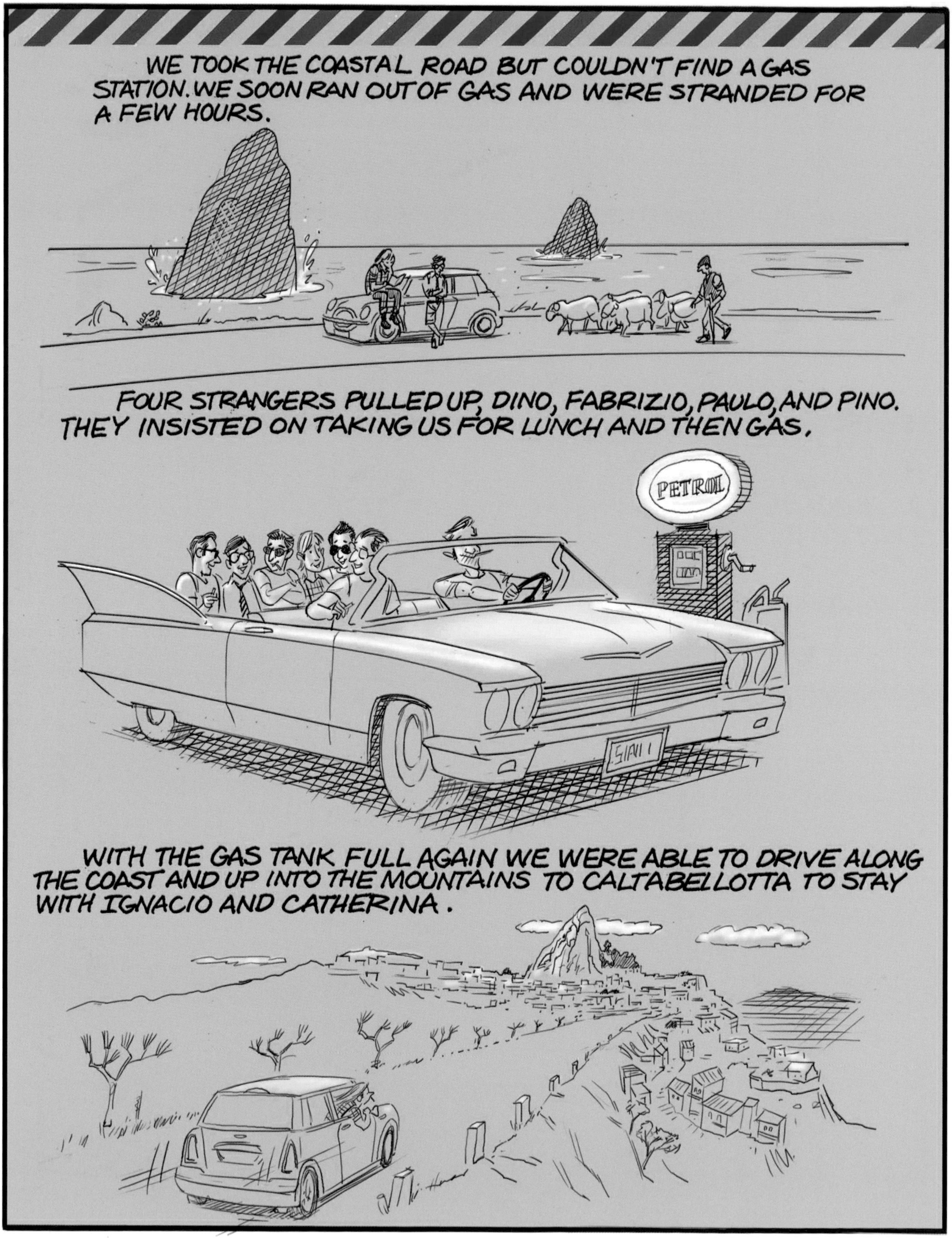
WE TOOK THE COASTAL ROAD BUT COULDN'T FIND A GAS STATION. WE SOON RAN OUT OF GAS AND WERE STRANDED FOR A FEW HOURS.
FOUR STRANGERS PULLED UP, DINO, FABRIZIO, PAULO, AND PINO. THEY INSISTED ON TAKING US FOR LUNCH AND THEN GAS.
PETROL
WITH THE GAS TANK FULL AGAIN WE WERE ABLE TO DRIVE ALONG THE COAST AND UP INTO THE MOUNTAINS TO CALTABELLOTTA TO STAY WITH IGNACIO AND CATHERINA.

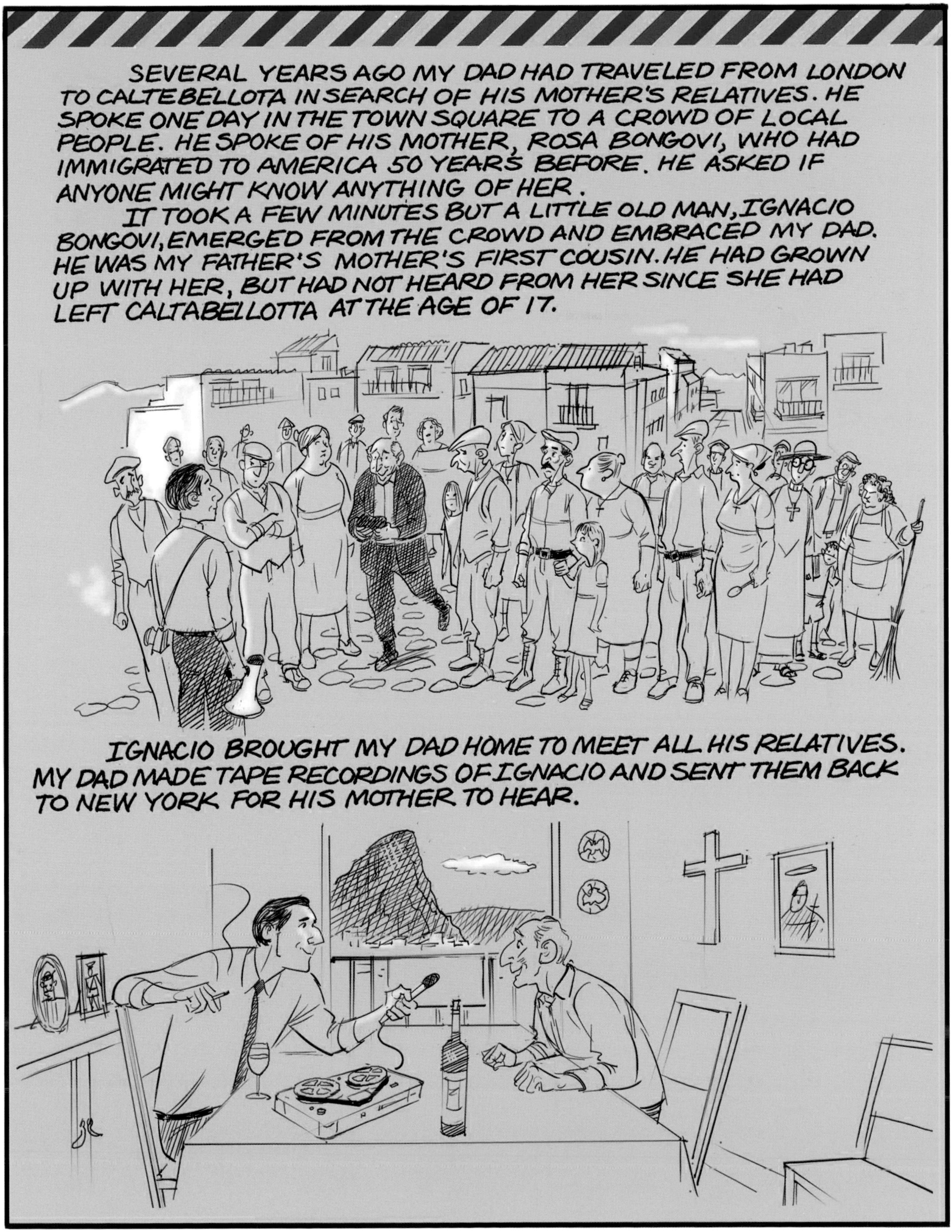
SEVERAL YEARS AGO MY DAD HAD TRAVELED FROM LONDON TO CALTEBELLOTA IN SEARCH OF HIS MOTHER'S RELATIVES. HE SPOKE ONE DAY IN THE TOWN SQUARE TO A CROWD OF LOCAL PEOPLE. HE SPOKE OF HIS MOTHER, ROSA BONGOVI, WHO HAD IMMIGRATED TO AMERICA 50 YEARS BEFORE. HE ASKED IF ANYONE MIGHT KNOW ANYTHING OF HER.
IT TOOK A FEW MINUTES BUT A LITTLE OLD MAN, IGNACIO BONGOVI, EMERGED FROM THE CROWD AND EMBRACED MY DAD. HE WAS MY FATHER'S MOTHER'S FIRST COUSIN. HE HAD GROWN UP WITH HER, BUT HAD NOT HEARD FROM HER SINCE SHE HAD LEFT CALTABELLOTTA AT THE AGE OF 17.
IGNACIO BROUGHT MY DAD HOME TO MEET ALL HIS RELATIVES. MY DAD MADE TAPE RECORDINGS OF IGNACIO AND SENT THEM BACK TO NEW YORK FOR HIS MOTHER TO HEAR.

IGNACIO AND CATHERINA WERE EXCITED TO SEE PAUL T. AND ME AND ARE FEEDING US LIKE ROYALTY. WE ARE ABLE TO COMMUNICATE WITH SIGN LANGUAGE AND THE LITTLE ITALIAN I KNOW.

EVERY DAY WE ESCORT IGNACIO DOWN THE MOUNTAIN TO HIS OLIVE ORCHARD WHERE WE GATHER FRESH OLIVES TO GO WITH FANTASTIC LUNCHES OF SWORDFISH, SALAD AND PASTA.

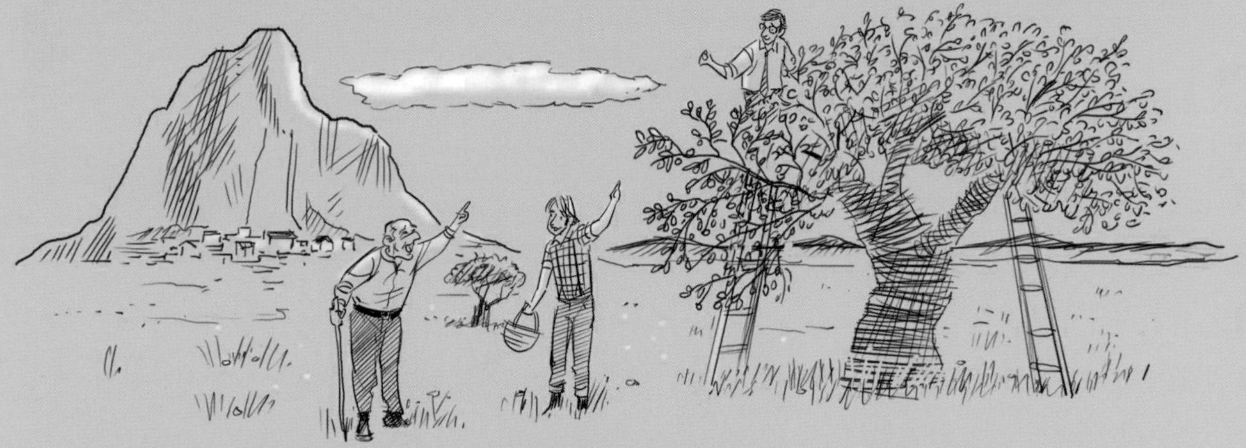

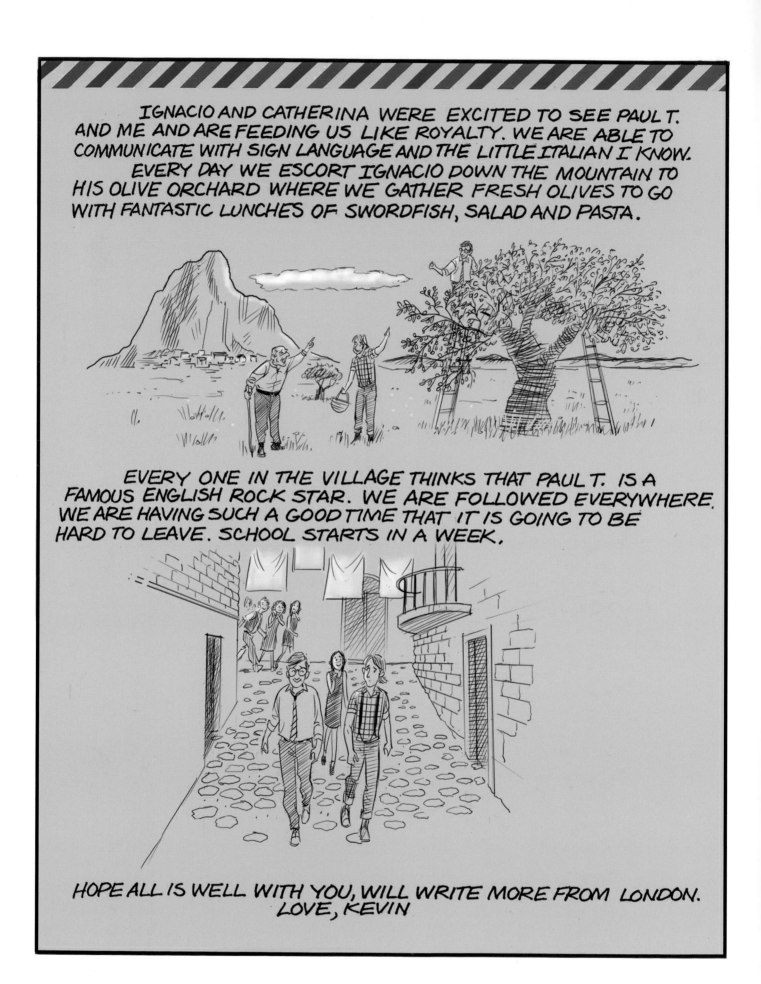

EVERY ONE IN THE VILLAGE THINKS THAT PAUL T. IS A FAMOUS ENGLISH ROCK STAR. WE ARE FOLLOWED EVERYWHERE. WE ARE HAVING SUCH A GOOD TIME THAT IT IS GOING TO BE HARD TO LEAVE. SCHOOL STARTS IN A WEEK.

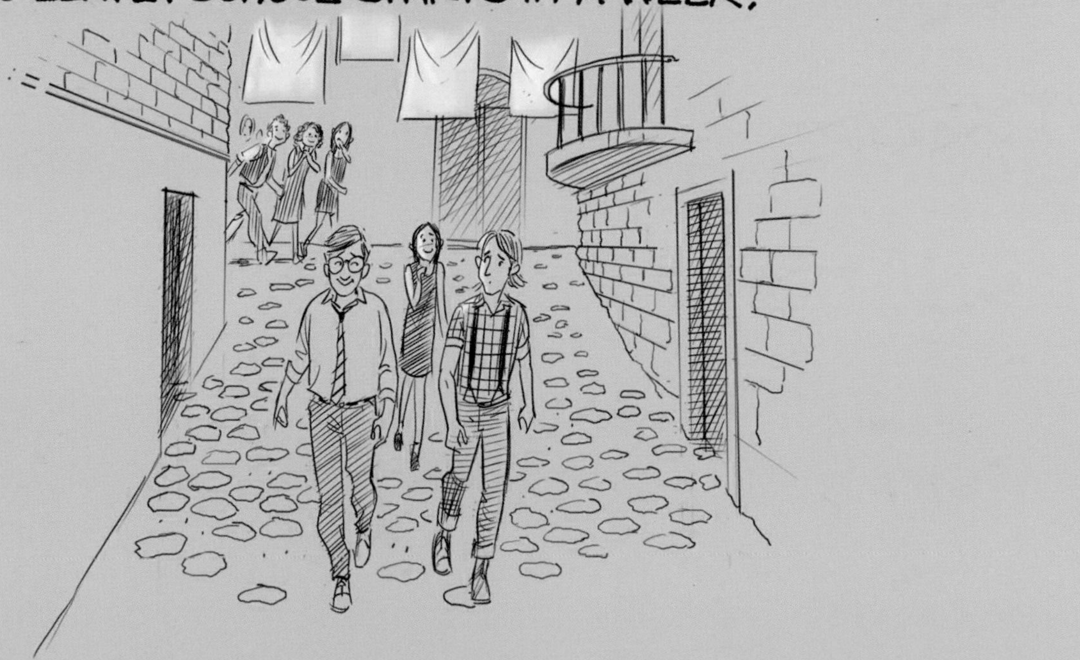

HOPE ALL IS WELL WITH YOU, WILL WRITE MORE FROM LONDON.
LOVE, KEVIN

DEAR ELIN, 10/3/71

I GUESS WE RUSHED TOO MUCH ON OUR WAY BACK TO SCHOOL. PAUL T. AND I LITERALLY RAN INTO AN ITALIAN COUPLE IN MILAN. NO ONE WAS HURT BUT OUR CAR WAS TOTALLED AND WE HAD TO TAKE THE TRAIN BACK TO LONDON.

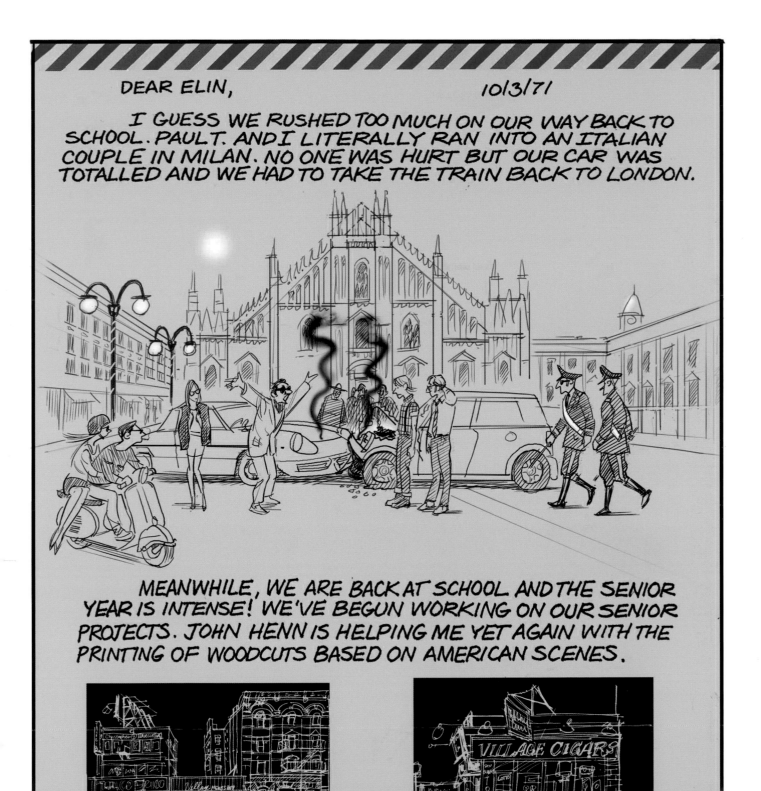

MEANWHILE, WE ARE BACK AT SCHOOL AND THE SENIOR YEAR IS INTENSE! WE'VE BEGUN WORKING ON OUR SENIOR PROJECTS. JOHN HENN IS HELPING ME YET AGAIN WITH THE PRINTING OF WOODCUTS BASED ON AMERICAN SCENES.

VILLAGE CIGARS
TOYS
LOTTO

HUGE THANK YOU FOR THE CHECK! HOPE ALL IS WELL.

LOVE, KEVIN

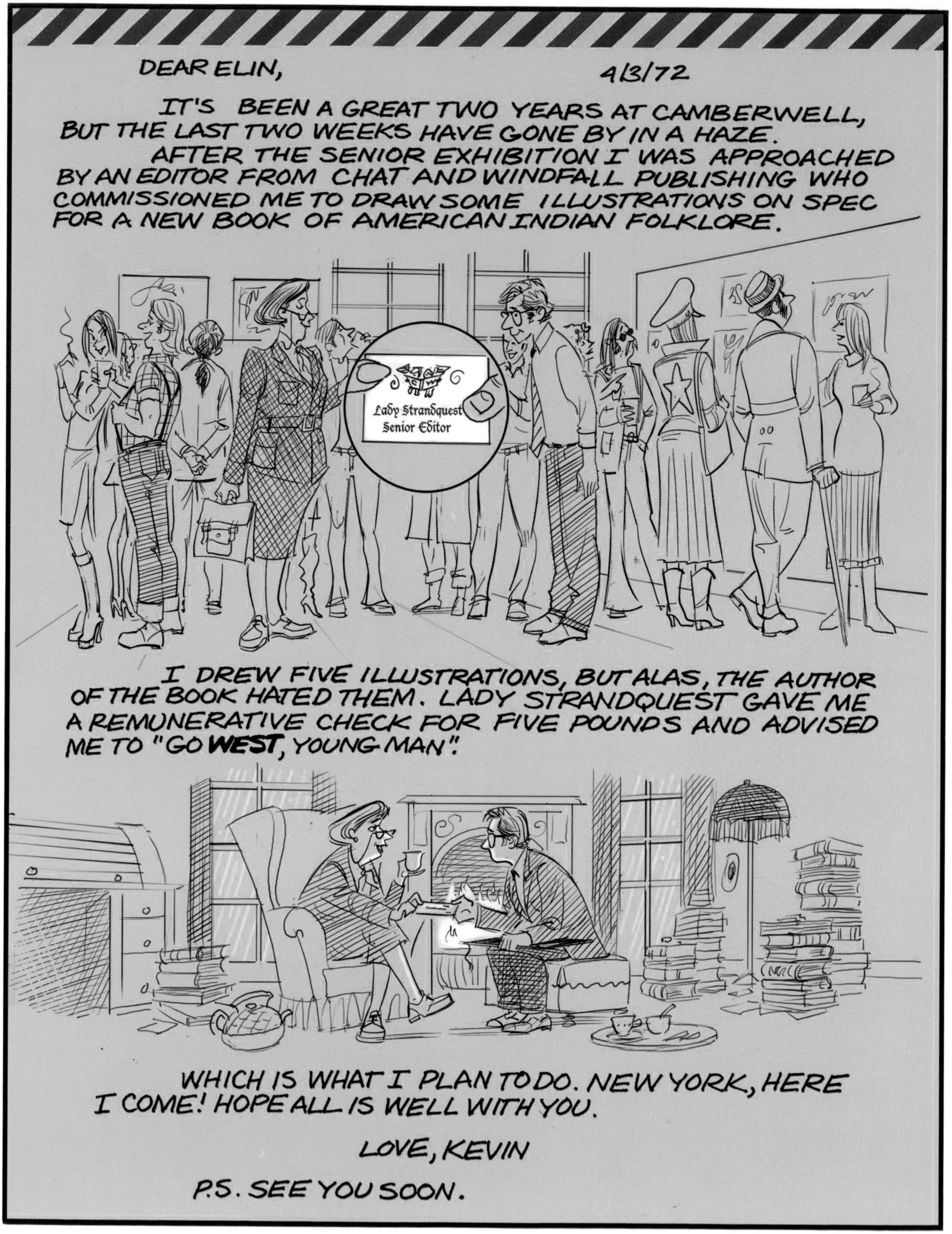
DEAR ELIN,
4/3/72
IT'S BEEN A GREAT TWO YEARS AT CAMBERWELL, BUT THE LAST TWO WEEKS HAVE GONE BY IN A HAZE.
AFTER THE SENIOR EXHIBITION I WAS APPROACHED BY AN EDITOR FROM CHAT AND WINDFALL PUBLISHING WHO COMMISSIONED ME TO DRAW SOME ILLUSTRATIONS ON SPEC FOR A NEW BOOK OF AMERICAN INDIAN FOLKLORE.
Lady Strandquest
Senior Editor
I DREW FIVE ILLUSTRATIONS, BUT ALAS, THE AUTHOR OF THE BOOK HATED THEM. LADY STRANDQUEST GAVE ME A REMUNERATIVE CHECK FOR FIVE POUNDS AND ADVISED ME TO "GO **WEST**, YOUNG MAN".
WHICH IS WHAT I PLAN TO DO. NEW YORK, HERE I COME! HOPE ALL IS WELL WITH YOU.
LOVE, KEVIN
P.S. SEE YOU SOON.

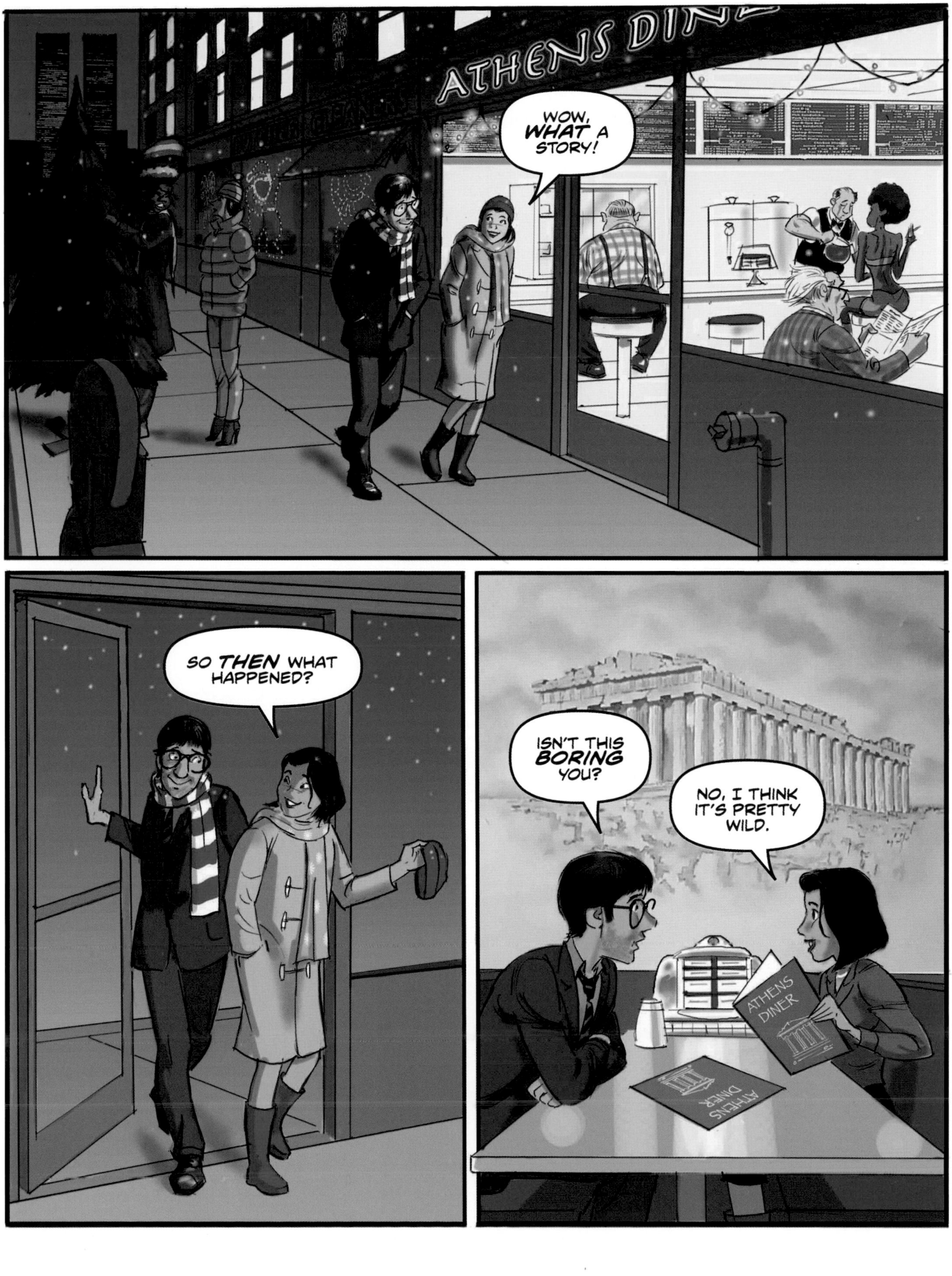
ATHENS DINE
WOW, WHAT A STORY!
SO THEN WHAT HAPPENED?
ISN'T THIS BORING YOU?
NO, I THINK IT'S PRETTY WILD.
ATHENS DINER
ATHENS DINER

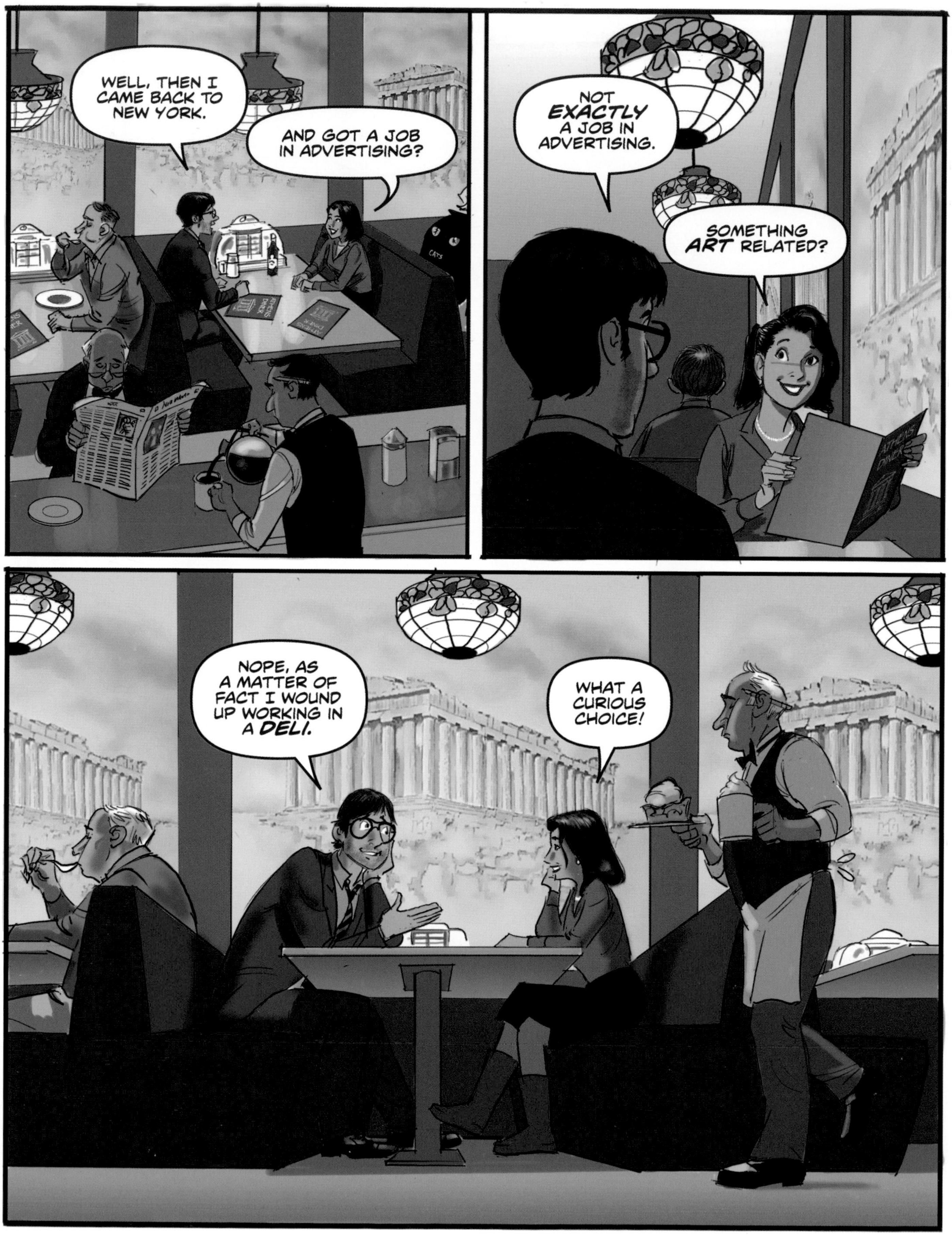

WELL, THEN I CAME BACK TO NEW YORK.
AND GOT A JOB IN ADVERTISING?
NOT *EXACTLY* A JOB IN ADVERTISING.
SOMETHING *ART* RELATED?
NOPE, AS A MATTER OF FACT I WOUND UP WORKING IN A *DELI*.
WHAT A CURIOUS CHOICE!

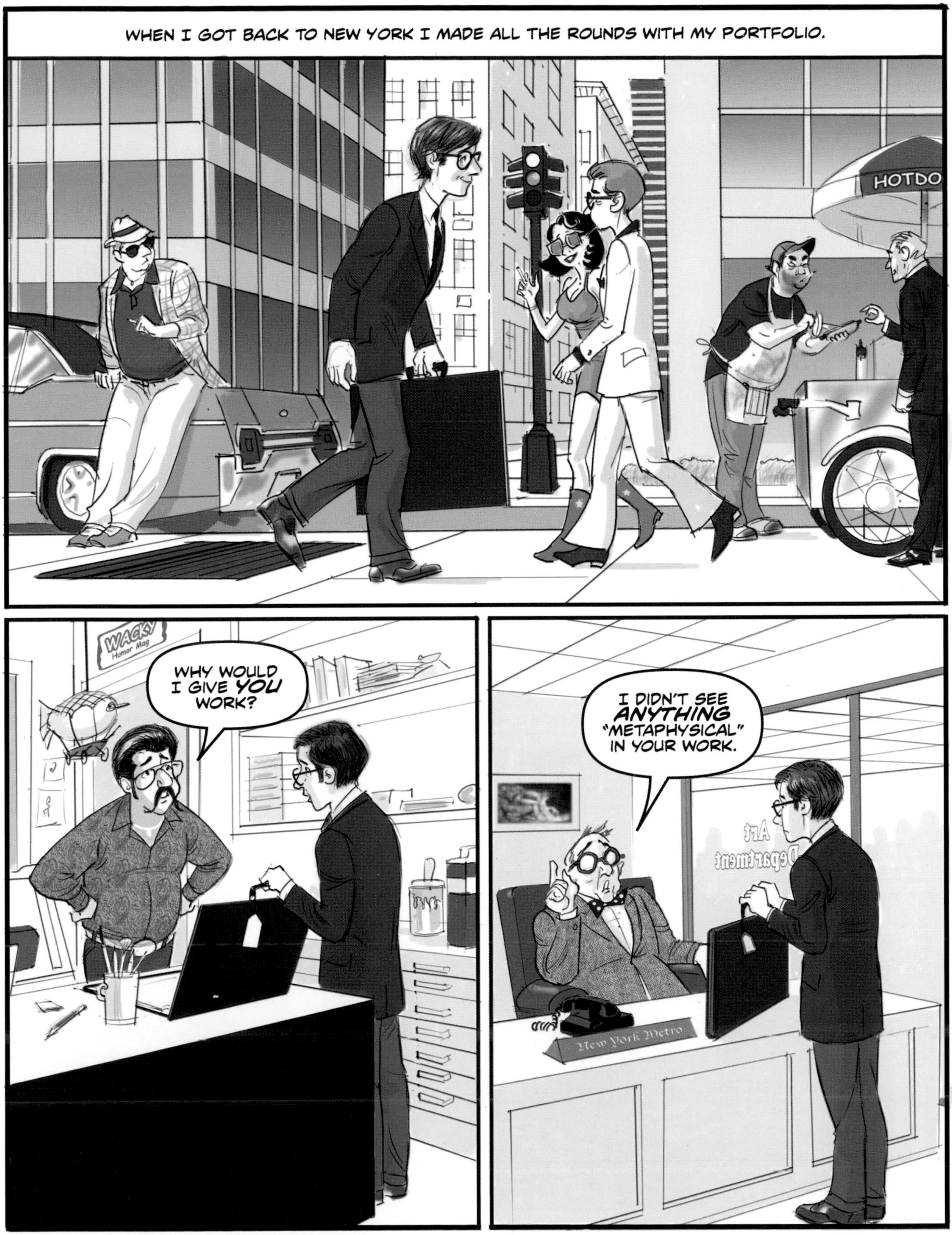
WHEN I GOT BACK TO NEW YORK I MADE ALL THE ROUNDS WITH MY PORTFOLIO.
HOTDO
WACKY Humor Mag
WHY WOULD I GIVE YOU WORK?
I DIDN'T SEE ANYTHING "METAPHYSICAL" IN YOUR WORK.
Art Department
New York Metro

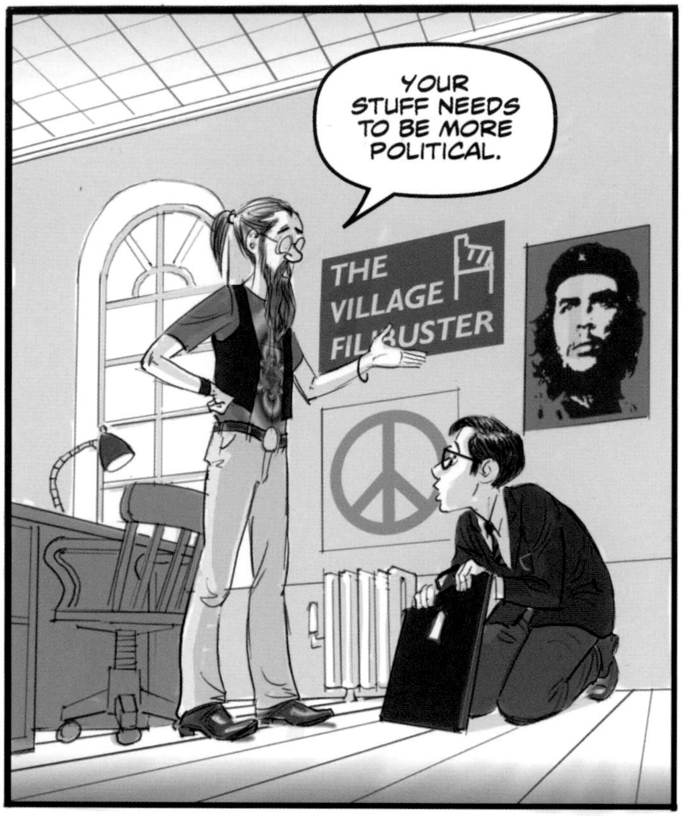
YOUR STUFF NEEDS TO BE MORE POLITICAL.
THE VILLAGE FILIBUSTER

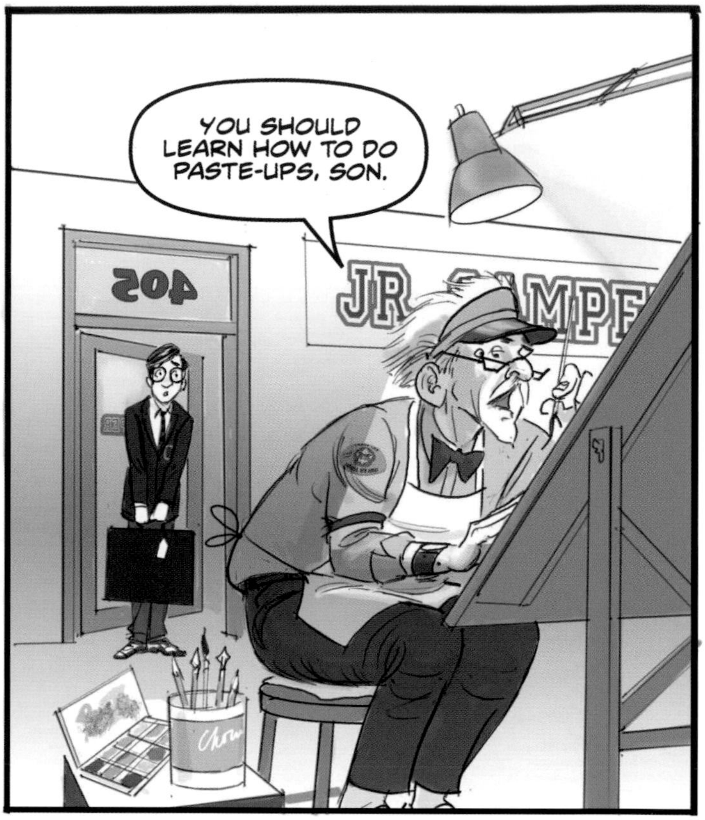
YOU SHOULD LEARN HOW TO DO PASTE-UPS, SON.
405

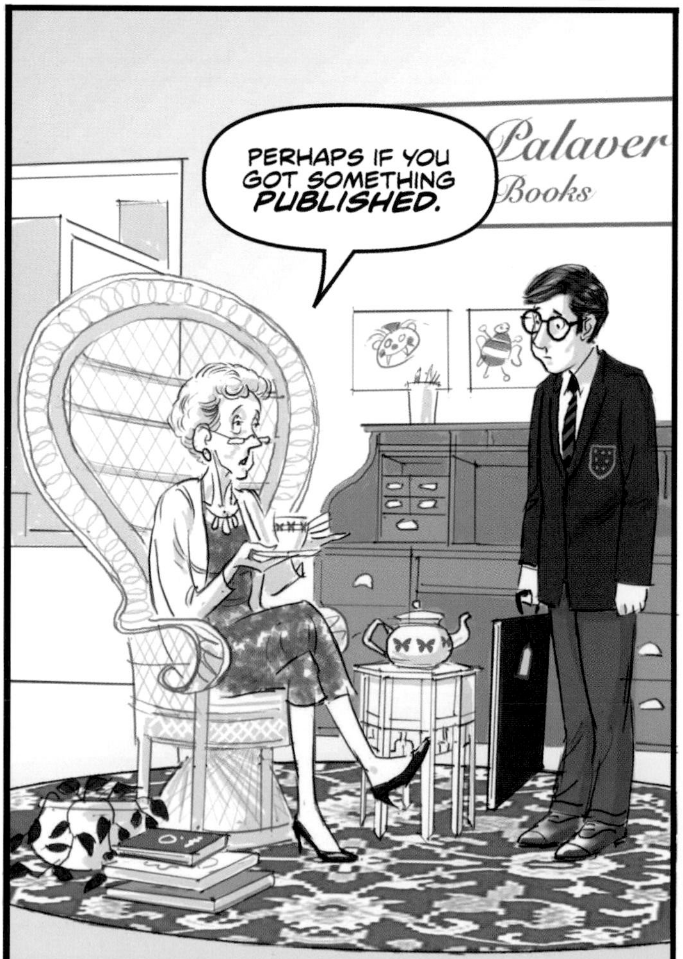
Palaver Books
PERHAPS IF YOU GOT SOMETHING ***PUBLISHED.***

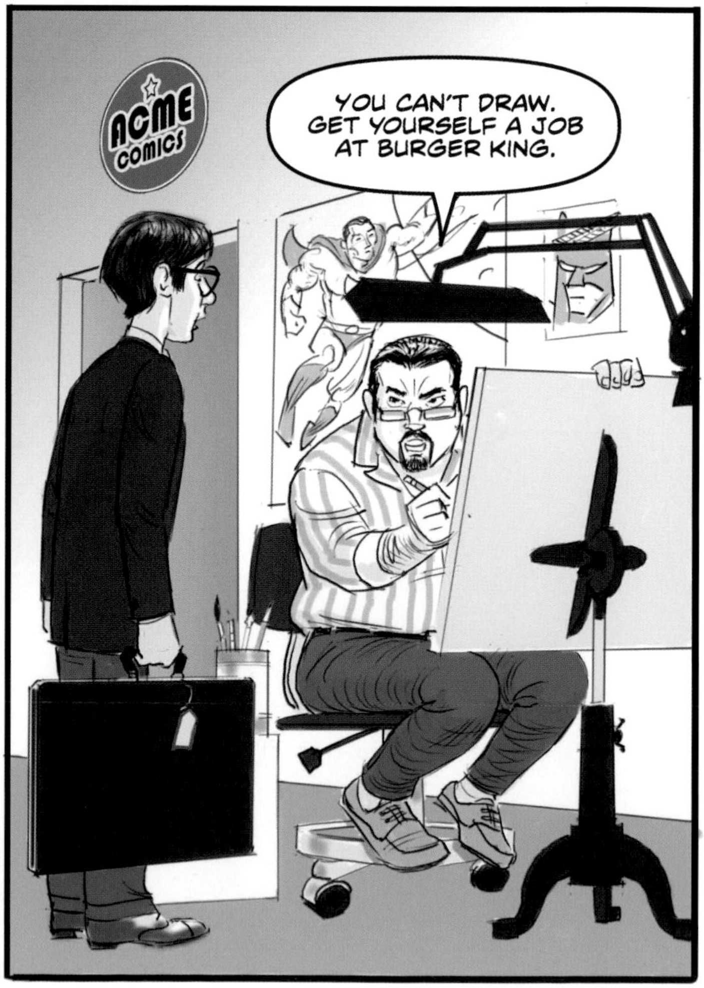
ACME COMICS
YOU CAN'T DRAW. GET YOURSELF A JOB AT BURGER KING.

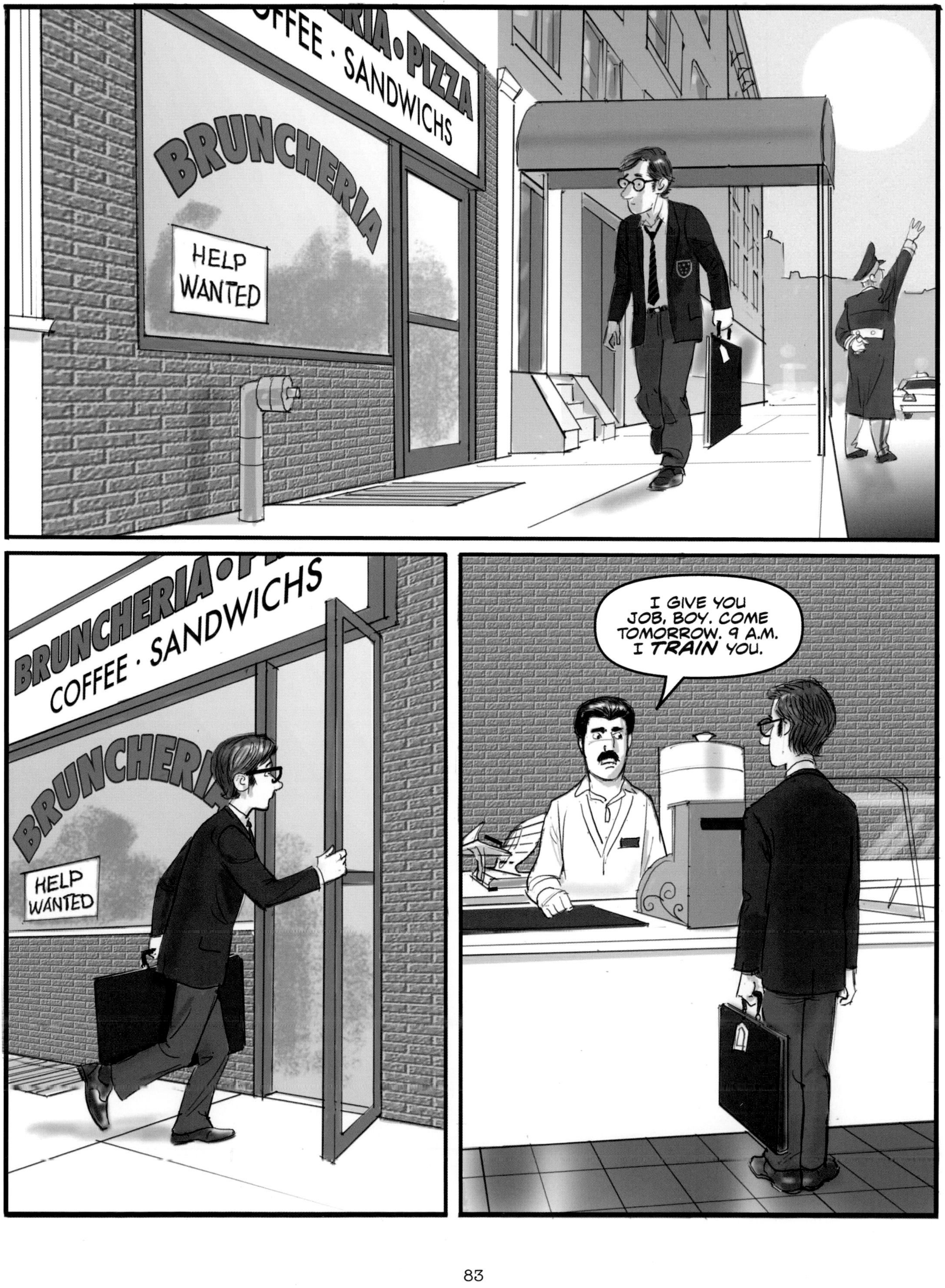

COFFEE · SANDWICHS
BRUNCHERIA
HELP WANTED
BRUNCHERIA
COFFEE · SANDWICHS
BRUNCHERIA
HELP WANTED
I GIVE YOU JOB, BOY. COME TOMORROW. 9 A.M. I *TRAIN* YOU.

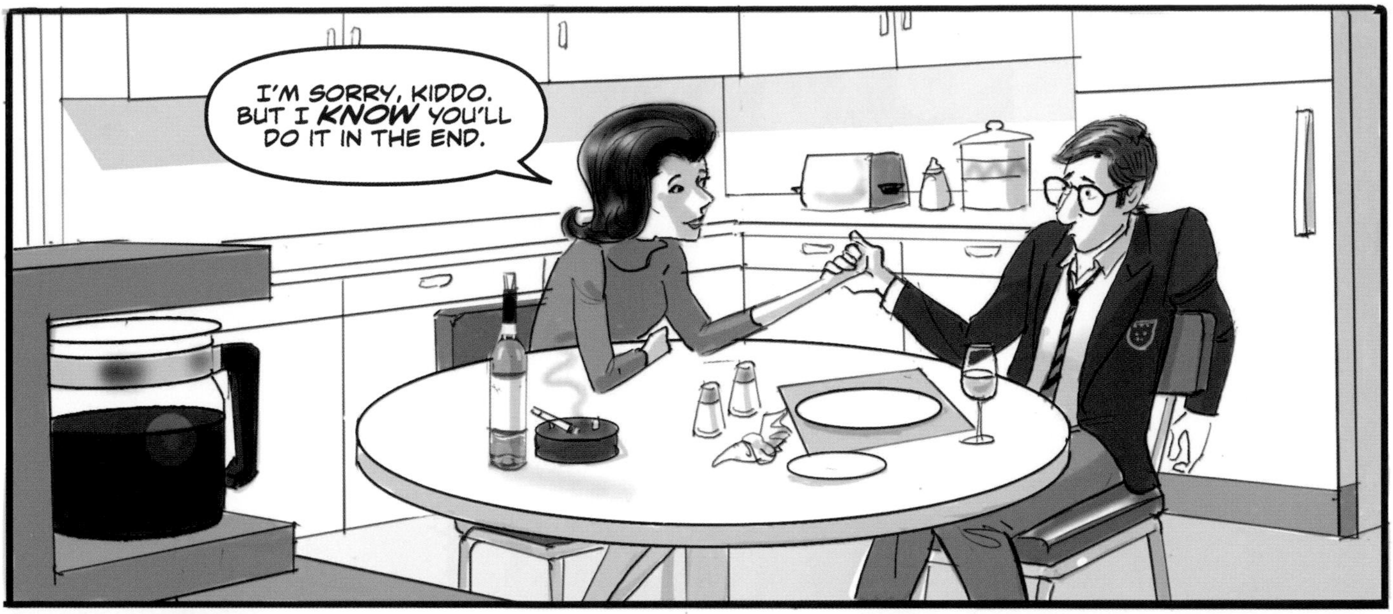
I'M SORRY, KIDDO. BUT I *KNOW* YOU'LL DO IT IN THE END.

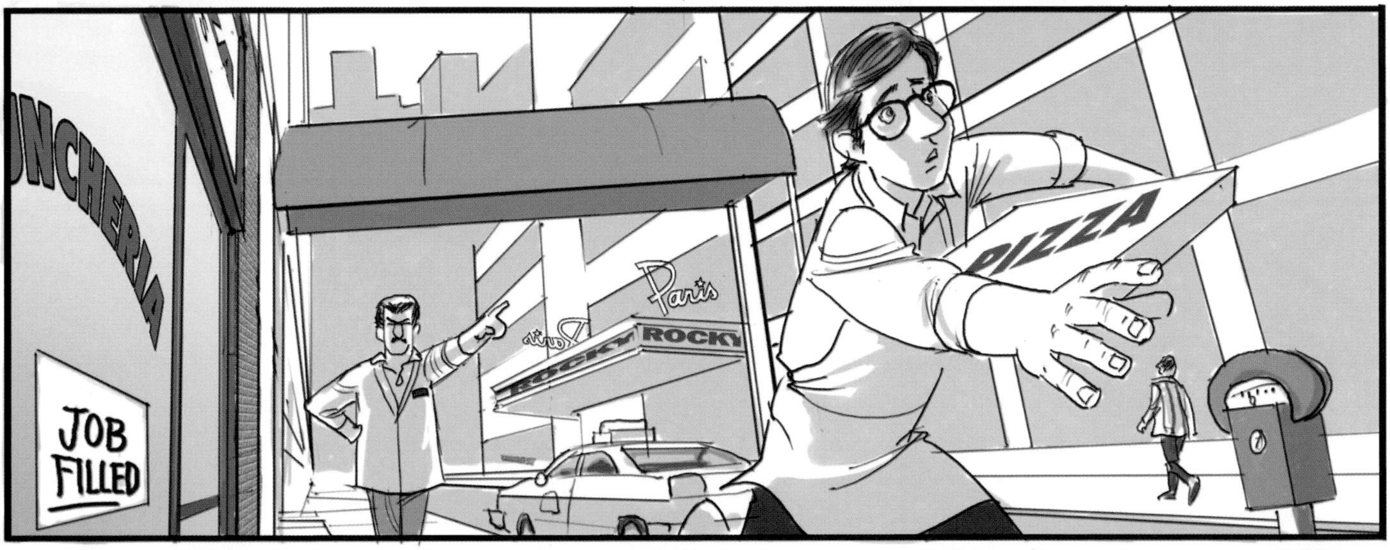
UNCHERIA
JOB FILLED
Paris
ROCKY
PIZZA

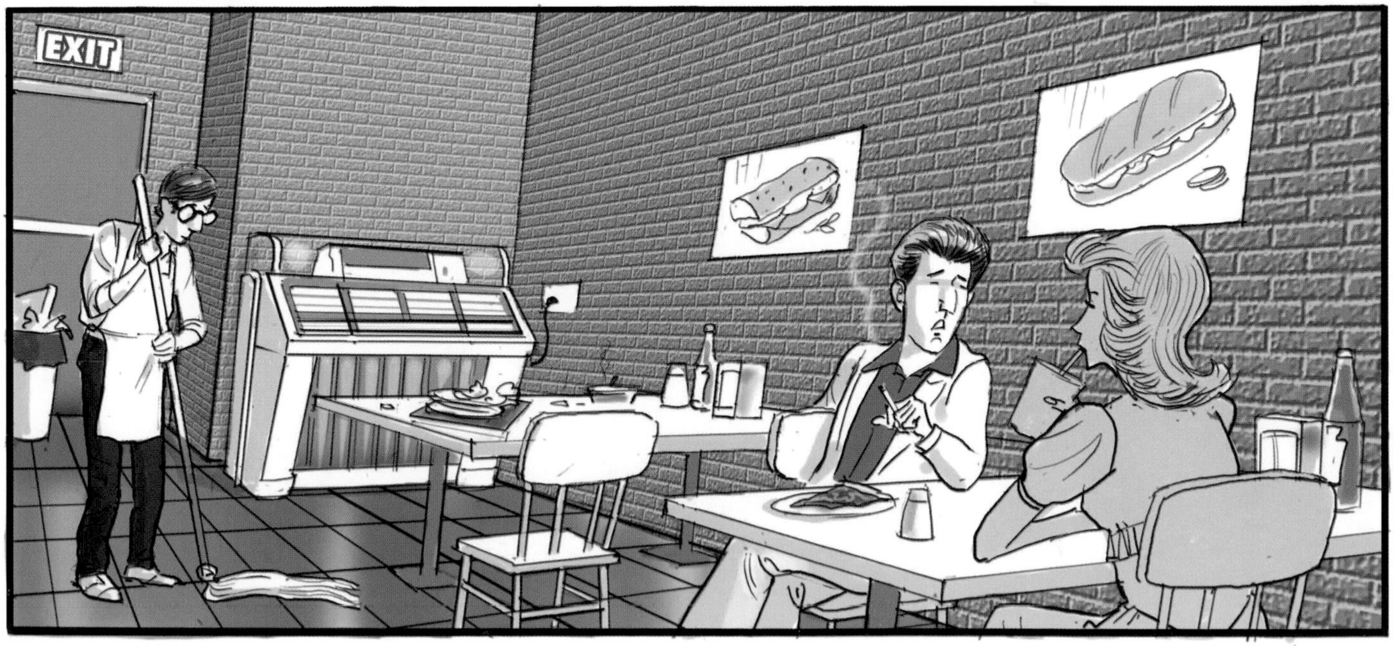
EXIT
PIZZA

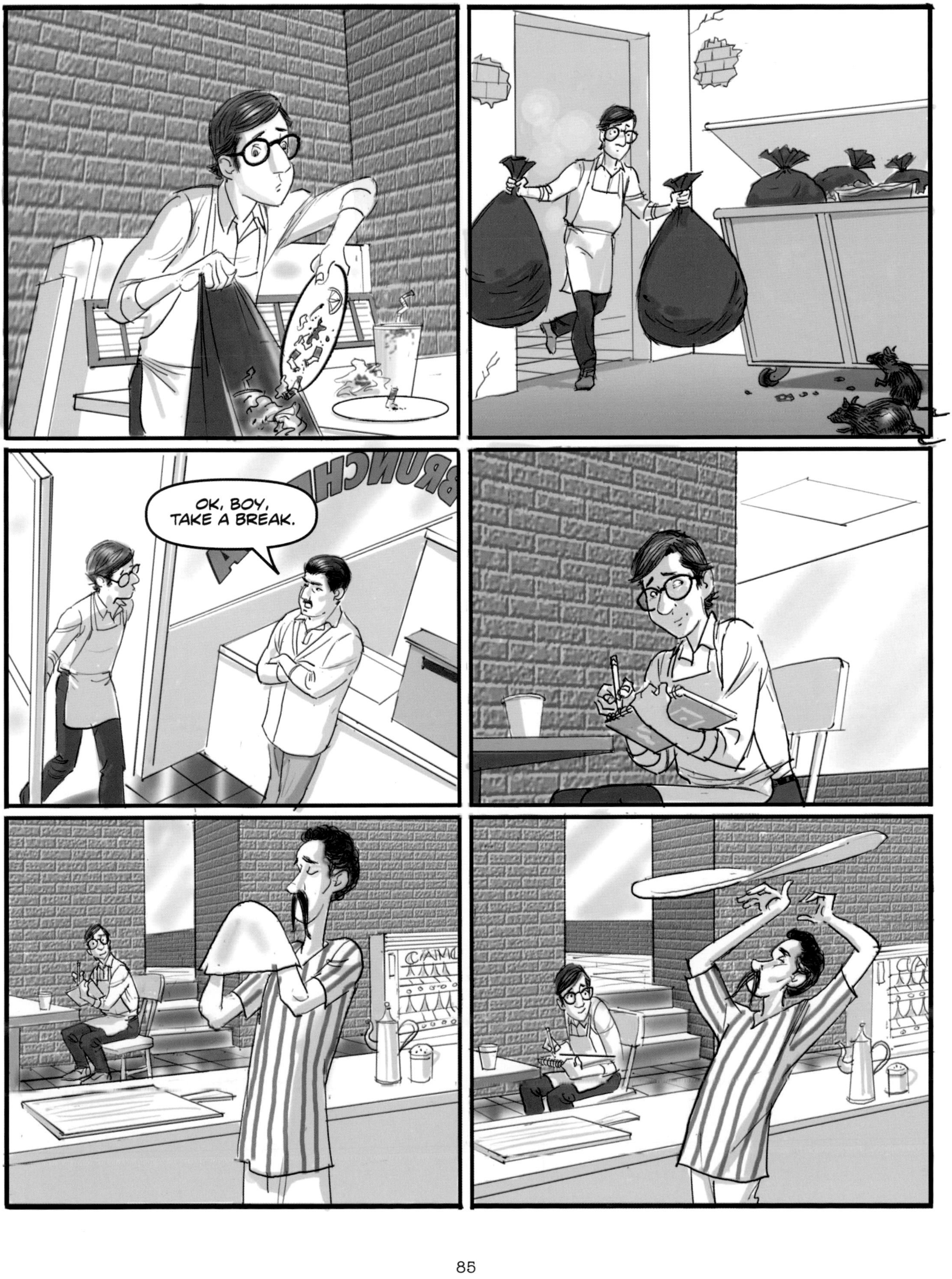
OK, BOY, TAKE A BREAK.

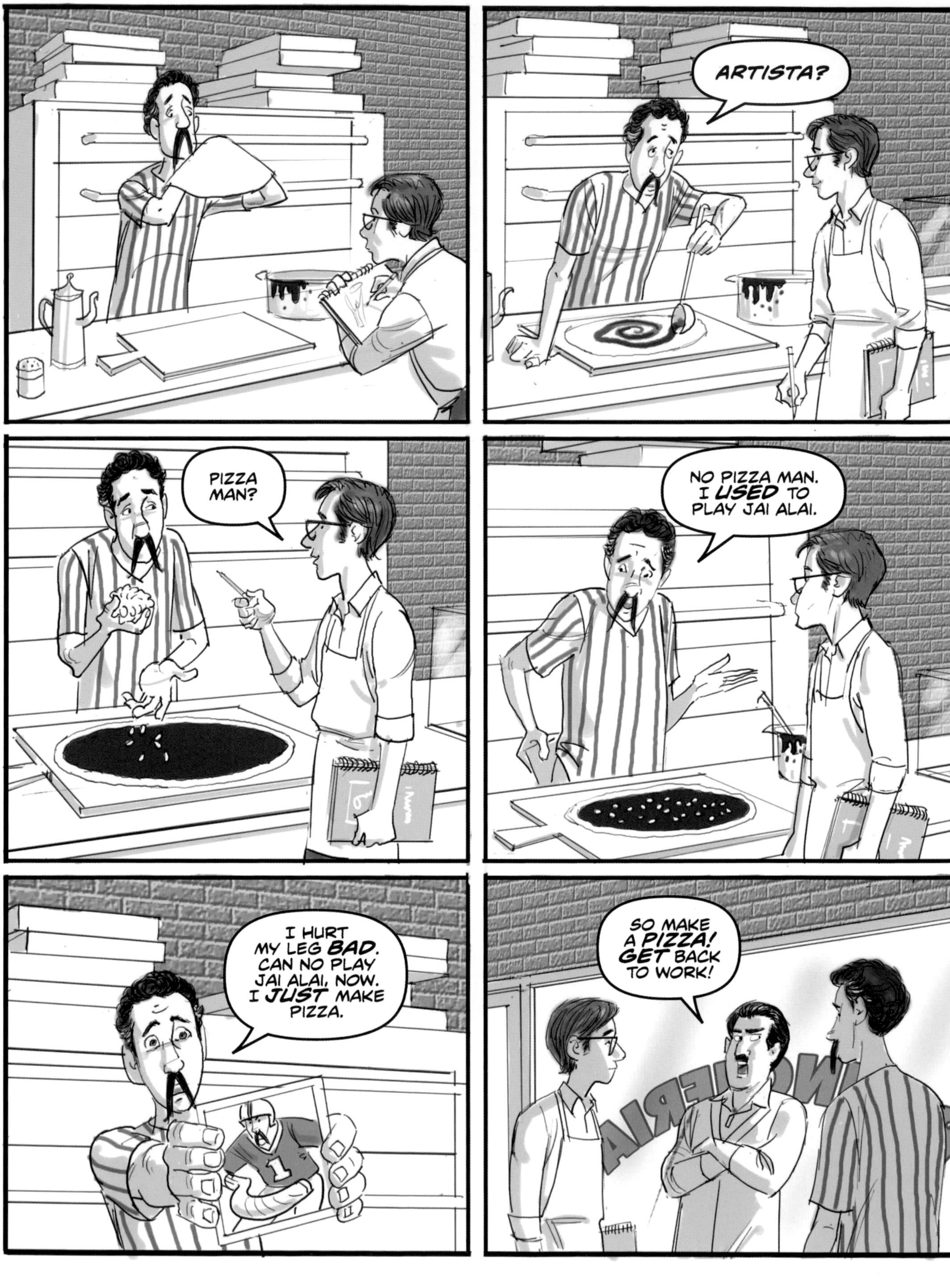
ARTISTA?
PIZZA MAN?
NO PIZZA MAN. I *USED* TO PLAY JAI ALAI.
I HURT MY LEG **BAD**. CAN NO PLAY JAI ALAI, NOW. I *JUST* MAKE PIZZA.
SO MAKE A *PIZZA!* **GET** BACK TO WORK!

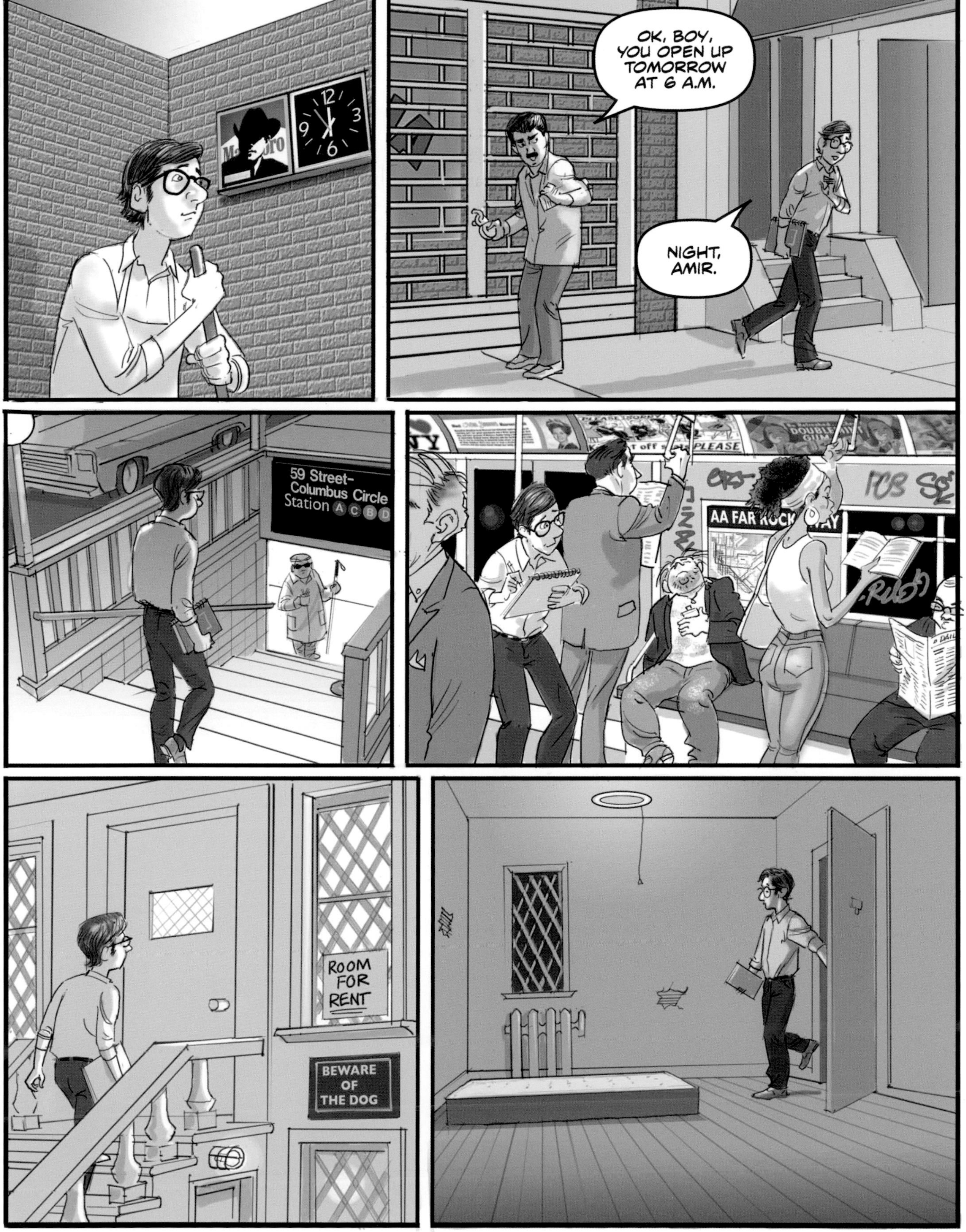
OK, BOY, YOU OPEN UP TOMORROW AT 6 A.M.
NIGHT, AMIR.
59 Street-
Columbus Circle
Station A C B D
ROOM FOR RENT
BEWARE OF THE DOG

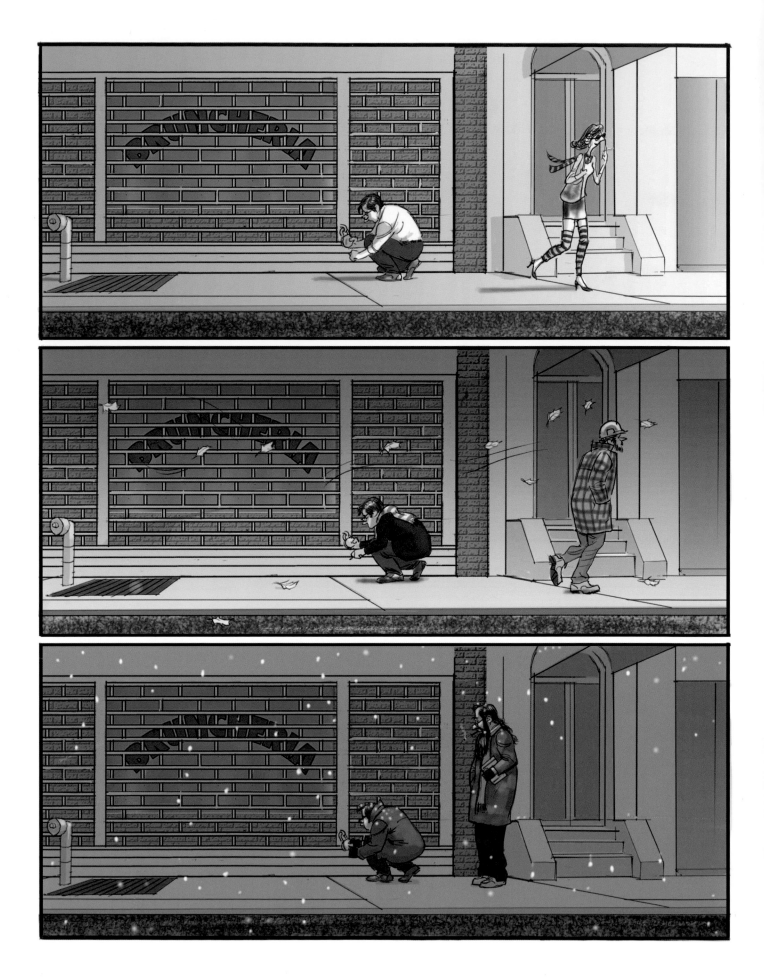

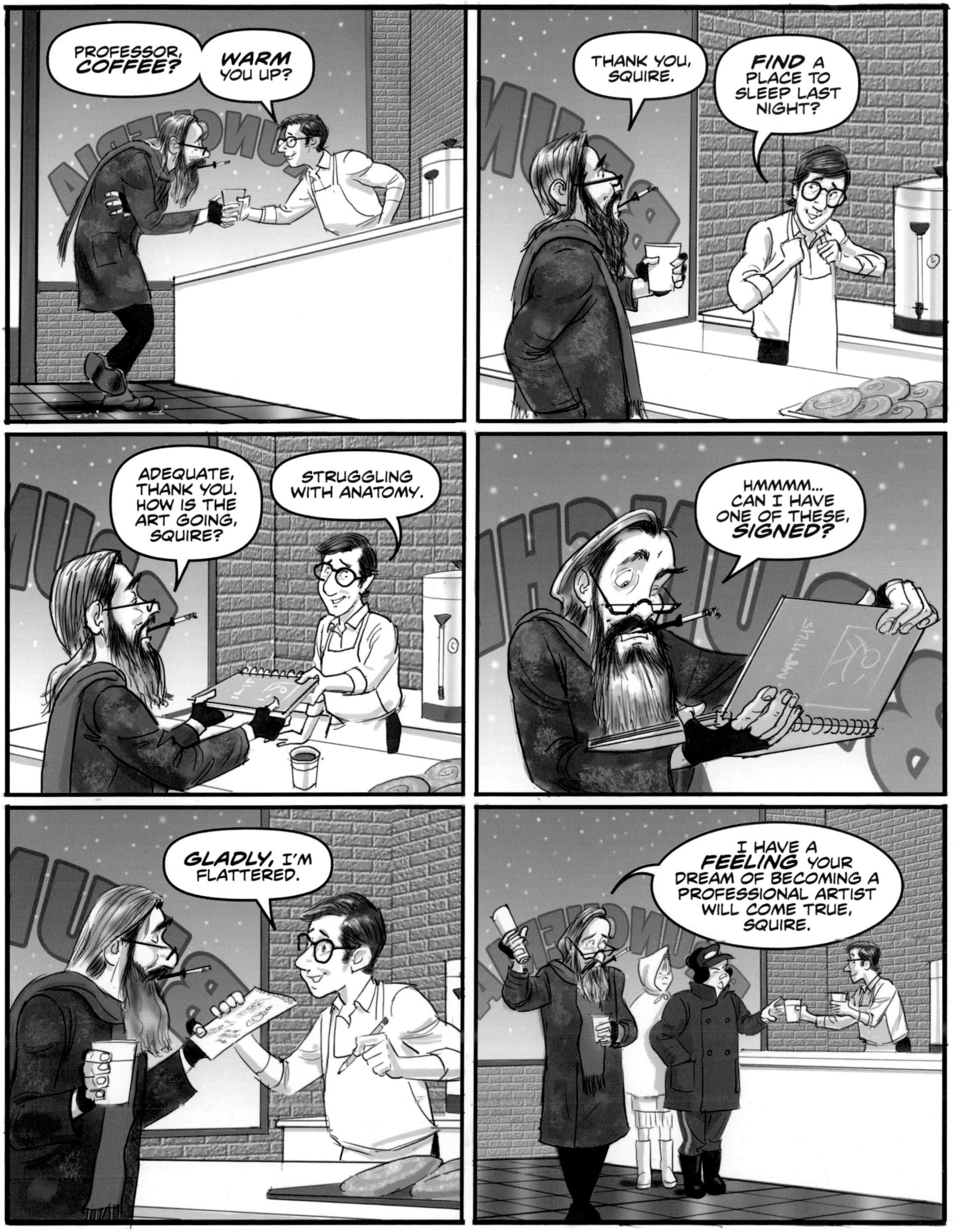
PROFESSOR, COFFEE?
WARM YOU UP?
THANK YOU, SQUIRE.
FIND A PLACE TO SLEEP LAST NIGHT?
ADEQUATE, THANK YOU. HOW IS THE ART GOING, SQUIRE?
STRUGGLING WITH ANATOMY.
HMMMM... CAN I HAVE ONE OF THESE, SIGNED?
GLADLY, I'M FLATTERED.
I HAVE A FEELING YOUR DREAM OF BECOMING A PROFESSIONAL ARTIST WILL COME TRUE, SQUIRE.

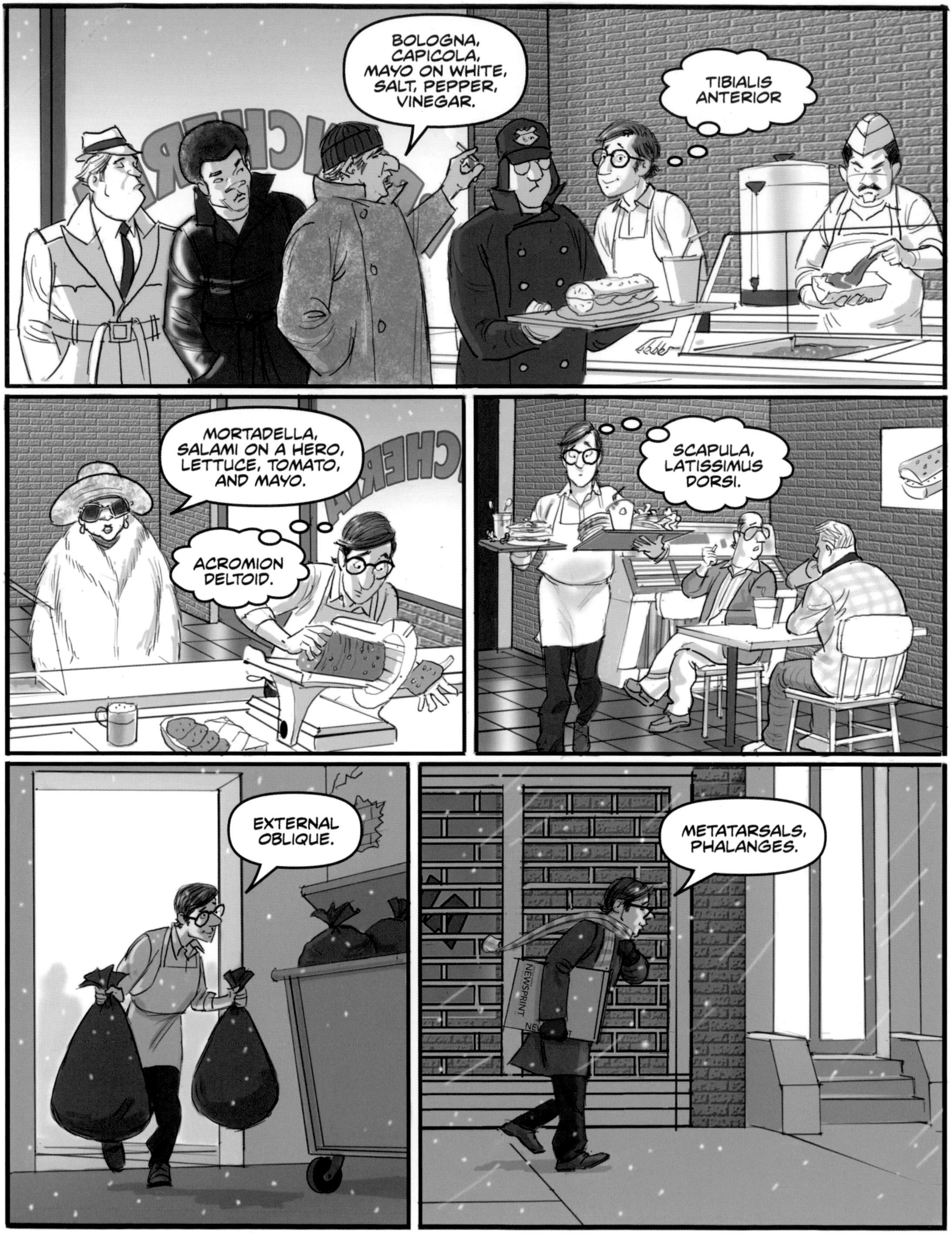
BOLOGNA, CAPICOLA, MAYO ON WHITE, SALT, PEPPER, VINEGAR.
TIBIALIS ANTERIOR
MORTADELLA, SALAMI ON A HERO, LETTUCE, TOMATO, AND MAYO.
ACROMION DELTOID.
SCAPULA, LATISSIMUS DORSI.
EXTERNAL OBLIQUE.
NEWSPRINT
METATARSALS, PHALANGES.

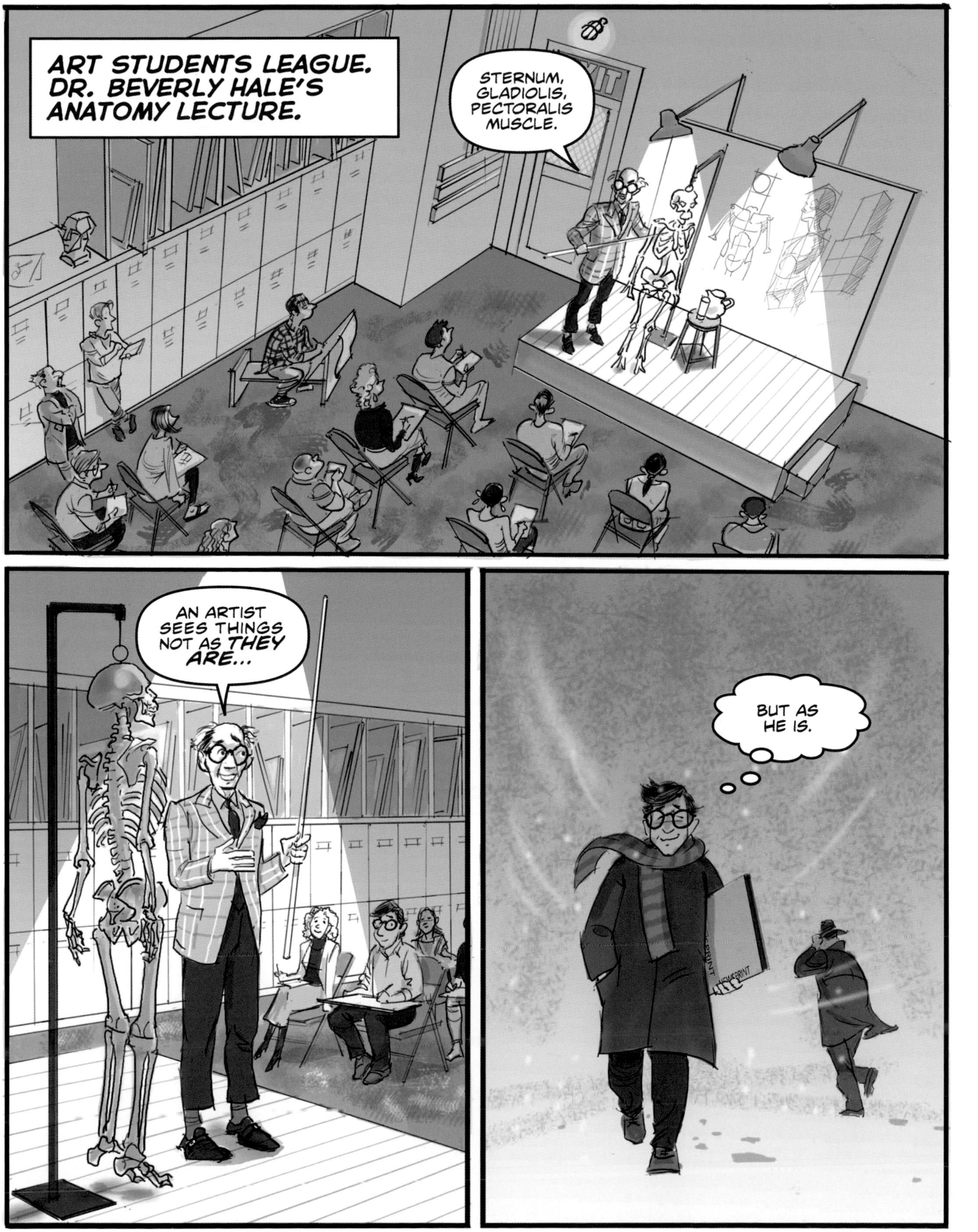
ART STUDENTS LEAGUE. DR. BEVERLY HALE'S ANATOMY LECTURE.
STERNUM, GLADIOLIS, PECTORALIS MUSCLE.
AN ARTIST SEES THINGS NOT AS *THEY ARE...*
BUT AS HE IS.
NEWSPRINT

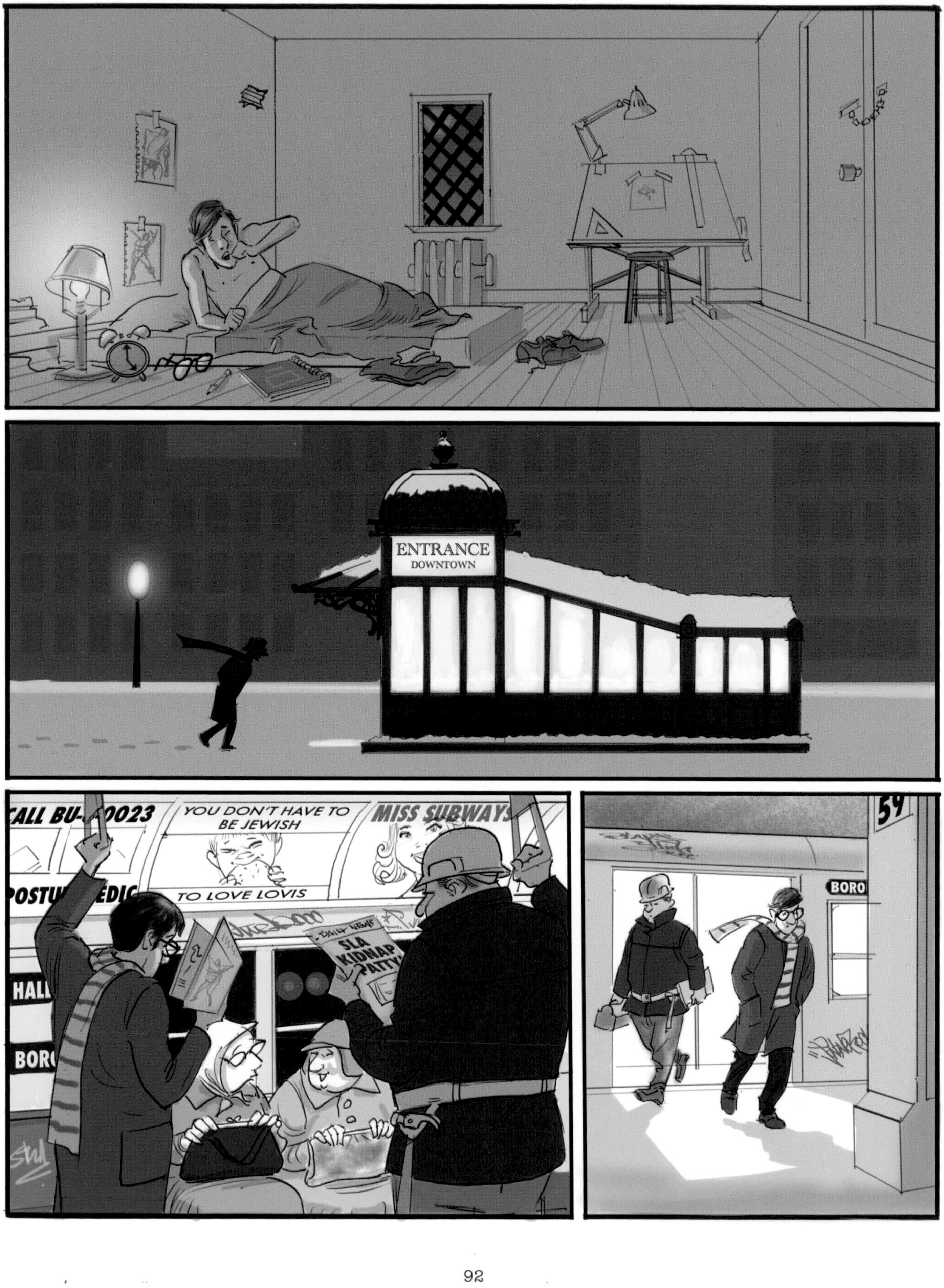
ENTRANCE
DOWNTOWN
CALL BU-
0023
YOU DON'T HAVE TO BE JEWISH
TO LOVE LOVIS
MISS SUBWAYS
POSTU
EDIC
DAILY NEWS
SLA KIDNAP PATTY
HALL
BORO
59
BORO

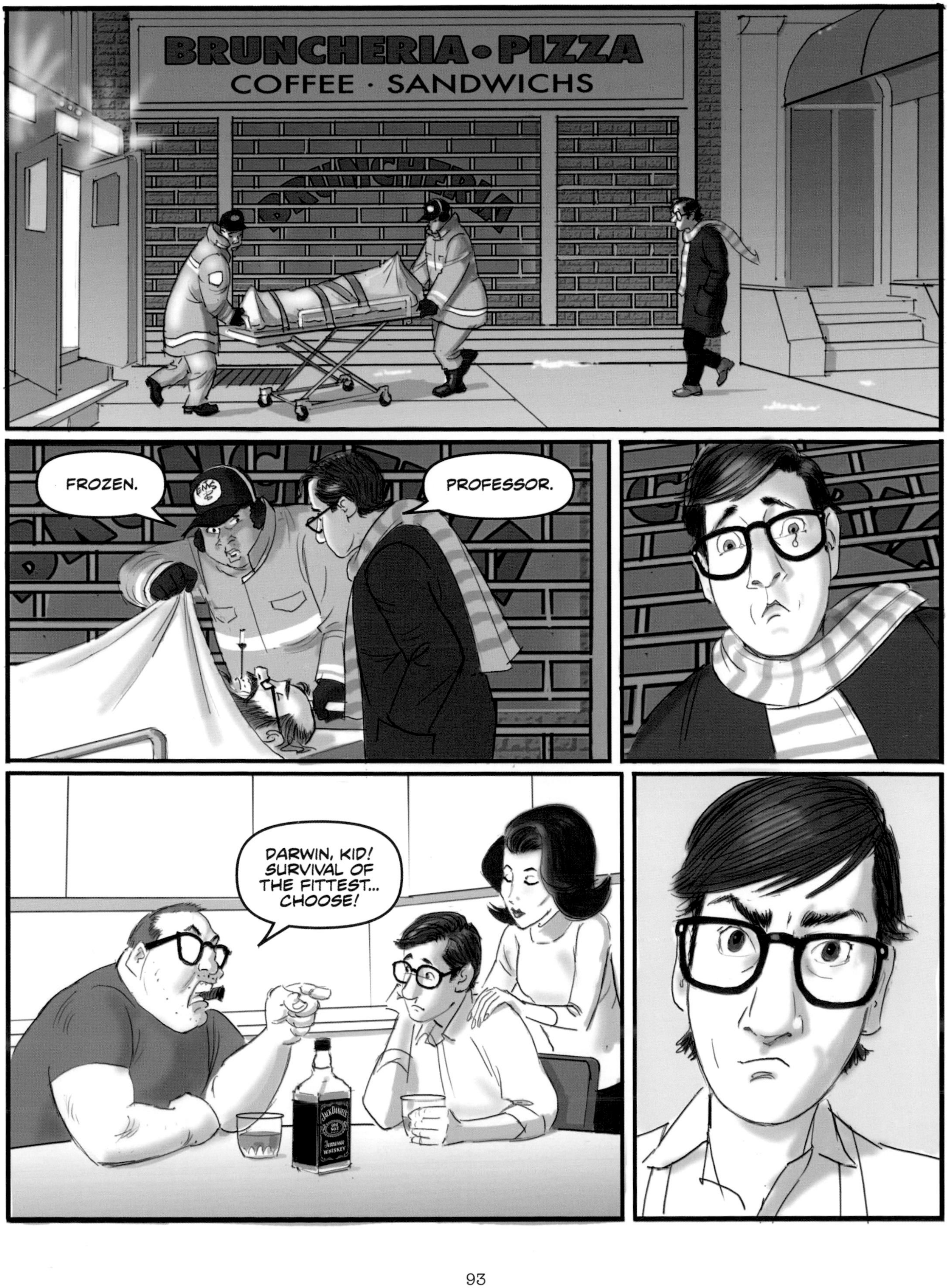
BRUNCHERIA • PIZZA
COFFEE · SANDWICHS
FROZEN.
PROFESSOR.
DARWIN, KID! SURVIVAL OF THE FITTEST... CHOOSE!

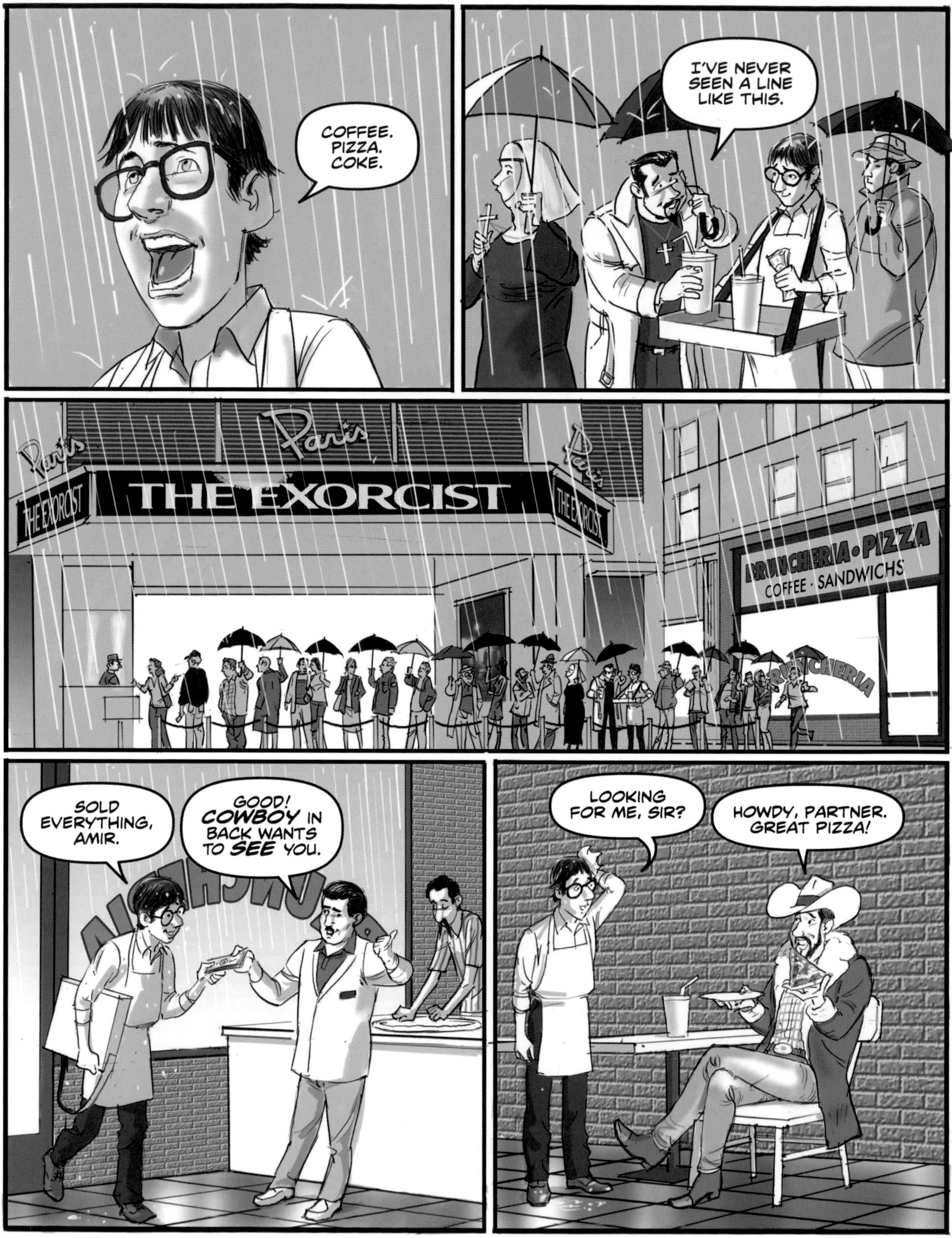
COFFEE. PIZZA. COKE.
I'VE NEVER SEEN A LINE LIKE THIS.
Paris
THE EXORCIST
BRUNCHERIA • PIZZA
COFFEE · SANDWICHS
BRUNCHERIA
SOLD EVERYTHING, AMIR.
GOOD! COWBOY IN BACK WANTS TO SEE YOU.
LOOKING FOR ME, SIR?
HOWDY, PARTNER. GREAT PIZZA!

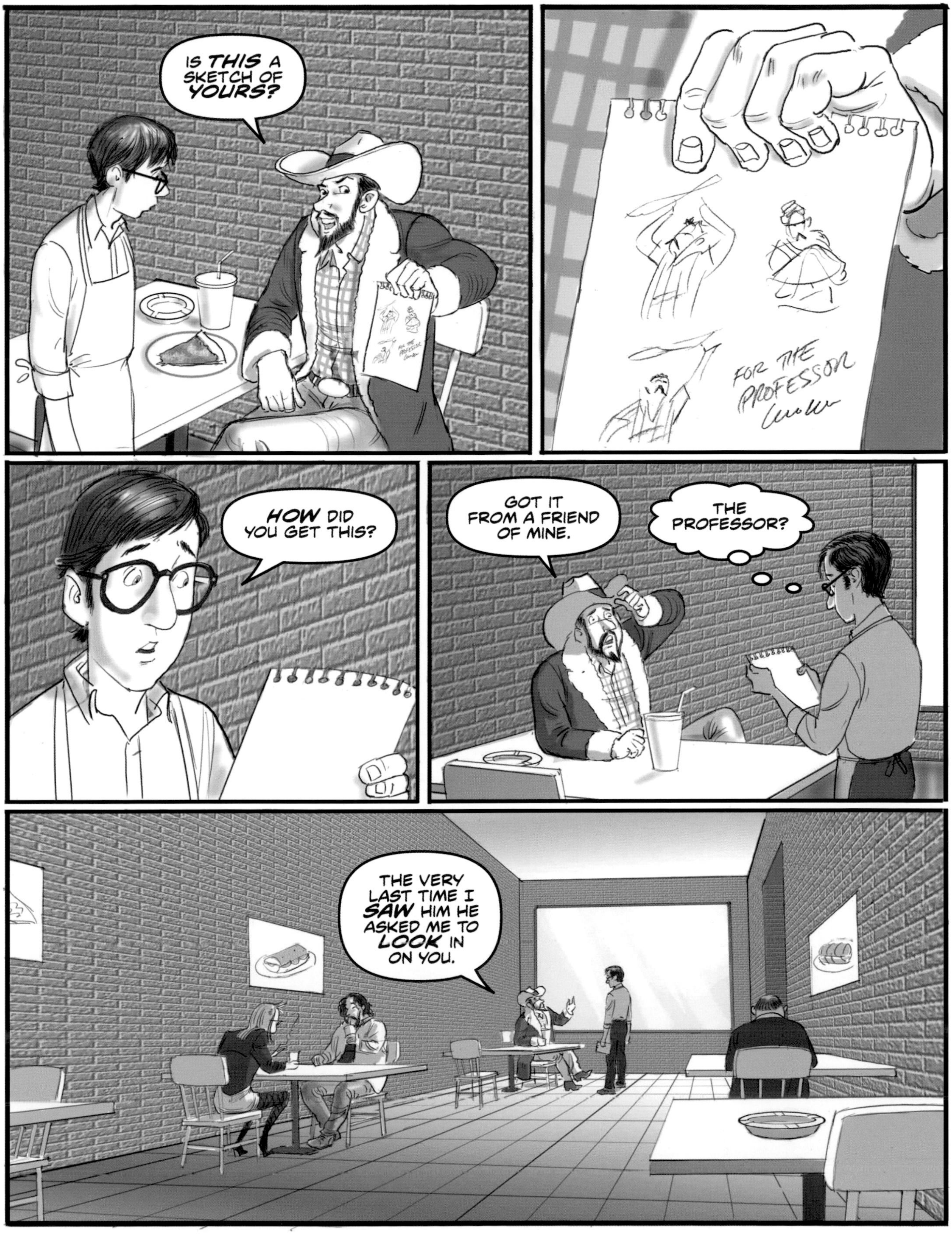
IS THIS A SKETCH OF YOURS?
FOR THE PROFESSOR
HOW DID YOU GET THIS?
GOT IT FROM A FRIEND OF MINE.
THE PROFESSOR?
THE VERY LAST TIME I SAW HIM HE ASKED ME TO LOOK IN ON YOU.

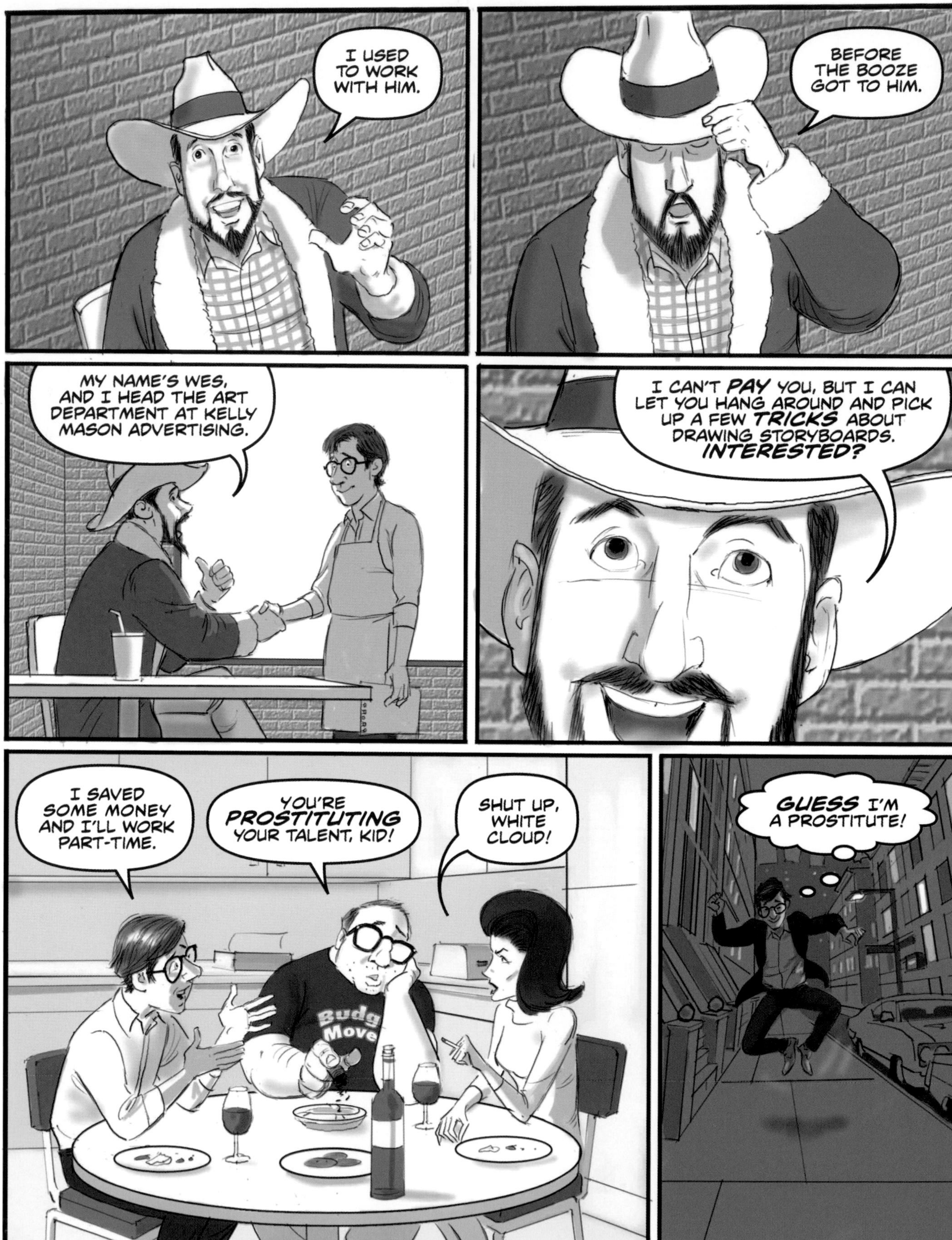
I USED TO WORK WITH HIM.
BEFORE THE BOOZE GOT TO HIM.
MY NAME'S WES, AND I HEAD THE ART DEPARTMENT AT KELLY MASON ADVERTISING.
I CAN'T PAY YOU, BUT I CAN LET YOU HANG AROUND AND PICK UP A FEW TRICKS ABOUT DRAWING STORYBOARDS. INTERESTED?
I SAVED SOME MONEY AND I'LL WORK PART-TIME.
YOU'RE PROSTITUTING YOUR TALENT, KID!
SHUT UP, WHITE CLOUD!
GUESS I'M A PROSTITUTE!

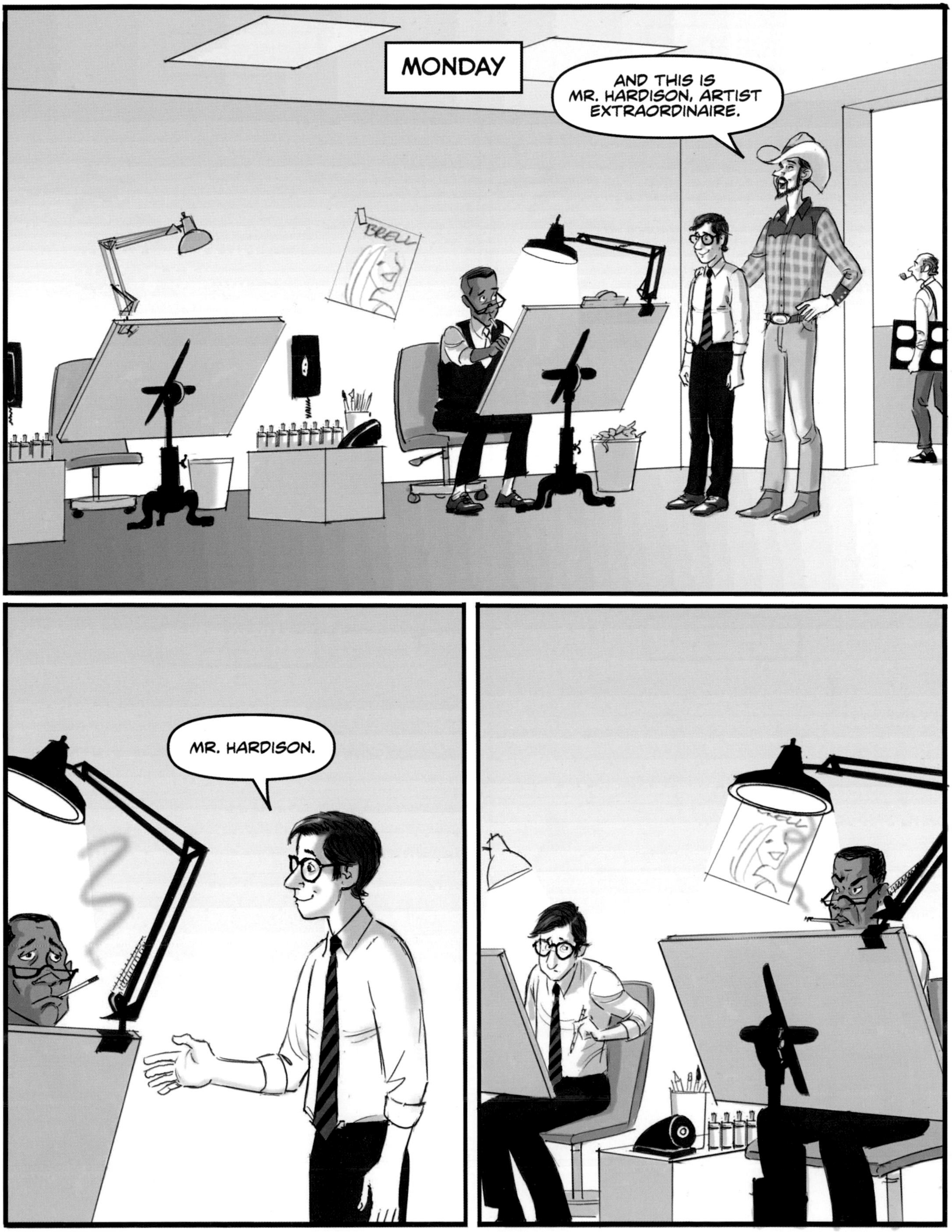
MONDAY
AND THIS IS MR. HARDISON, ARTIST EXTRAORDINAIRE.
MR. HARDISON.

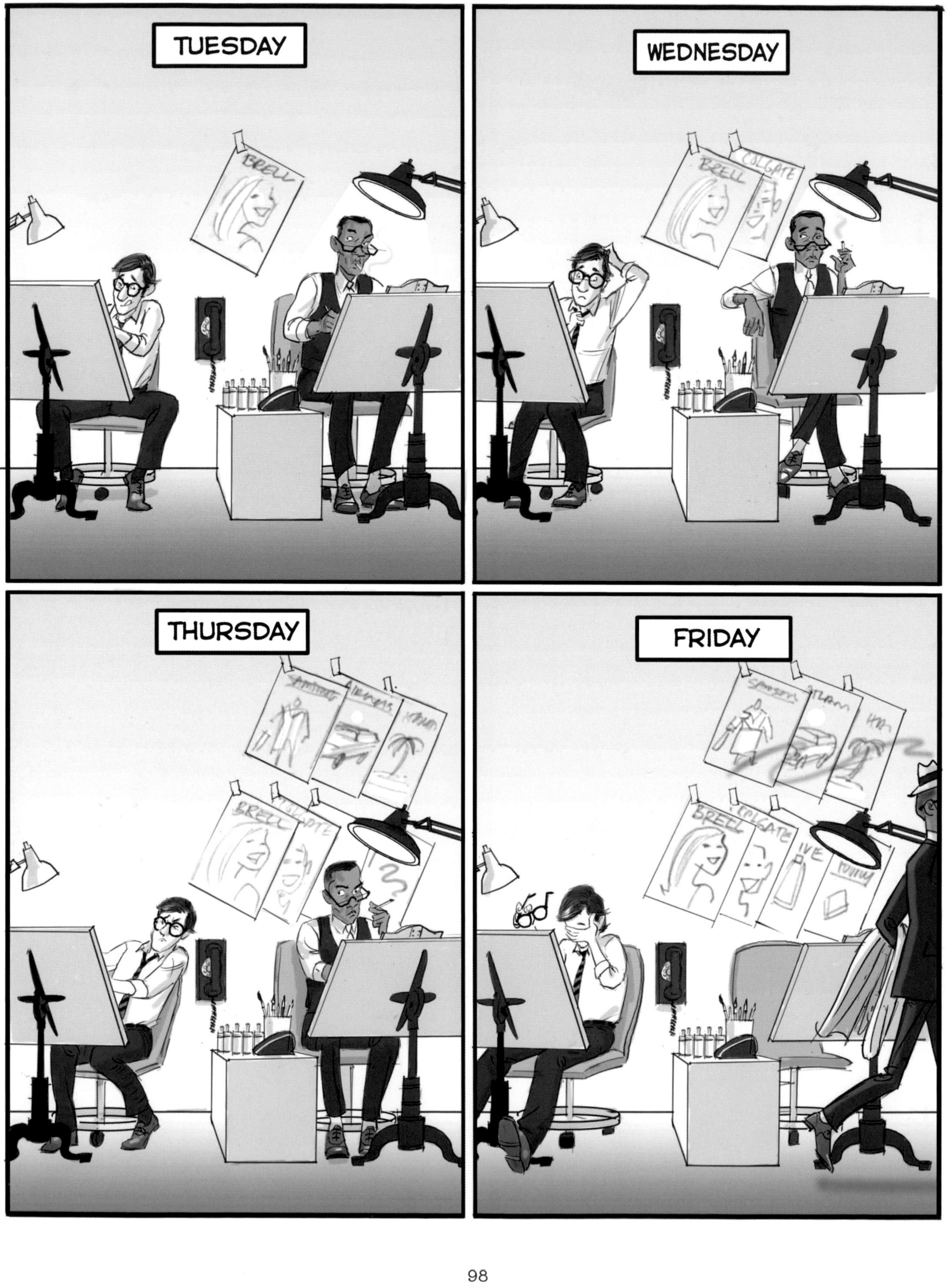
TUESDAY
BRELL
WEDNESDAY
BRELL
COLGATE
THURSDAY
BRELL
FRIDAY
BRELL
COLGATE

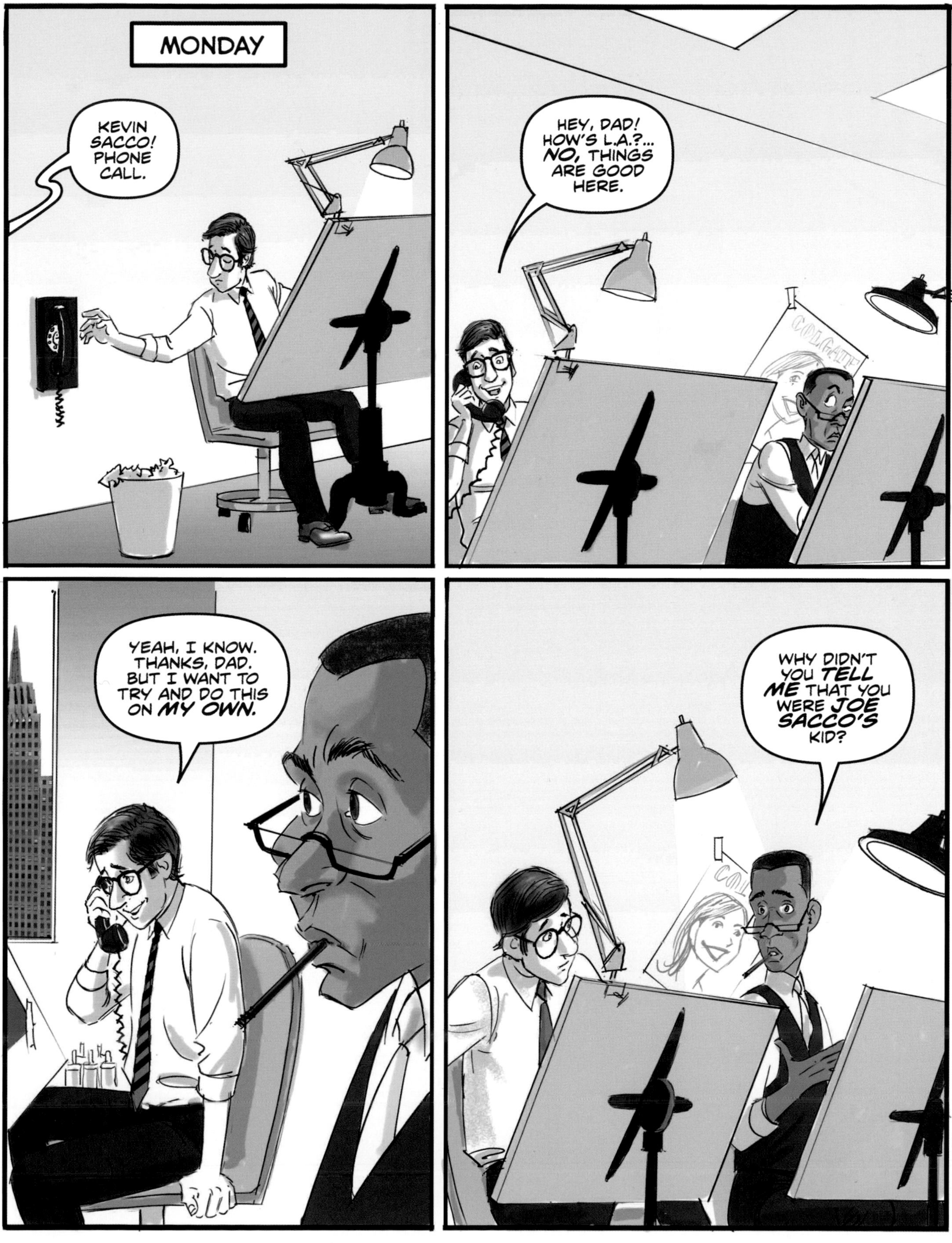
MONDAY
KEVIN SACCO! PHONE CALL.
HEY, DAD! HOW'S L.A.?... NO, THINGS ARE GOOD HERE.
COLGATE
YEAH, I KNOW. THANKS, DAD. BUT I WANT TO TRY AND DO THIS ON MY OWN.
WHY DIDN'T YOU TELL ME THAT YOU WERE JOE SACCO'S KID?

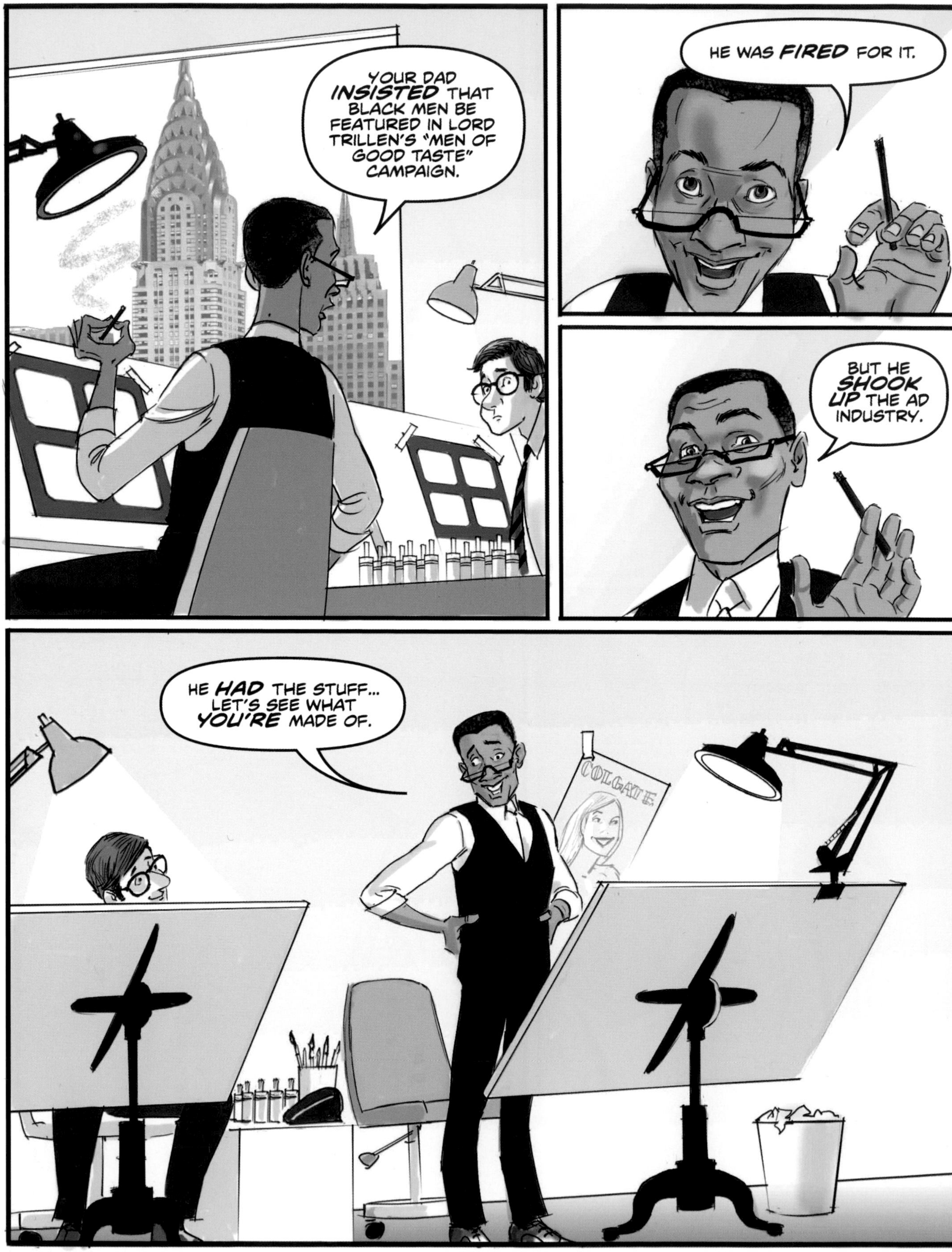
YOUR DAD INSISTED THAT BLACK MEN BE FEATURED IN LORD TRILLEN'S "MEN OF GOOD TASTE" CAMPAIGN.
HE WAS FIRED FOR IT.
BUT HE SHOOK UP THE AD INDUSTRY.
HE HAD THE STUFF... LET'S SEE WHAT YOU'RE MADE OF.
COLGATE

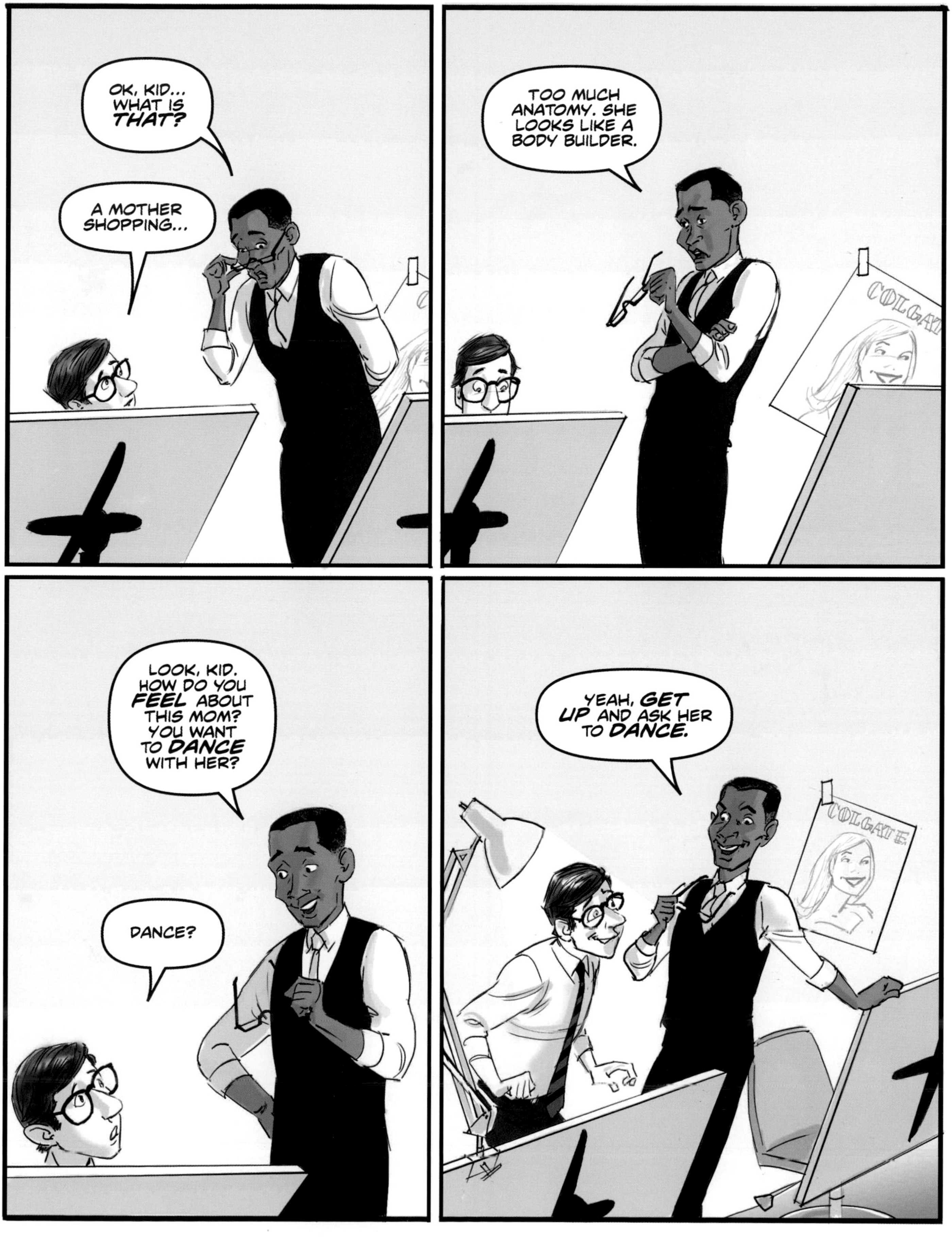
OK, KID... WHAT IS *THAT?*
A MOTHER SHOPPING...
TOO MUCH ANATOMY. SHE LOOKS LIKE A BODY BUILDER.
COLGATE
LOOK, KID. HOW DO YOU *FEEL* ABOUT THIS MOM? YOU WANT TO *DANCE* WITH HER?
DANCE?
YEAH, *GET UP* AND ASK HER TO *DANCE.*
COLGATE

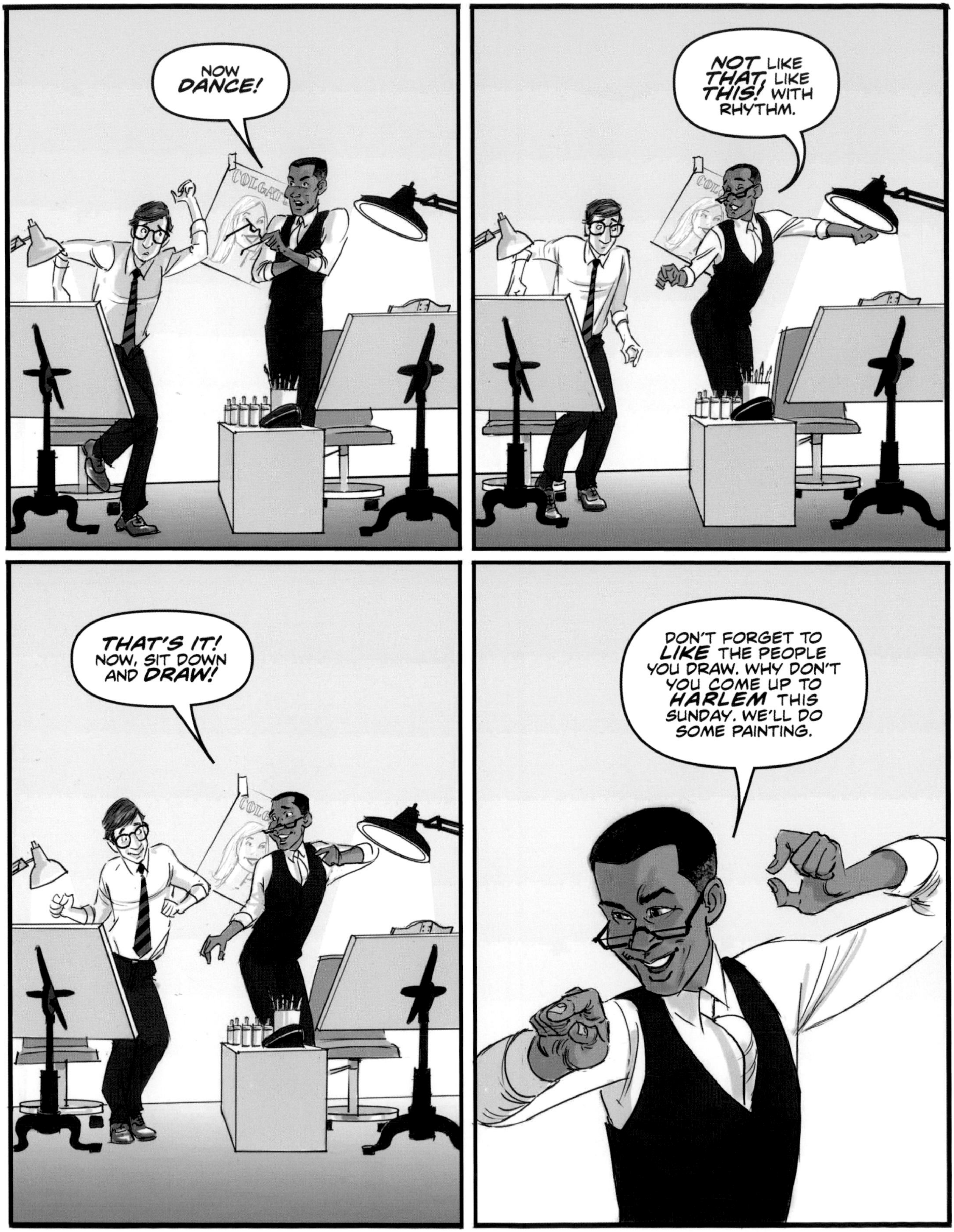
NOW DANCE!
NOT LIKE THAT, LIKE THIS! WITH RHYTHM.
THAT'S IT! NOW, SIT DOWN AND DRAW!
DON'T FORGET TO LIKE THE PEOPLE YOU DRAW. WHY DON'T YOU COME UP TO HARLEM THIS SUNDAY. WE'LL DO SOME PAINTING.

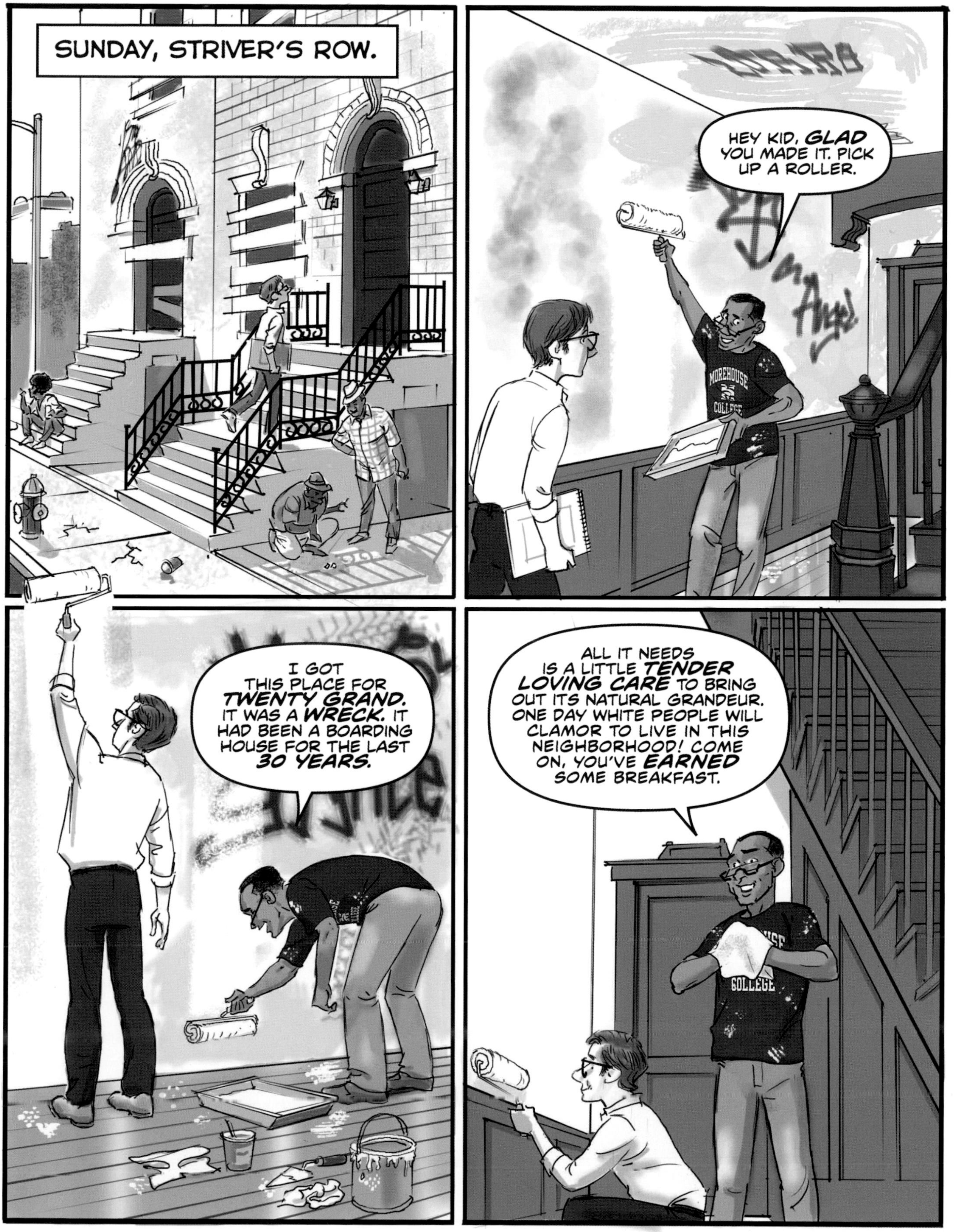
SUNDAY, STRIVER'S ROW.
HEY KID, GLAD YOU MADE IT. PICK UP A ROLLER.
I GOT THIS PLACE FOR TWENTY GRAND. IT WAS A WRECK. IT HAD BEEN A BOARDING HOUSE FOR THE LAST 30 YEARS.
ALL IT NEEDS IS A LITTLE TENDER LOVING CARE TO BRING OUT ITS NATURAL GRANDEUR. ONE DAY WHITE PEOPLE WILL CLAMOR TO LIVE IN THIS NEIGHBORHOOD! COME ON, YOU'VE EARNED SOME BREAKFAST.

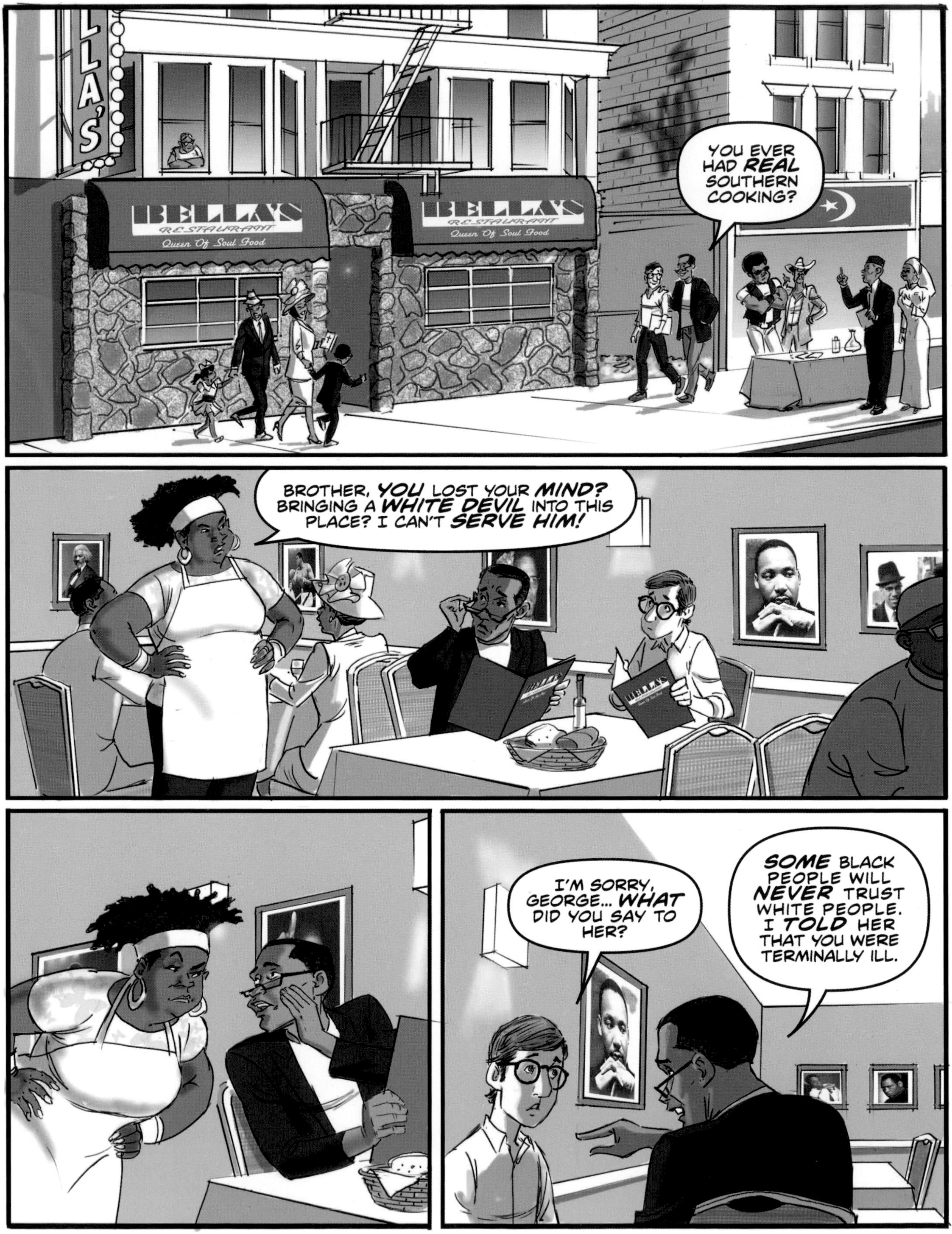
LLA'S
BELLA'S
RE-STAURANT
Queen Of Soul Food
YOU EVER HAD **REAL** SOUTHERN COOKING?
BROTHER, ***YOU*** LOST YOUR ***MIND?*** BRINGING A ***WHITE DEVIL*** INTO THIS PLACE? I CAN'T ***SERVE HIM!***
I'M SORRY, GEORGE... ***WHAT*** DID YOU SAY TO HER?
SOME BLACK PEOPLE WILL ***NEVER*** TRUST WHITE PEOPLE. I ***TOLD*** HER THAT YOU WERE TERMINALLY ILL.

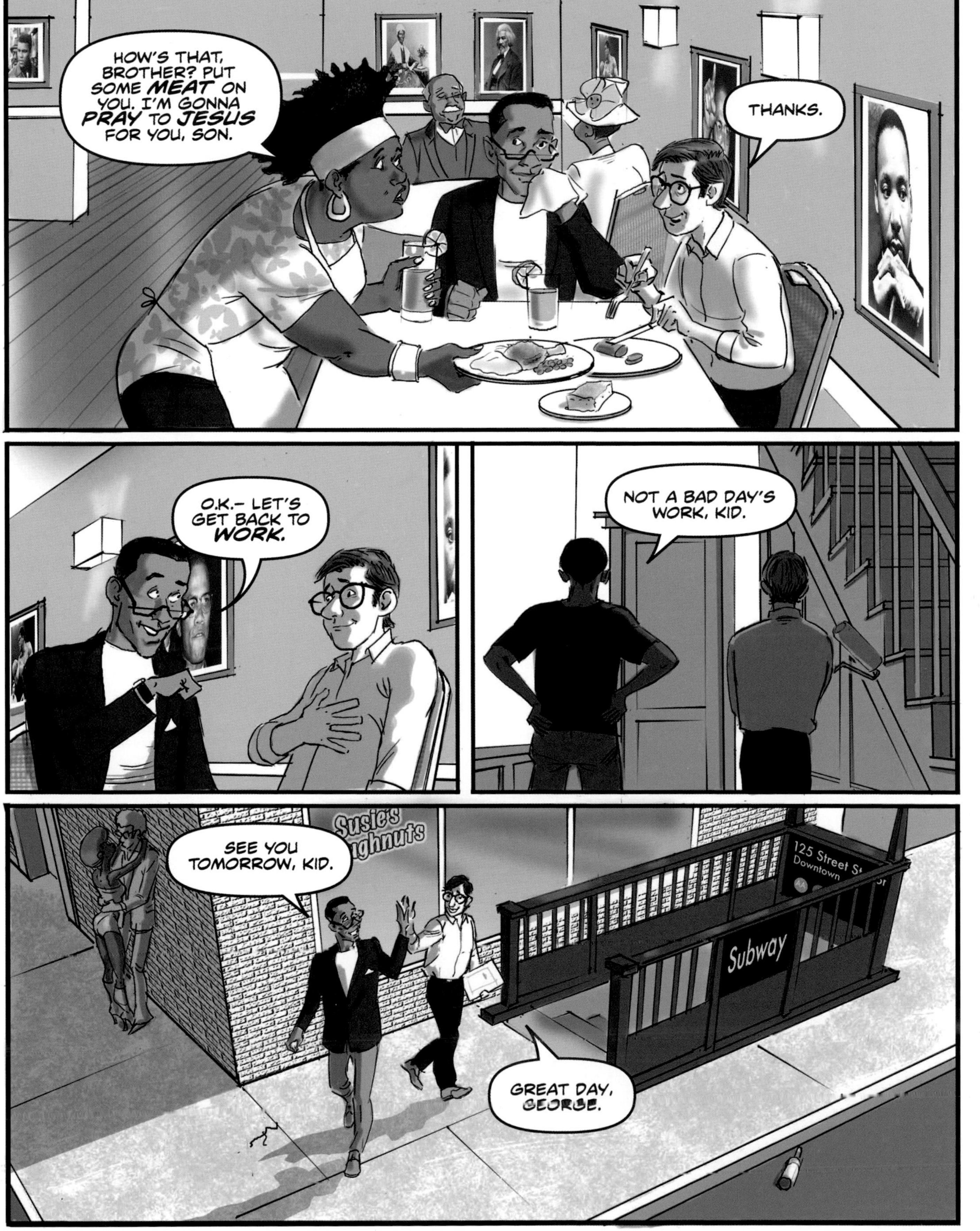
HOW'S THAT, BROTHER? PUT SOME MEAT ON YOU. I'M GONNA PRAY TO JESUS FOR YOU, SON.
THANKS.
O.K.– LET'S GET BACK TO WORK.
NOT A BAD DAY'S WORK, KID.
Susie's
SEE YOU TOMORROW, KID.
125 Street
Downtown
Subway
GREAT DAY, GEORGE.

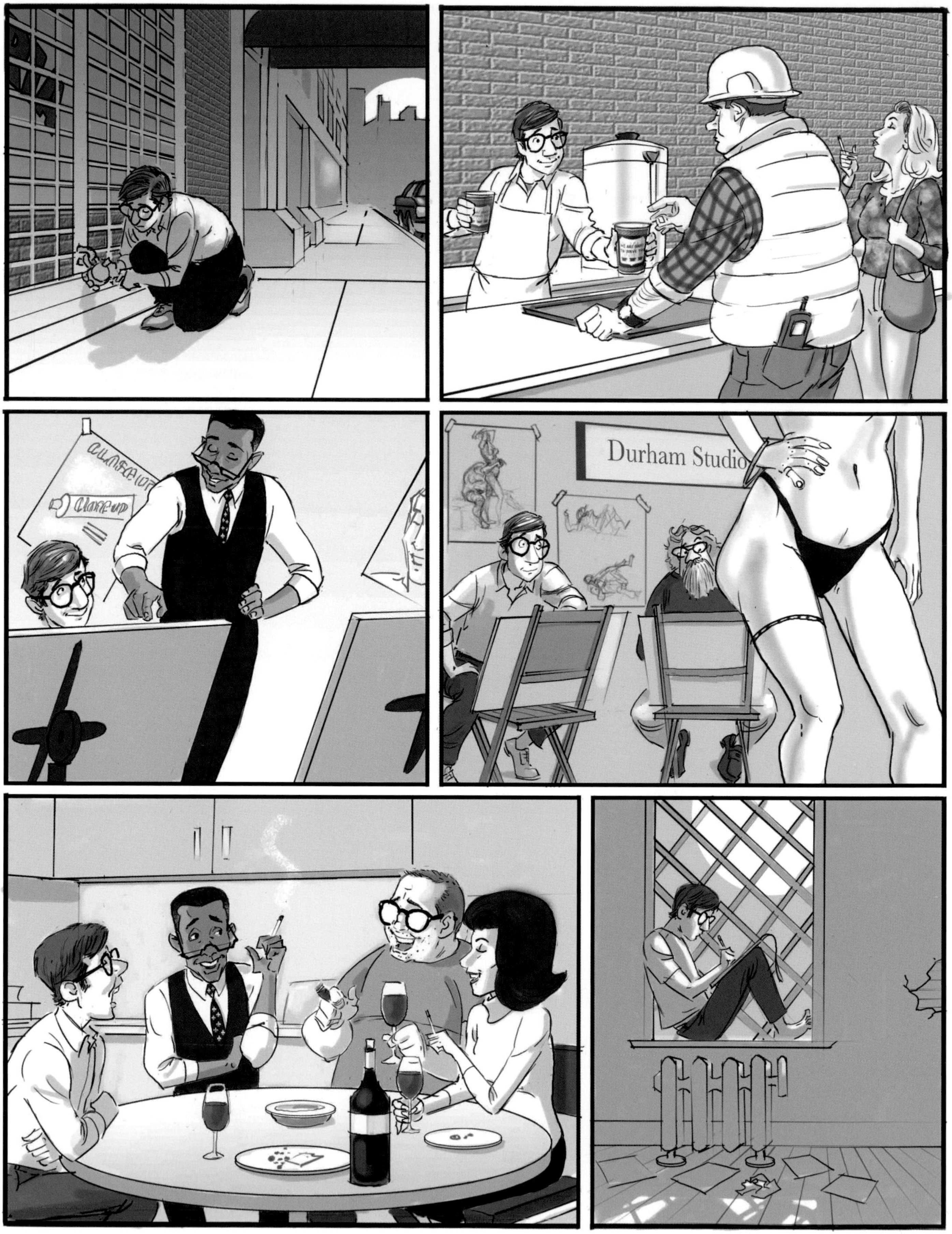
Durham Studio

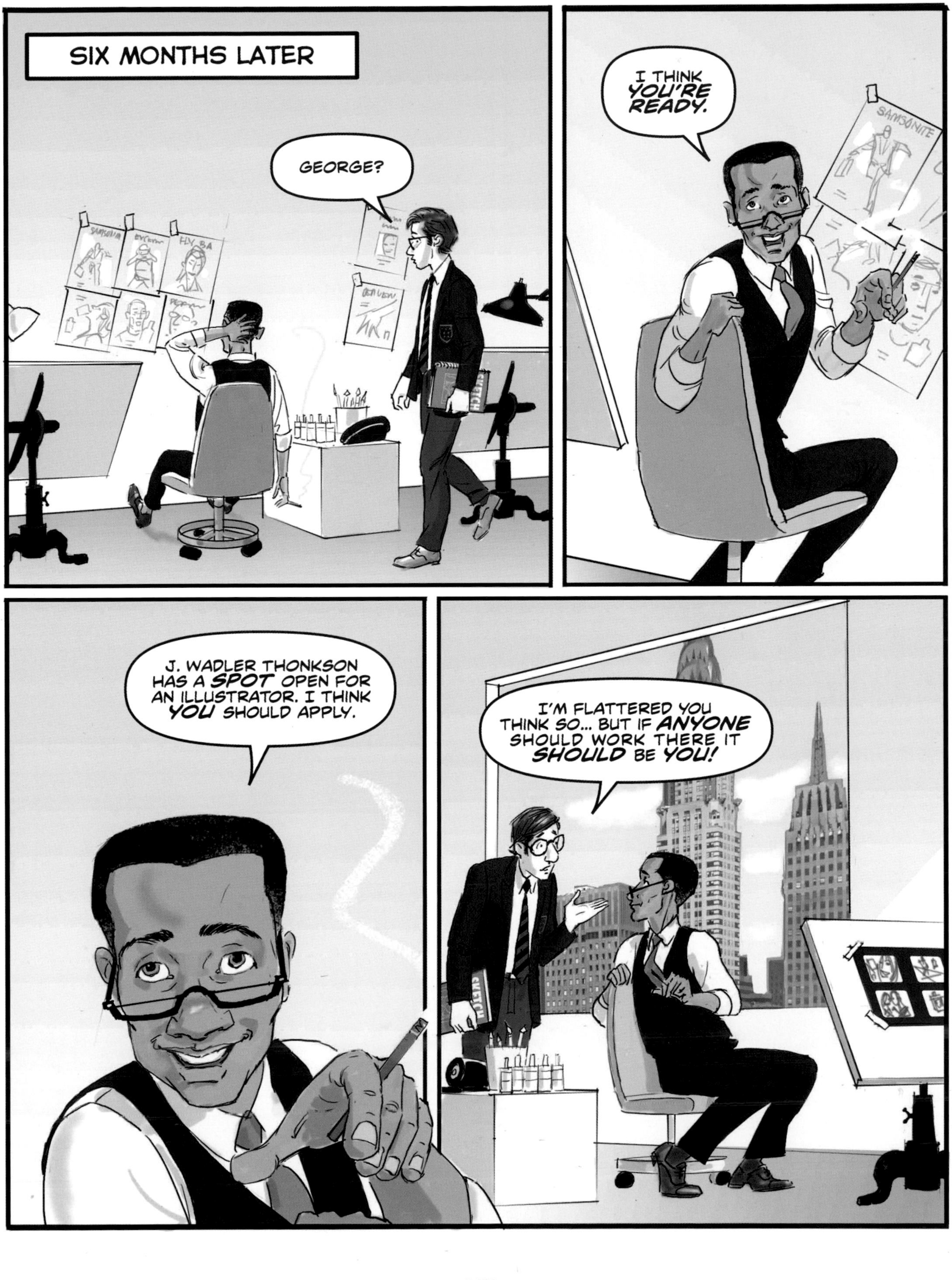
SIX MONTHS LATER
GEORGE?
I THINK YOU'RE READY.
J. WADLER THONKSON HAS A SPOT OPEN FOR AN ILLUSTRATOR. I THINK YOU SHOULD APPLY.
I'M FLATTERED YOU THINK SO... BUT IF ANYONE SHOULD WORK THERE IT SHOULD BE YOU!

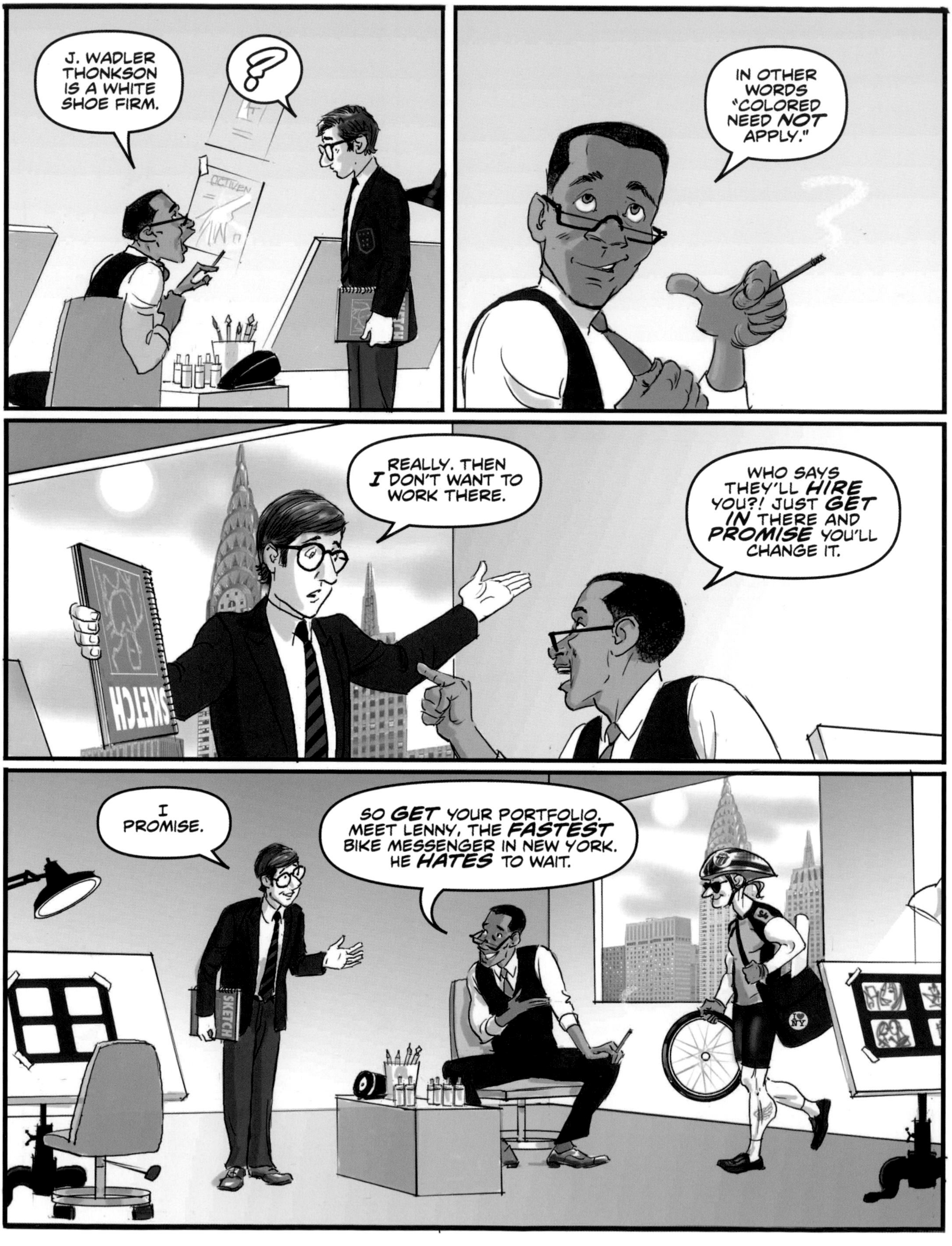
J. WADLER THONKSON IS A WHITE SHOE FIRM.
?
IN OTHER WORDS "COLORED NEED NOT APPLY."
REALLY. THEN I DON'T WANT TO WORK THERE.
WHO SAYS THEY'LL HIRE YOU?! JUST GET IN THERE AND PROMISE YOU'LL CHANGE IT.
I PROMISE.
SO GET YOUR PORTFOLIO. MEET LENNY, THE FASTEST BIKE MESSENGER IN NEW YORK. HE HATES TO WAIT.
SKETCH
SKETCH
SKETCH

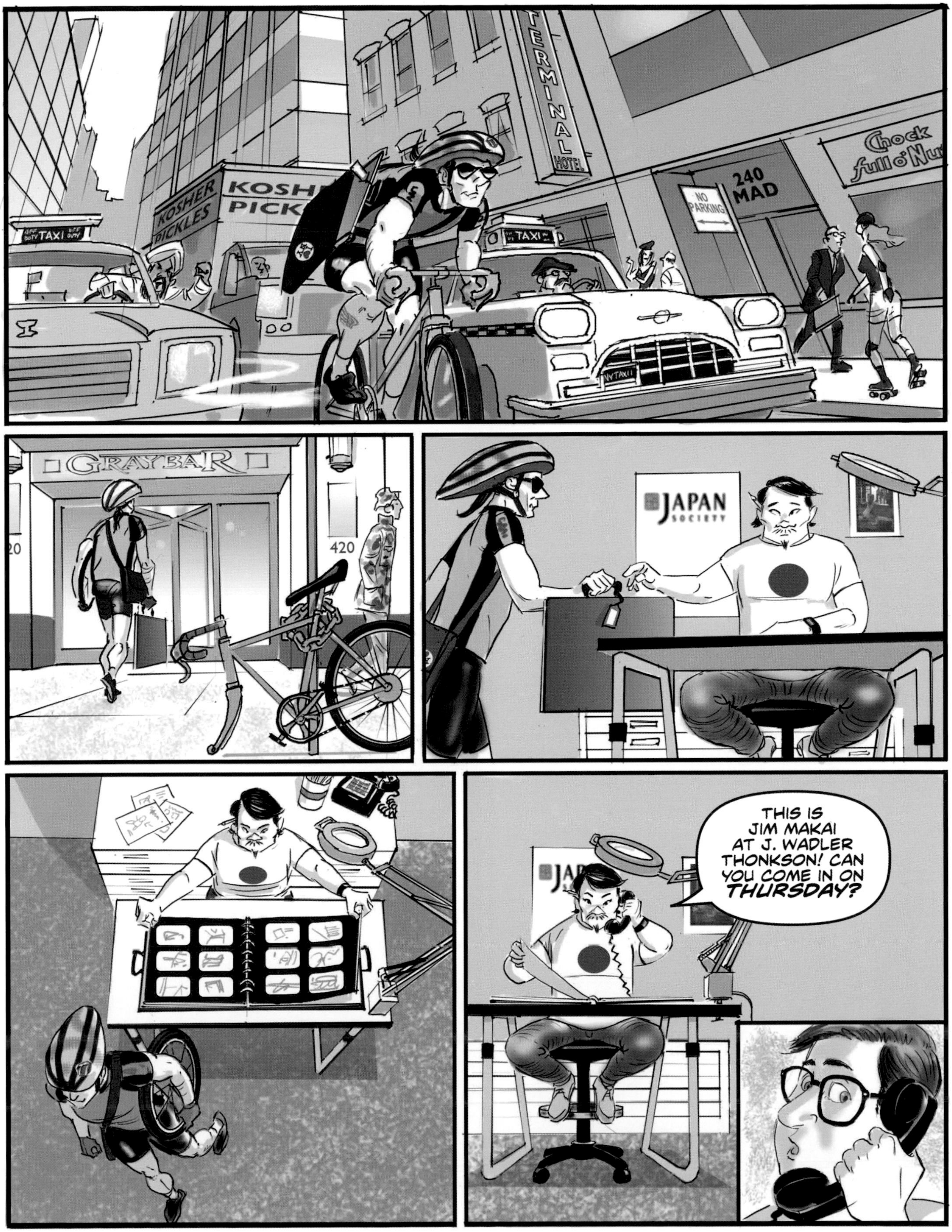
TERMINAL
HOTEL
KOSHER PICKLES
TAXI
NO PARKING
240 MAD
GRAYBAR
420
JAPAN SOCIETY
THIS IS JIM MAKAI AT J. WADLER THONKSON! CAN YOU COME IN ON THURSDAY?

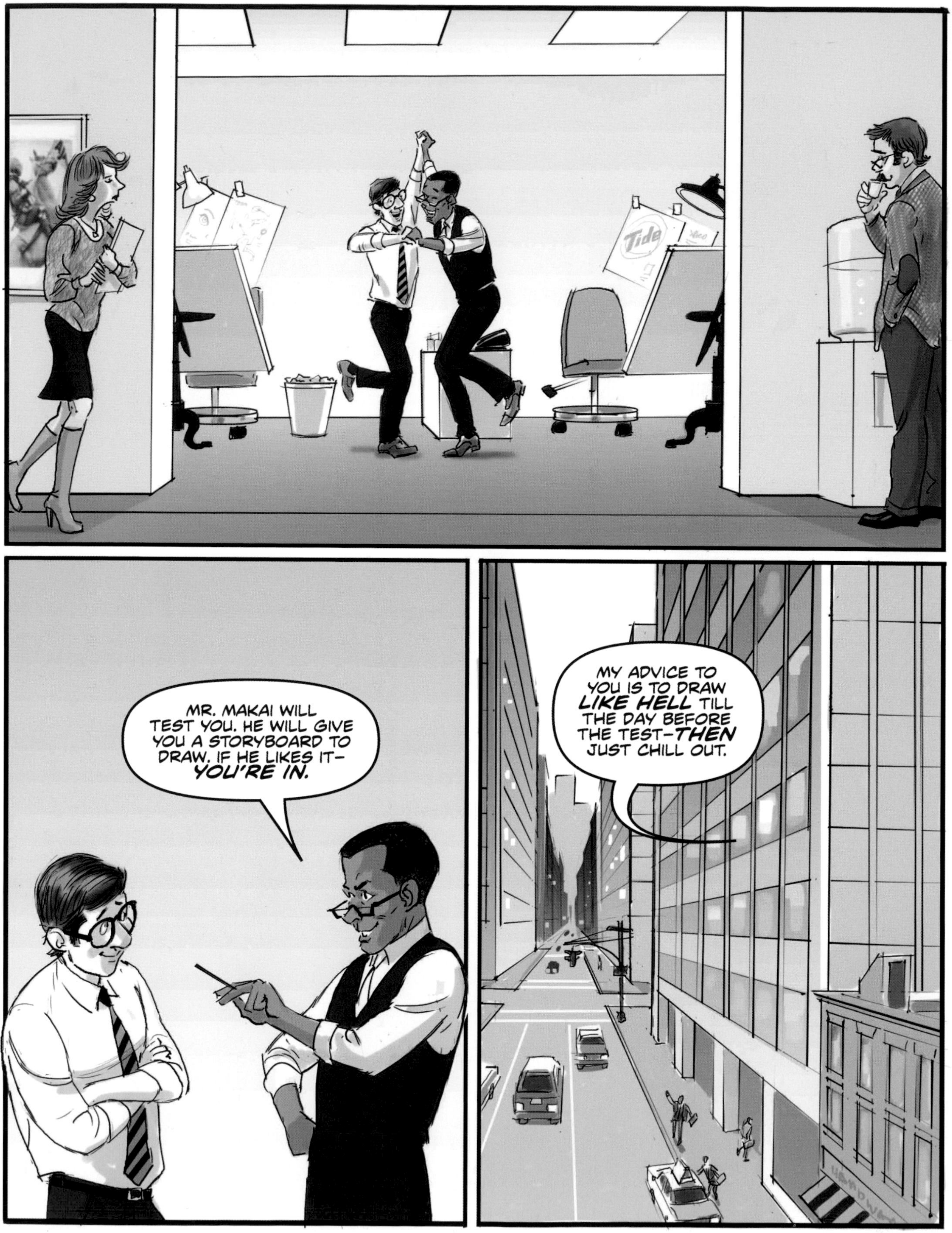
Tide
MR. MAKAI WILL TEST YOU. HE WILL GIVE YOU A STORYBOARD TO DRAW. IF HE LIKES IT– ***YOU'RE IN.***
MY ADVICE TO YOU IS TO DRAW ***LIKE HELL*** TILL THE DAY BEFORE THE TEST–***THEN*** JUST CHILL OUT.

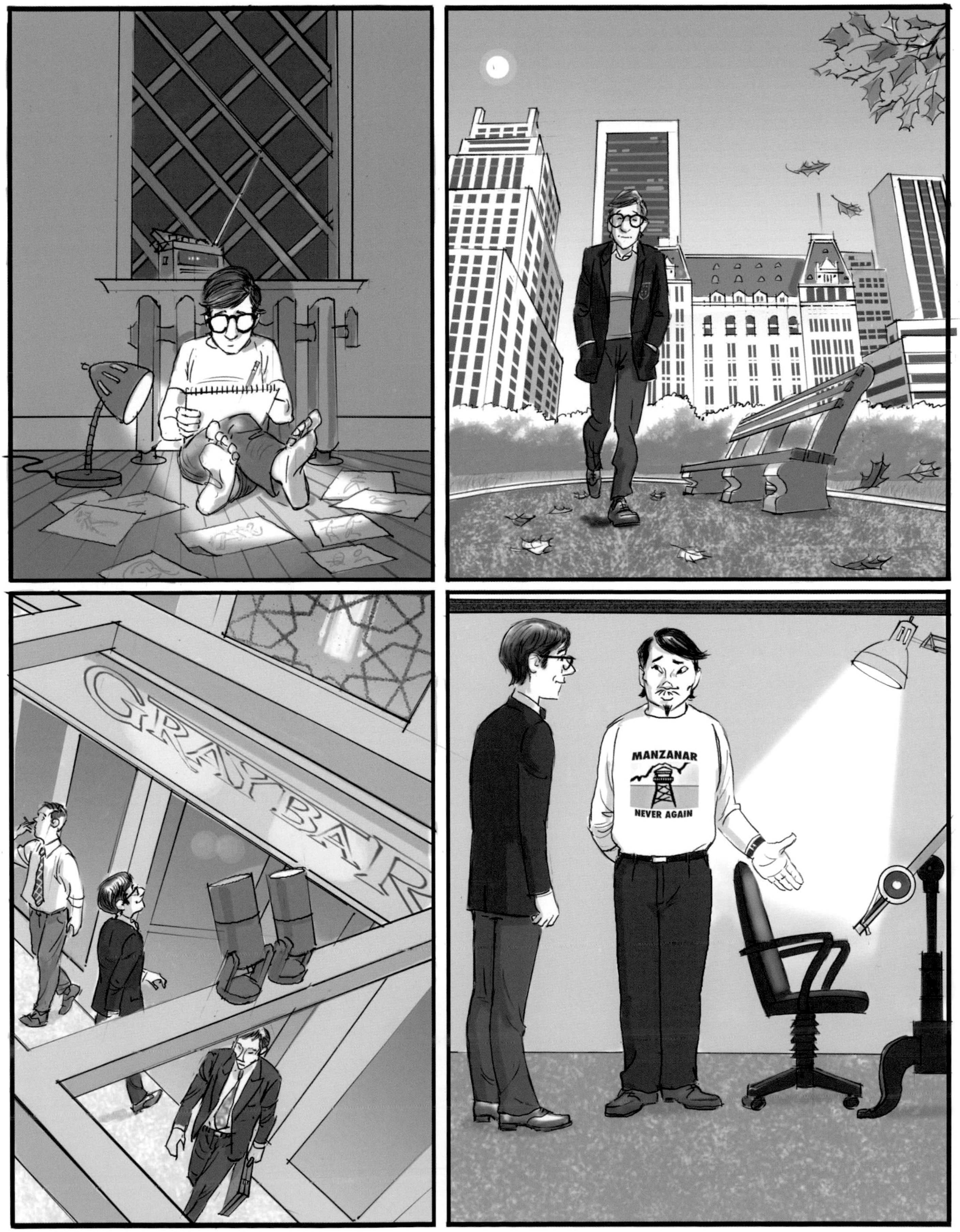
GRAYBAR
MANZANAR
NEVER AGAIN

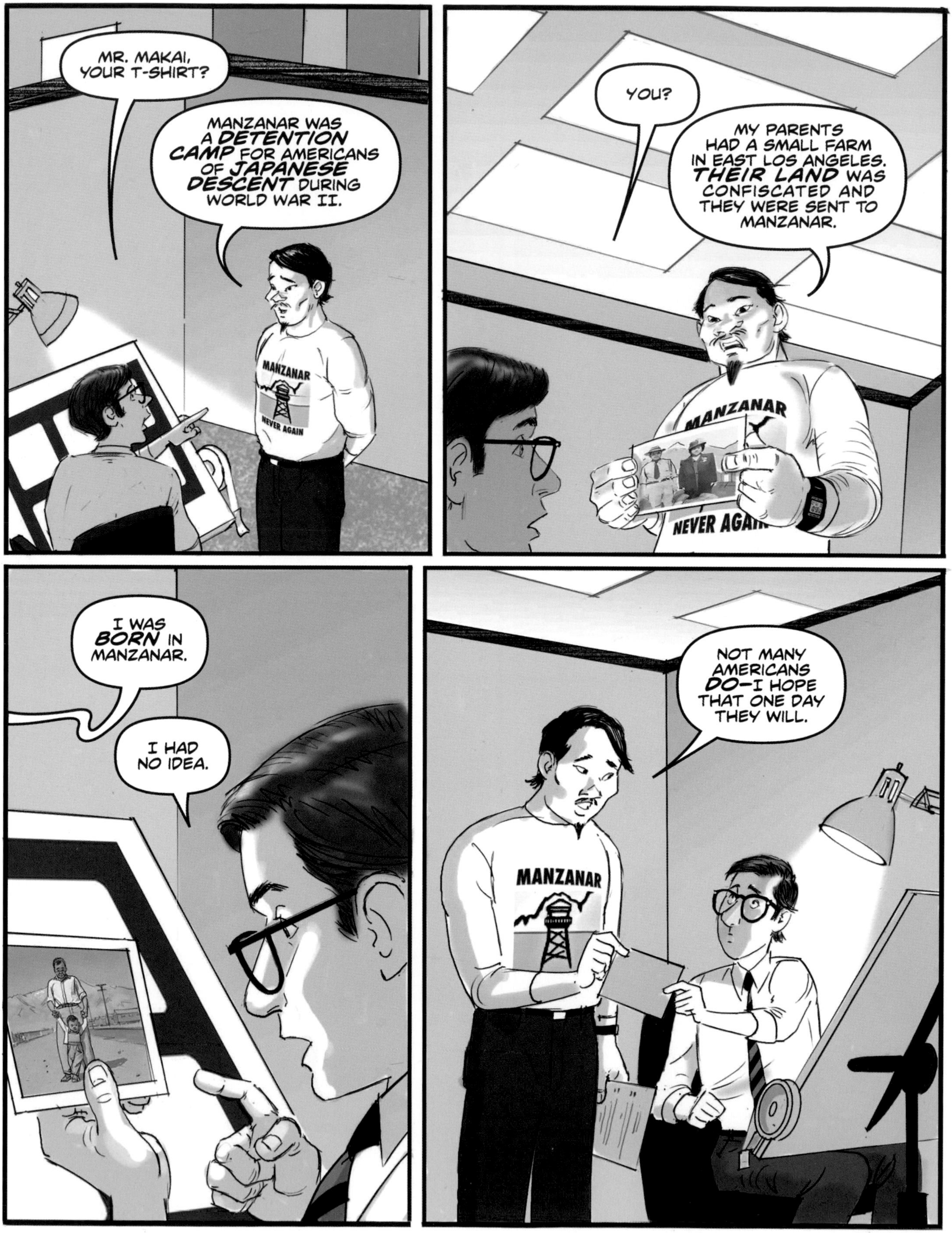
MR. MAKAI, YOUR T-SHIRT?
MANZANAR WAS A DETENTION CAMP FOR AMERICANS OF JAPANESE DESCENT DURING WORLD WAR II.
MANZANAR
NEVER AGAIN
YOU?
MY PARENTS HAD A SMALL FARM IN EAST LOS ANGELES. THEIR LAND WAS CONFISCATED AND THEY WERE SENT TO MANZANAR.
MANZANAR
NEVER AGAI
I WAS BORN IN MANZANAR.
I HAD NO IDEA.
NOT MANY AMERICANS DO—I HOPE THAT ONE DAY THEY WILL.
MANZANAR

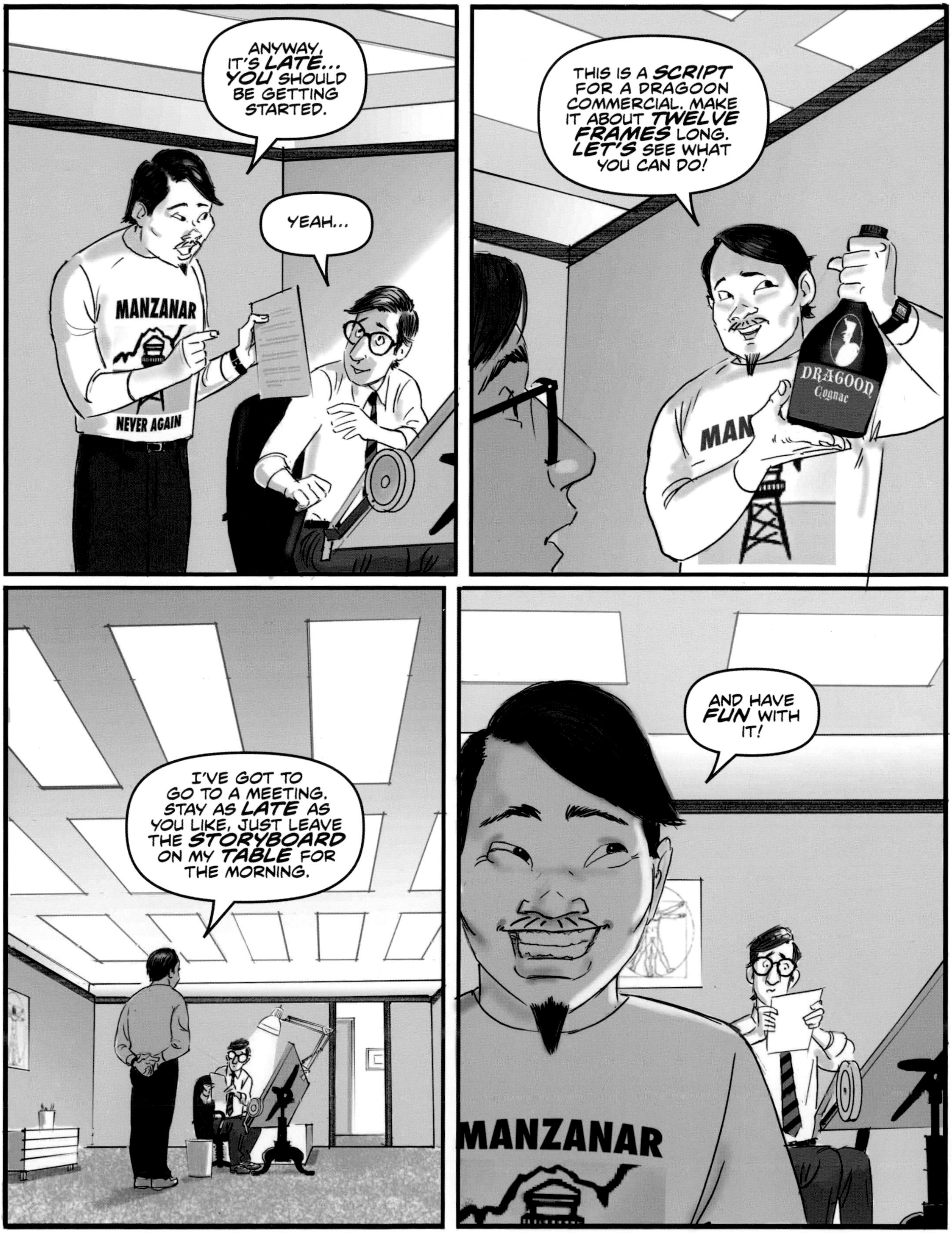
ANYWAY, IT'S LATE... YOU SHOULD BE GETTING STARTED.
MANZANAR
NEVER AGAIN
YEAH...
THIS IS A SCRIPT FOR A DRAGOON COMMERCIAL. MAKE IT ABOUT TWELVE FRAMES LONG. LET'S SEE WHAT YOU CAN DO!
DRAGOON
Cognac
I'VE GOT TO GO TO A MEETING. STAY AS LATE AS YOU LIKE, JUST LEAVE THE STORYBOARD ON MY TABLE FOR THE MORNING.
AND HAVE FUN WITH IT!
MANZANAR

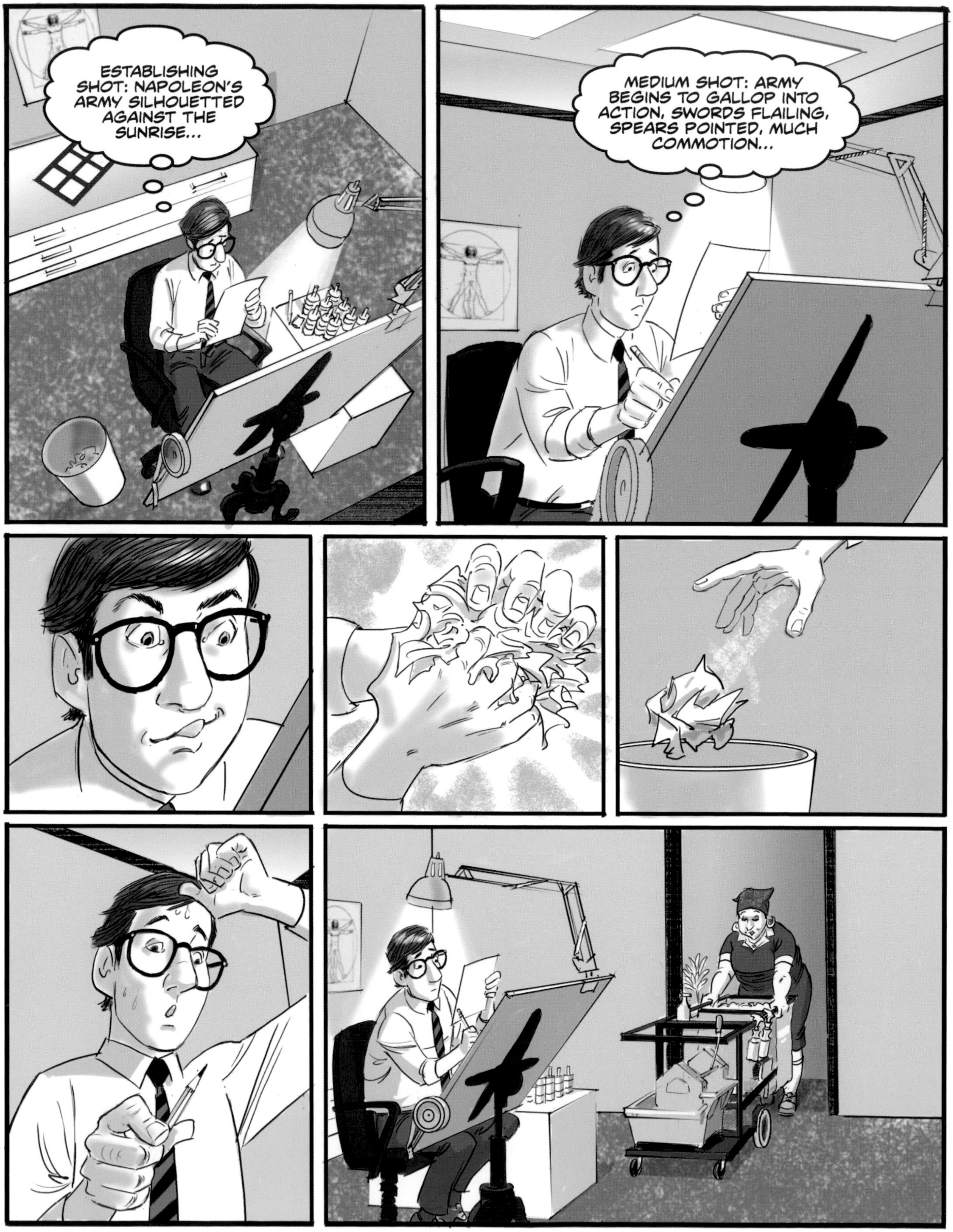
ESTABLISHING SHOT: NAPOLEON'S ARMY SILHOUETTED AGAINST THE SUNRISE...
MEDIUM SHOT: ARMY BEGINS TO GALLOP INTO ACTION, SWORDS FLAILING, SPEARS POINTED, MUCH COMMOTION...

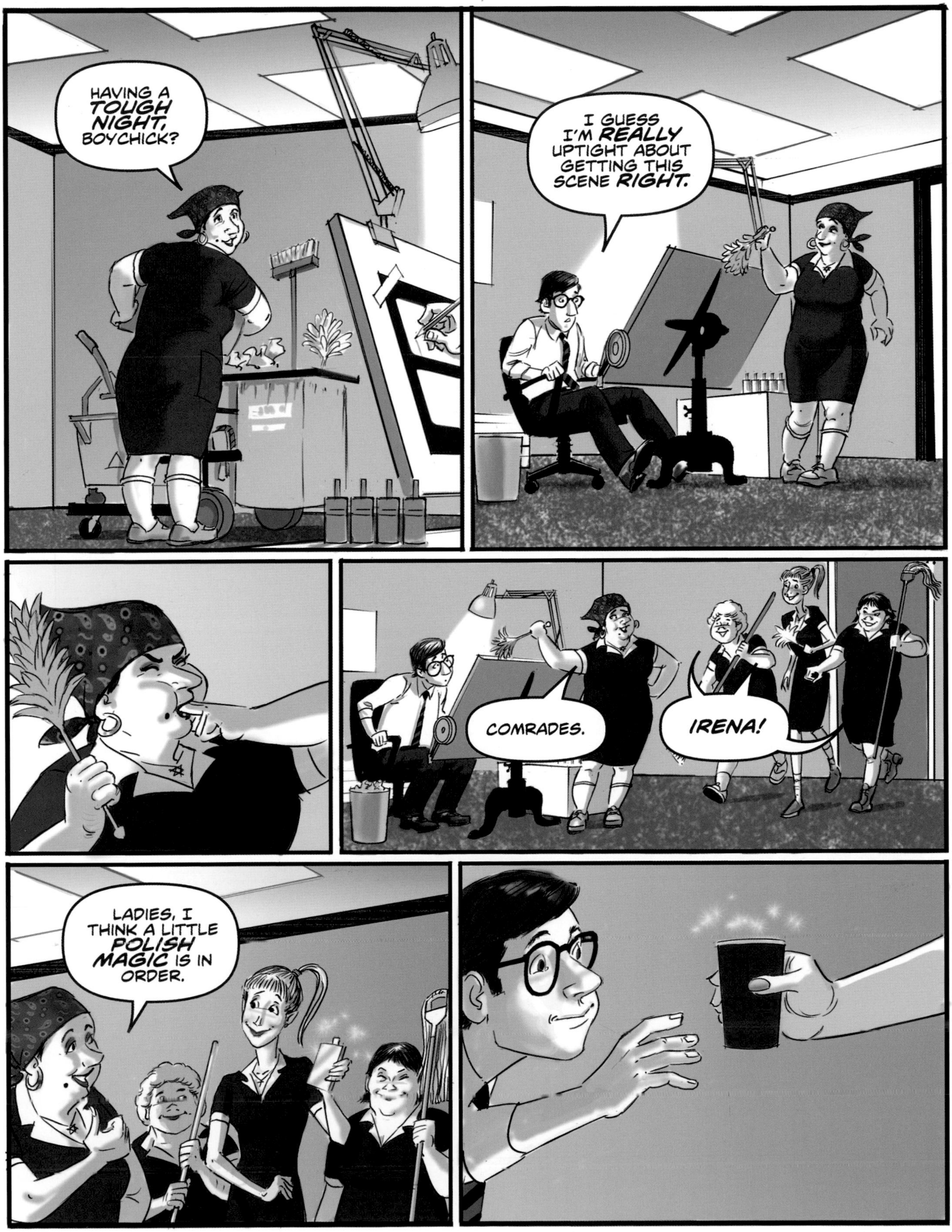
HAVING A TOUGH NIGHT, BOYCHICK?
I GUESS I'M REALLY UPTIGHT ABOUT GETTING THIS SCENE RIGHT.
COMRADES.
IRENA!
LADIES, I THINK A LITTLE POLISH MAGIC IS IN ORDER.

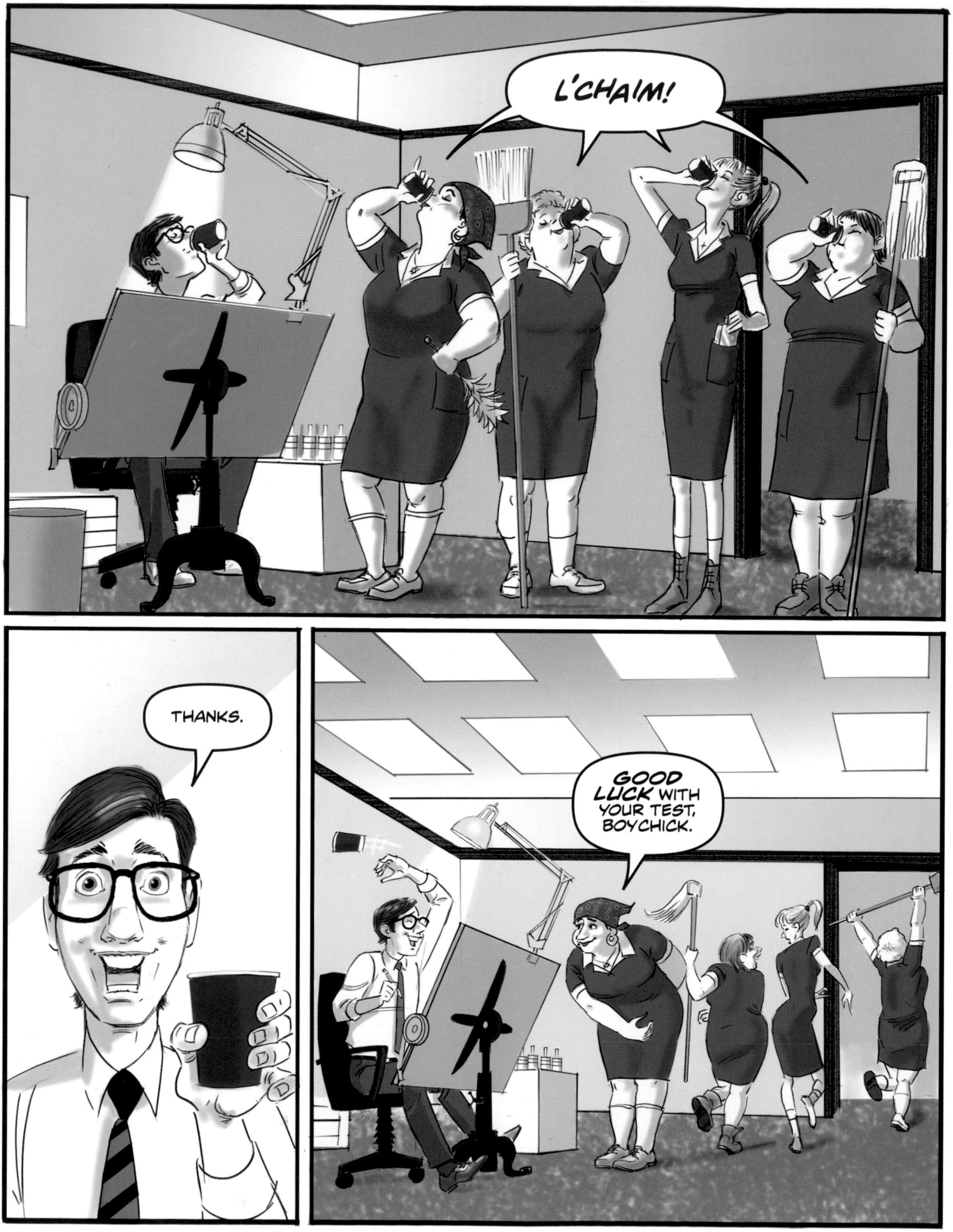
L'CHAIM!
THANKS.
GOOD LUCK WITH YOUR TEST, BOYCHICK.

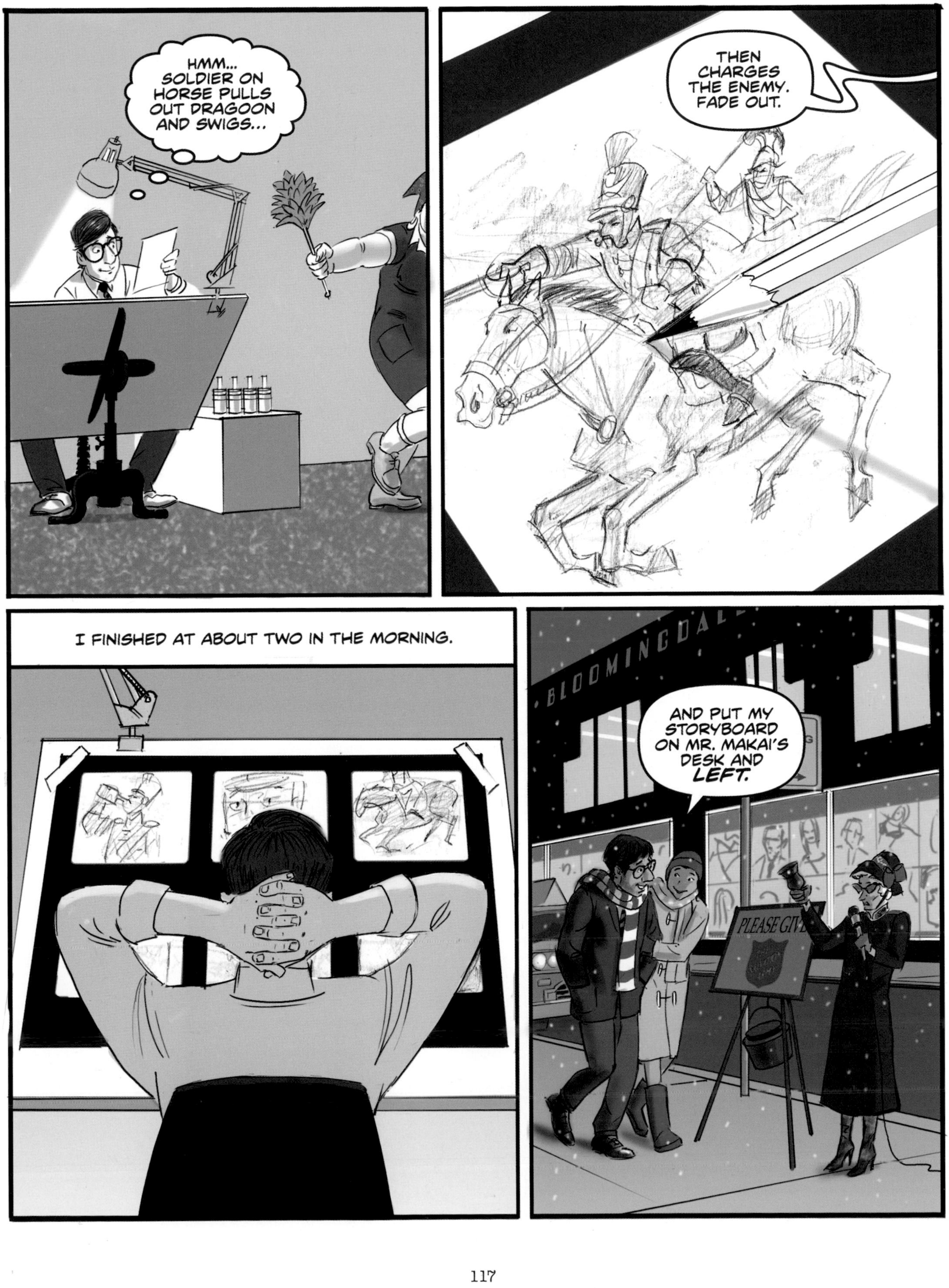
HMM... SOLDIER ON HORSE PULLS OUT DRAGOON AND SWIGS...
THEN CHARGES THE ENEMY. FADE OUT.
I FINISHED AT ABOUT TWO IN THE MORNING.
AND PUT MY STORYBOARD ON MR. MAKAI'S DESK AND *LEFT.*

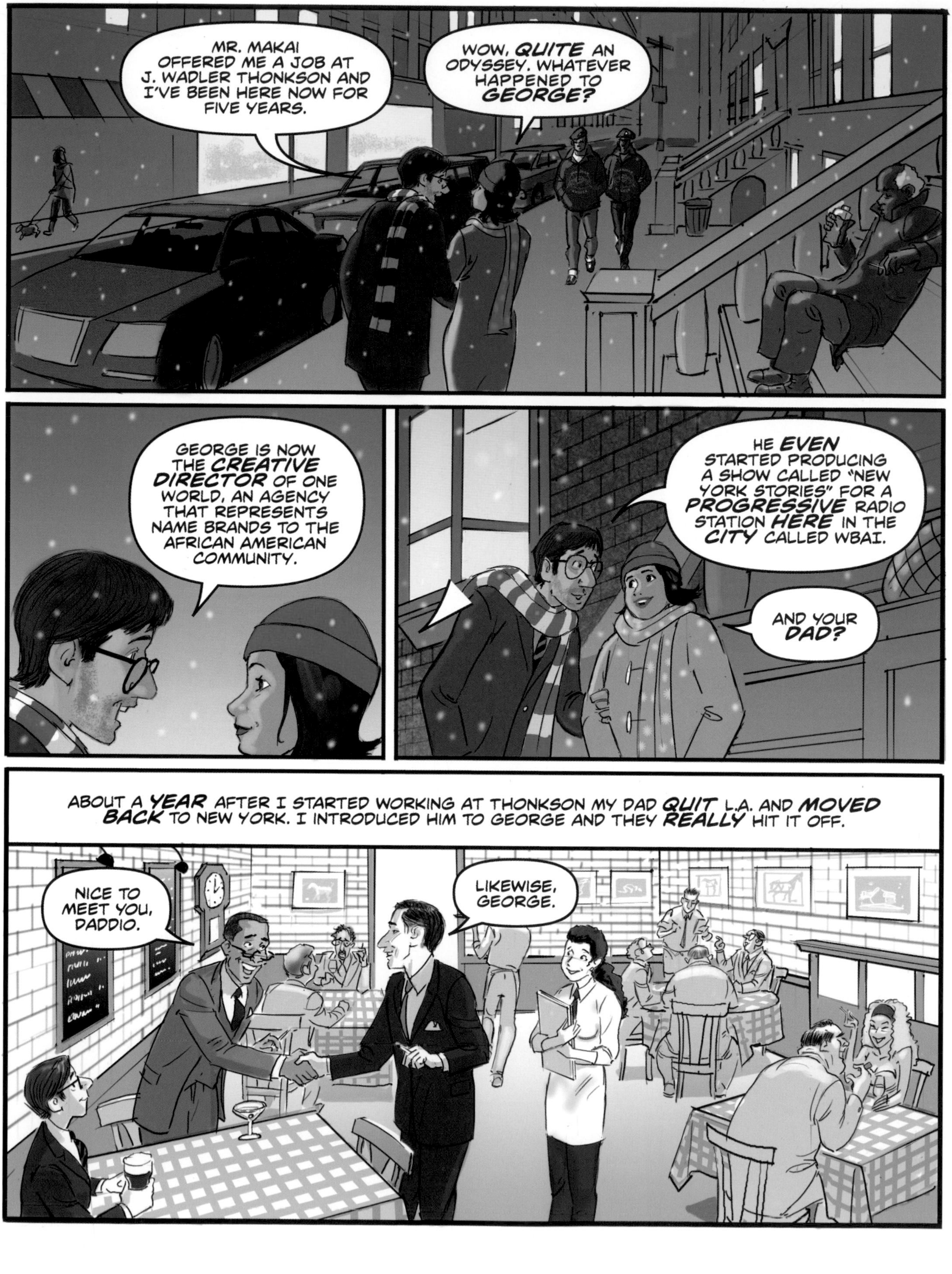
MR. MAKAI OFFERED ME A JOB AT J. WADLER THONKSON AND I'VE BEEN HERE NOW FOR FIVE YEARS.
WOW, QUITE AN ODYSSEY. WHATEVER HAPPENED TO GEORGE?
GEORGE IS NOW THE CREATIVE DIRECTOR OF ONE WORLD, AN AGENCY THAT REPRESENTS NAME BRANDS TO THE AFRICAN AMERICAN COMMUNITY.
HE EVEN STARTED PRODUCING A SHOW CALLED "NEW YORK STORIES" FOR A PROGRESSIVE RADIO STATION HERE IN THE CITY CALLED WBAI.
AND YOUR DAD?
ABOUT A YEAR AFTER I STARTED WORKING AT THONKSON MY DAD QUIT L.A. AND MOVED BACK TO NEW YORK. I INTRODUCED HIM TO GEORGE AND THEY REALLY HIT IT OFF.
NICE TO MEET YOU, DADDIO.
LIKEWISE, GEORGE.

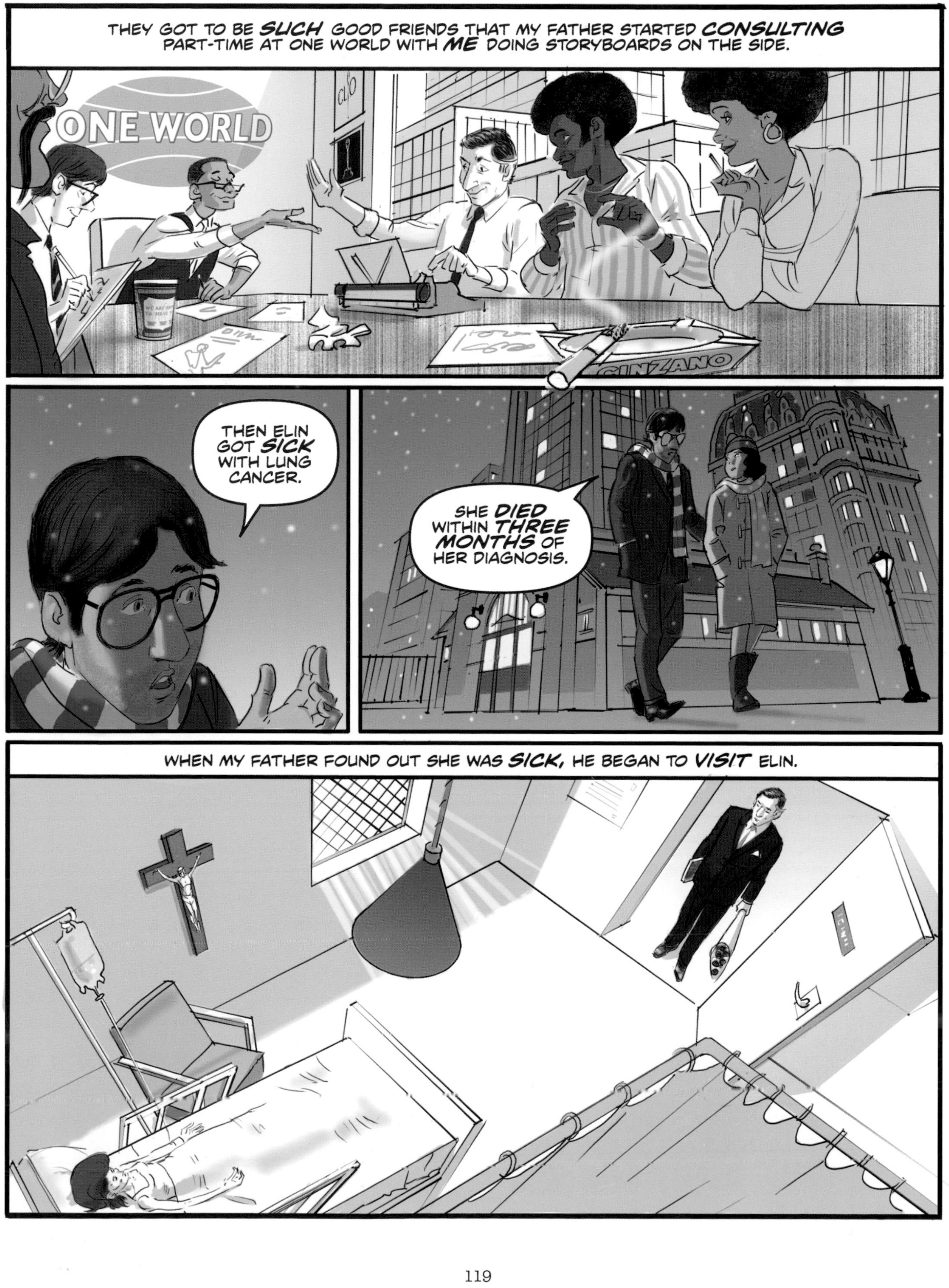
THEY GOT TO BE SUCH GOOD FRIENDS THAT MY FATHER STARTED CONSULTING PART-TIME AT ONE WORLD WITH ME DOING STORYBOARDS ON THE SIDE.
ONE WORLD
CINZANO
THEN ELIN GOT SICK WITH LUNG CANCER.
SHE DIED WITHIN THREE MONTHS OF HER DIAGNOSIS.
WHEN MY FATHER FOUND OUT SHE WAS SICK, HE BEGAN TO VISIT ELIN.

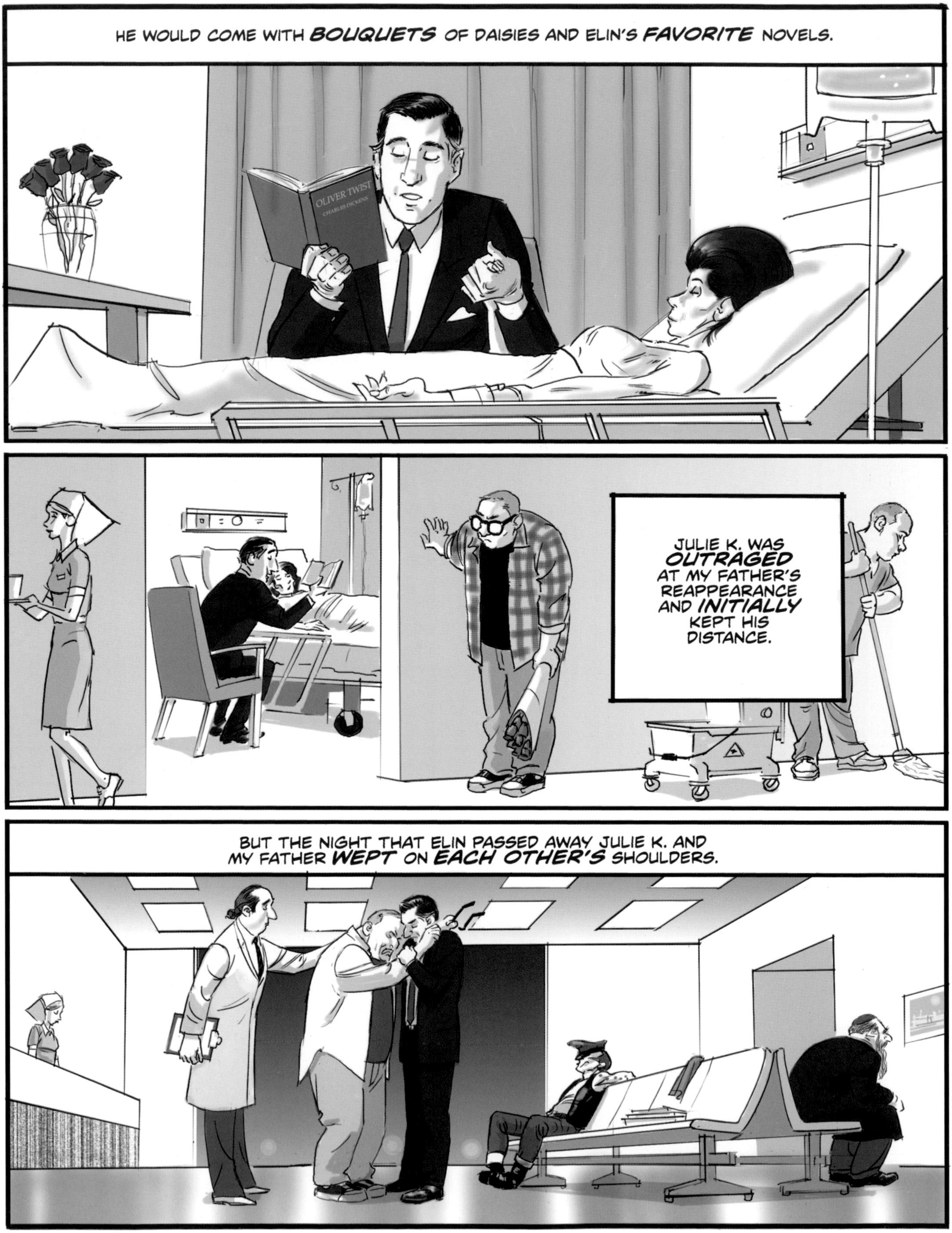
HE WOULD COME WITH BOUQUETS OF DAISIES AND ELIN'S FAVORITE NOVELS.
OLIVER TWIST
CHARLES DICKENS
JULIE K. WAS OUTRAGED AT MY FATHER'S REAPPEARANCE AND INITIALLY KEPT HIS DISTANCE.
BUT THE NIGHT THAT ELIN PASSED AWAY JULIE K. AND MY FATHER WEPT ON EACH OTHER'S SHOULDERS.

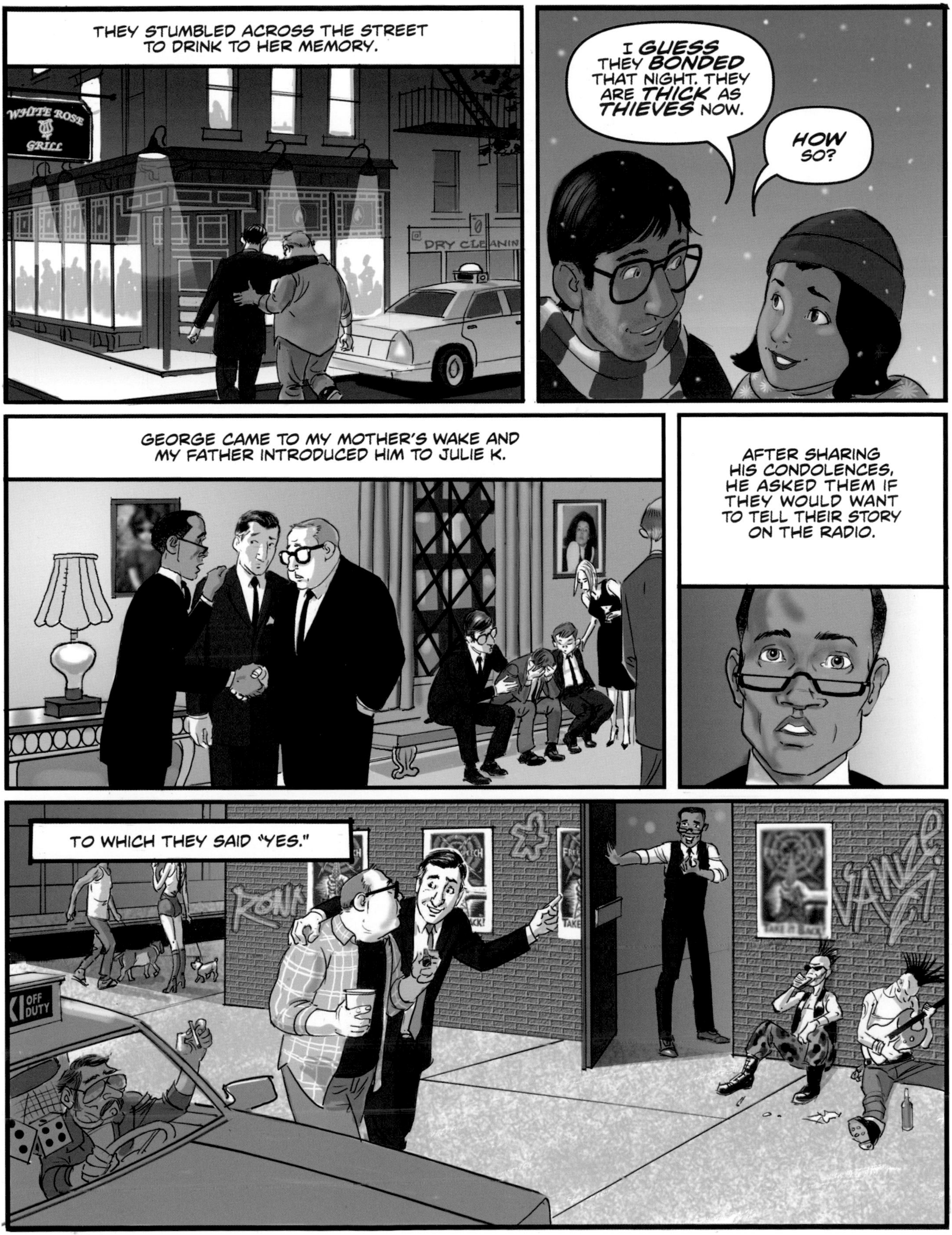
THEY STUMBLED ACROSS THE STREET TO DRINK TO HER MEMORY.
WHITE ROSE GRILL
DRY CLEANIN
I GUESS THEY BONDED THAT NIGHT. THEY ARE THICK AS THIEVES NOW.
HOW SO?
GEORGE CAME TO MY MOTHER'S WAKE AND MY FATHER INTRODUCED HIM TO JULIE K.
AFTER SHARING HIS CONDOLENCES, HE ASKED THEM IF THEY WOULD WANT TO TELL THEIR STORY ON THE RADIO.
TO WHICH THEY SAID "YES."
OFF DUTY

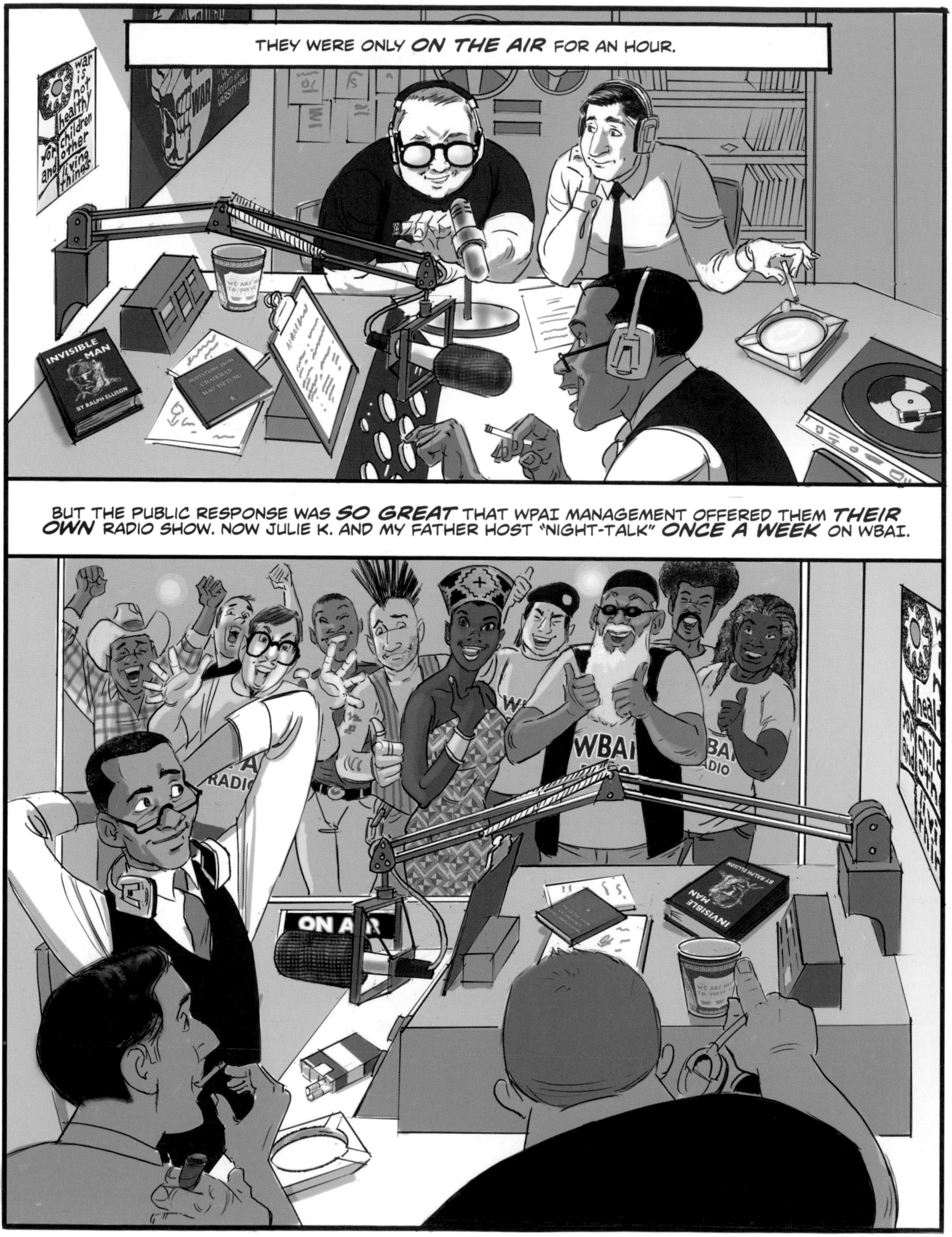
THEY WERE ONLY ON THE AIR FOR AN HOUR.
war is not healthy for children and other living things
INVISIBLE MAN
BY RALPH ELLISON
QUOTATIONS FROM CHAIRMAN MAO TSETUNG
BUT THE PUBLIC RESPONSE WAS SO GREAT THAT WPAI MANAGEMENT OFFERED THEM THEIR OWN RADIO SHOW. NOW JULIE K. AND MY FATHER HOST "NIGHT-TALK" ONCE A WEEK ON WBAI.
WBAI
RADIO
ON AIR
INVISIBLE MAN
BY RALPH ELLISON

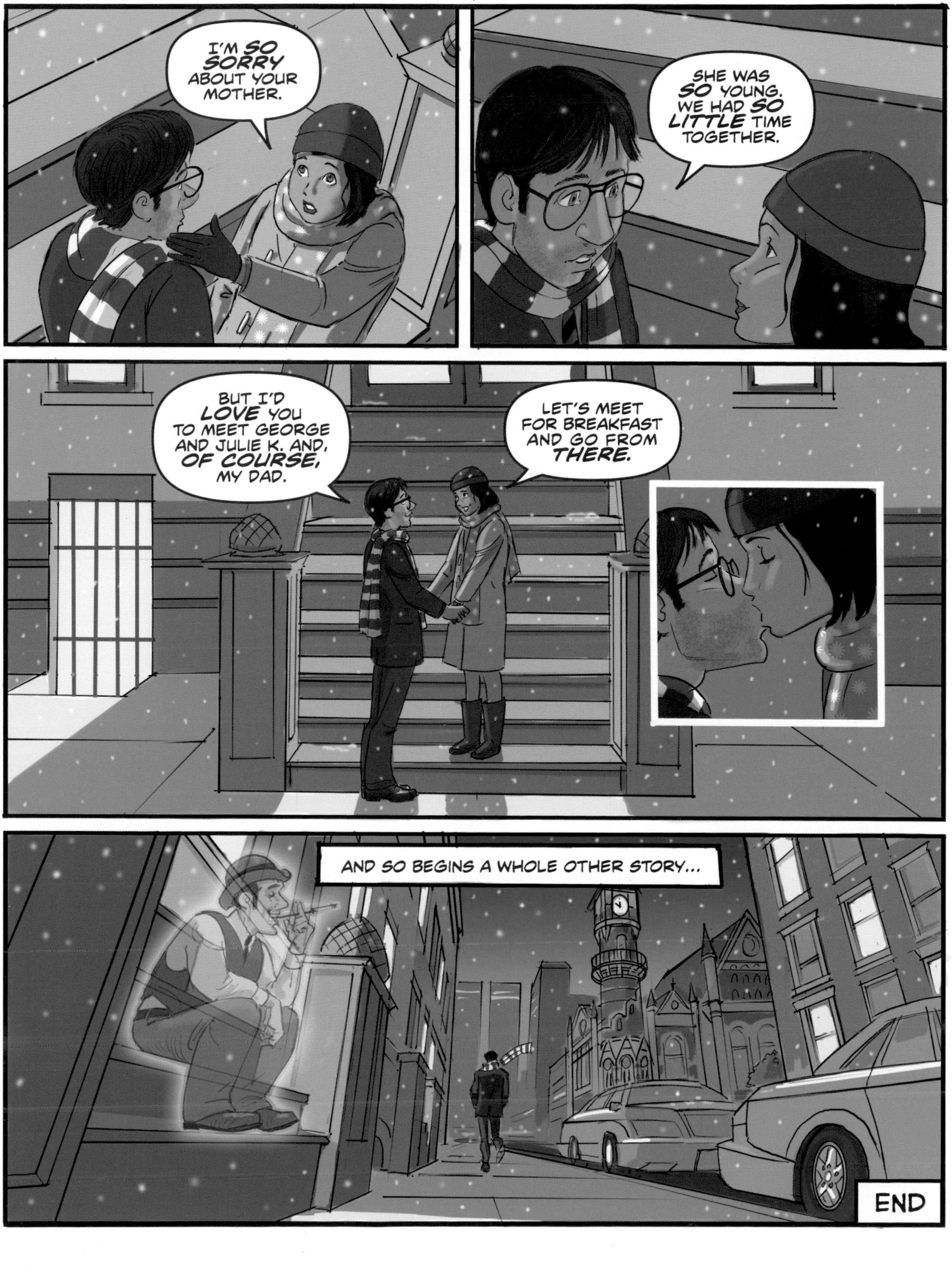
I'M SO SORRY ABOUT YOUR MOTHER.
SHE WAS SO YOUNG. WE HAD SO LITTLE TIME TOGETHER.
BUT I'D LOVE YOU TO MEET GEORGE AND JULIE K. AND, OF COURSE, MY DAD.
LET'S MEET FOR BREAKFAST AND GO FROM THERE.
AND SO BEGINS A WHOLE OTHER STORY...
END

ACKNOWLEDGEMENTS

When I was 21, I went to see Ralph Bakshi's "Heavy Traffic" with my dad. We were both stunned by the sophisticated and adult story Mr. Bakshi told in the form of a cartoon. It's bittersweet that I can't have my dad read the cartoon I finally managed to make of him. He would probably insist, in his garrulous way, on taking all my friends out for a huge Italian meal, hugging and kissing everyone while smoking Camels and sipping wine.

So, for both of us, let me express my gratitude to my friend Marilyn Adams and my mentor Neal Adams, who saw something in the story and passed it along to the wonderful Bob Schreck, my new friend and editor who brought it to IDW. My thanks to Justin Eisinger who "brought it across the Finish line" and to Chris Ryall, a fellow veteran of the advertising business for his support.

Thanks to my fellow artists Tom Fluharty, Ray Ketchem, John Wohland, Tim Shinn and Dan Zollinger for their almost daily enlightenment and inspiration over the last twenty years.

Thanks to my fellow New Yorkers Andy Field and Meryl Rosner, the Queen of Perspective, for their Enthusiasm and Encouragement.

Thanks to my friends in England, Sandra Grantham, John Henn, Andy Dodd and Kenny Penman.

Thanks to "Mr. Movies" Noah Sacco and "Miss Emergency Rescue Tech" Isabella Sacco for being my captive audience.

And lastly thanks to my constant muse and best friend Ronnie Sacco for helping to live and write this.